Colonel Roosevelt

Theodore Roosevelt Goes to War, 1897–1898

H. PAUL JEFFERS

JOHN WILEY & SONS, INC.

New York • Chichester • Brisbane • Toronto • Singapore

Copyright © 1996 by H. Paul Jeffers
Published by John Wiley & Sons, Inc.

Library of Congress Cataloging-in-Publication Data:

Jeffers, H. Paul (Harry Paul).
  Colonel Roosevelt : Theodore Roosevelt goes to war, 1897–1898 / by
H. Paul Jeffers.
    p.   cm.
  Includes bibliographical references and index.
  ISBN 0-471-12678-0 (cloth : alk. paper)
  1. Roosevelt, Theodore, 1858–1919—Military leadership.
  2. Spanish-American War, 1898. I. Title.
  E757.J44 1996
  973.8'9'092—dc20   95-23544

Printed in the United States of America

10 9 8 7 6 5 4 3 2 1

For my nephew, Michael Paul Jeffers

I had very deeply felt that it was our duty to free Cuba, and
I had publicly expressed this feeling; and when a man takes
such a position, he ought to be willing to make his words good
by his deeds. He should pay with his body.

—THEODORE ROOSEVELT

Caspar Whitney of *Harper's Weekly* mapped the defenses at Santiago, Cuba.
Note that north is to the right.

Contents

Preface

From George Washington to George Bush, men who had gone to war before becoming president of the United States had done so reluctantly and with revulsion. But Theodore Roosevelt eagerly encouraged a war and happily joined the fight. "He was so overflowing with patriotism, so certain that war was at hand," observed a close friend, "that he could not restrain himself."

The war he fought is little noted, yet enormously important in the history of the United States: the Spanish-American War.

Colonel Roosevelt details the dramatic story of how and why Theodore Roosevelt almost single-handedly turned a crisis over Cuba into a war that transformed the United States into a world power. It also assured his political career. Four months after he led a charge up San Juan Hill he was elected governor of New York. In less than three years he was president.

"San Juan," he would say, "was the great day of my life."

Drawing on the diaries, letters, and memoirs of Roosevelt and those closest to him, as well as on contemporary news reports, government archives, military histories, and biographies, this book details the crisis that led to the war, reveals the personalities of those who became involved, traces the preparations for the war, and describes all aspects of the fighting. It shows that much of the responsibility for the conflict and its consequences must be attributed to the character and personal objectives of Theodore Roosevelt.

"For Roosevelt," wrote his biographer Nathan Miller, "the war had been a vindication of his physical courage and his abilities as a leader, and it thrust him into the national limelight." Another Roosevelt chronicler, Alvin F. Harlow, noted that after the war "the name of Roosevelt was on every tongue. He was very nearly the top-ranking hero of the war. His career had been helped, not hindered, by his military venture, for the people love to give military heroes high political preference."

Roosevelt's friend, novelist Owen Wister, found the war to be a whirl of history that put the United States among the great nations of the world. Because of the war—the shortest declared war in American history—the United States became a colonial power, having secured the Philippines, Puerto Rico, and Hawaii. The country assumed the role of a major fighting force with a two-ocean navy, established itself as the sole arbiter of affairs in the Western Hemisphere, and planted seeds for a war with Japan some forty years later.

Roosevelt himself said, "The young giant of the West stands on a continent and clasps the crest of an ocean in either hand. Our nation, glorious in youth and strength, looks into the future with eager eyes and rejoices as a strong man to run a race."

"It has been," said the American ambassador to England, John Hay, "a splendid little war."

Prologue

Ships, Ships, Ships

To a native Rhode Islander strolling the Newport waterfront on Wednesday morning, June 2, 1897, the short, stocky man of middle years with an impressive mustache and pince-nez glasses might have appeared to be just another wealthy vacationer up from New York. He scurried down the gangway of the Fall River steamer and bounded to the dock, much as men had been doing for decades upon arriving by way of Long Island Sound aboard the overnight boat from New York. Free to laze away their summers, these men came to enjoy the cooling breezes on the broad and shady porches and manicured lawns and croquet greens of the palatial mansions known as "cottages," which dotted the picturesque shores and yacht-crowded waters of Narragansett Bay.

Described in 1893's *Baedeker's United States* as the undisputed "Queen of American seaside resorts," Newport had long since left behind the puritanism of religious dissenters who in 1639 had fled there because Massachusetts was not religious enough for them. By the next century the settlement they created had become a lucrative base for the rum-molasses-slave trade and for colorful freebooting ocean-going privateers. Following the Civil War, its pleasant summer sea vistas had attracted intellectuals and artists down by train from Boston and the wealthy over water from New York, led by social pace-setters Mrs. John Jacob Astor and Mrs. August Belmont.

But the destination of the energetic figure who debarked on that June 2 was not one of the stately mansions along Bellevue Avenue, the membership-by-introduction-only casino where the lawn tennis championship of America was decided each September, nor one of the posh hotels or any of the town's attractive beaches. As the new assistant secretary of the navy, Theodore Roosevelt did not have opulence and leisure on his mind. He was on his way to the poorhouse.

1

Topped with a graceful cupola, the federal-style red brick building on Coaster's Island had been a place of last resort for the down-and-out until it was taken over by the navy in October 1884 to accommodate the Naval War College. The grand ambition of Admiral Stephen B. Luce, the college had as its purpose advanced training and instruction for commissioned naval officers in science and the history of marine warfare. Between 1886 and 1889 and again from 1892 to 1893 its president had been a brilliant but quirky naval strategist who, despite a forty-year career, thoroughly disliked naval service and could not board even the largest ship in the fleet without suffering severely from seasickness. Yet Captain Alfred Thayer Mahan was the foremost propagandist for an American navy that he thought should be second to none in the world. Led by the most formidable assemblage of battleships that money could buy, the United States Navy of Mahan's dream would not only defend and secure America's coasts but project American interests, prestige, and power to the four corners of the world. On these vital issues, in Roosevelt's opinion, "there was no one else in his class, or anywhere near it."

Although Mahan had retired from active duty and been succeeded as commanding officer of the Naval War College, his idea of a first-class American fleet plying all the world's oceans and seas had been given wide circulation by scores of his articles, letters to newspaper editors, and books, the most important of which, *The Influence of Sea Power upon History, 1660–1783,* had been published in 1890. Among its many readers, none had been so admiring, nor had agreed so wholeheartedly, as Theodore Roosevelt.

October 1890's issue of the *Atlantic Monthly* had afforded Roosevelt an opportunity to review the book. The critic noted that the author clearly proved the "tremendous effect which seapower has had upon the development of certain of the great nations of the world, especially at momentous crises in their history." He declared that "one or two of the points which Captain Mahan brings out have a very important bearing on our present condition." These were the need for a secure base of operations for action against an enemy's commerce and some kind of line of battle to fall back on.

It was not enough for the United States to rely on coastal fortifications for defense. Roosevelt wrote, "Forts alone could not prevent the occupation of any town or territory outside the range of their guns, or the general wasting of the seaboard, while a squadron of heavy battleships, able to sail out and attack the enemy's vessels as they approached, and possessing the great advantage of being near their own base of supplies, would effectively guard a thousand miles of coast."

The meaning was clear. "We need a large navy, composed not merely of cruisers, but containing also a full proportion of powerful battleships, able to meet those of any nation."

Between the lines one could read Roosevelt's proposition that the closer this powerful fleet was stationed in the way of any potential routes of attack on the United States, the better; ideal sites would be islands such as Puerto Rico and Cuba in the Atlantic and the Hawaiian Islands in the Pacific.

Another Roosevelt review of a Mahan book—this one on the life of Britain's naval hero Admiral Horatio Nelson—was scheduled for publication in *The Bookman* during the very month that Roosevelt traveled to Newport to address the Naval War College. In this essay he would assert, "No triumph of peace can equal the armed triumph over malice domestic or foreign levy. No qualities called out by a purely peaceful life can stand on a level with those stern and virile virtues which move the men of stout heart and strong hand who uphold the honor of their flag in battle. It is better for a nation to produce one [General Ulysses S.] Grant or one [Admiral David] Farragut than a thousand shrewd manufacturers or successful speculators."

While Roosevelt certainly placed Captain Mahan in such a category, Mahan was not at the war college to greet his admirer. He had been succeeded by Captain Casper B. Goodrich, who, shortly before Roosevelt's arrival, had received an order from the assistant secretary to engage the college's staff and student officers in deliberating a "Special Confidential Problem." It centered on two of the most debated policy issues facing the administration of President William McKinley. The first involved the Hawaiian Islands.

Since American residents there had overthrown the regime of Queen Liliuokalani, they had been agitating for formal union with the United States, and in 1893 they had included in Hawaii's constitution an authorization for a treaty of annexation. Roosevelt's problem posited a pair of breathtaking assumptions: (1) Japan makes demands upon the Hawaiian Islands; (2) the United States intervenes militarily. Because as assistant secretary of the navy he was directly in charge of fleet operations, Roosevelt wanted to know what force would be necessary to uphold the intervention and how it should be employed. He added that the problem should be considered while "keeping in mind possible complications with another Power on the Atlantic Coast," referring to Spain and its colonies, Puerto Rico and Cuba.

That the author of the provocative request had followed up by actually coming to Newport served to underscore that the problem meant more to Roosevelt than an interesting exercise in naval strategy. Neither was it lost to the college faculty and student officers that the speech would be Roosevelt's first public pronouncement since becoming assistant secretary on April 19. Nor could they have been unaware of the dramatic emergence on the national political stage of a man who was one of the country's most fascinating and controversial public figures.

In June 1897, Theodore Roosevelt was four months shy of his thirty-ninth birthday and seventeen years out of college, yet he already had been a leader of the New York state legislature, a candidate for mayor of New York City (defeated in 1886), a member of the United States Civil Service Commission, and president of the New York City Board of Police Commissioners (1895-97). When the potentates of the Republican Party pondered the future and combed party rolls for prospective candidates for president of the United States, they placed his name high on their list.

Upon Roosevelt's appointment as assistant secretary of the navy by McKinley, the *Chicago Times-Herald's* Washington correspondent had noted, "He is by long odds one of the most interesting of the younger men seen here in recent years."

A prolific writer, Roosevelt had established himself as an essayist and author of books, including *The Winning of the West,* published in four volumes between 1889 and 1896, and *The Naval War of 1812,* published in 1882. The latter had been started in the form of his senior thesis while he was at Harvard University.

"When the professor thought I ought to be on mathematics and the languages," Roosevelt recalled, "my mind was running to ships that were fighting each other."

This fascination with warring ships had surfaced long before Roosevelt went to Cambridge. Born in New York City on October 27, 1858, and nicknamed Teedie, he had been a sickly child about whom his doctors had expressed grave doubts that he could survive to adulthood. Because he was often confined to bed, he read voraciously and listened eagerly to his mother's stories about the Civil War exploits of an uncle, James Bulloch, who had built the Confederate warship

Alabama. When not telling him about Uncle James, he recalled, his mother would "talk to me as a little shaver about ships, ships, ships, and fighting ships, till they sank into the depths of my soul."

Begun in 1880 when Roosevelt was twenty years of age, *The Naval War of 1812* was completed and published two years after his graduation from Harvard. According to his friend and classmate Owen Wister, Roosevelt's postcollege writing had been pursued in Roosevelt's New York City house. In *Roosevelt, the Story of a Friendship, 1880–1919,* Wister described Roosevelt's new wife, Alice, looking in at her husband's "oblivious back" and exclaiming in a plaintive drawl: "We're dining out in twenty minutes, and Teedie's drawing little ships."

In a room crammed with ships' log books, navigational charts, and stacks of other source material, Wister watched Roosevelt doing his work "mostly standing on one leg at the bookcases . . . the other leg crossed behind, toe touching the floor, heedless of dinner engagements and the flight of time. A slide drew out from the bookcase. On this he had open the leading authorities on navigation, of which he knew nothing. He knew that when a ship's course was one way, with the wind another, the ship had to sail at right angles, and this was called tacking or beating. By exhaustive study and drawing of models, he pertinaciously got it all right, whatever of it came into the naval engagements he was writing about."

Book critics agreed. A reviewer for the *New York Times* hailed the work as an excellent one in every respect, showing "in so young an author the best promises for a good historian—fearlessness of statement, caution, endeavor to be impartial, and a brisk and interesting way of telling events." *Harper's* extolled the book "as the most accurate, as it is certainly the most cool and impartial, and in some respects the most intrepid, account that has yet appeared of the naval actions of the War of 1812."

These judgments have withstood the test of time. In *Theodore Roosevelt, A Life,* Nathan Miller wrote, "A century after its appearance, [Roosevelt's book] is still a standard work on the subject." In *The Rise of Theodore Roosevelt,* Edmund Morris noted that it remained the definitive work in its field, "an extraordinary achievement," its merits "as simple as those of any serious piece of academic writing: clarity, accuracy and completeness, backed by massive documentation." But it is also an exciting adventure story brimming with vivid accounts of ships at war on the high seas.

The book had also impressed the Navy Department. It ordered a copy placed aboard every ship in the fleet and designated it a textbook at the Naval War College.

Fifteen years later, here was the book's author taking to a podium at the college, when he could have had his choice of speaking venues in Washington and New York. Surely, anyone might rightly reason, he had not traveled all the way up to Rhode Island from the capital simply to deliver a pep talk to the Naval War College, class of '97. He was, after all, the man who would, said the *Washington Post* at the time of his appointment to the Navy Department, bring to Washington "all that machinery of disturbance and upheaval which is as much a part of his *entourage* as the air he breathes. He is a fighter, a man of indomitable pluck and energy, a potent and forceful factor in any equation into which he may be introduced. A field of immeasurable usefulness awaits him—will he find it?"

Typically, the robust Roosevelt had answered the query with dramatic action. Early in May he seized the occasion of a mishap involving a navy torpedo boat to conduct a personal inspection and write a report for the secretary of the navy, John D. Long. This on-the-scene investigation by an assistant secretary of the navy was a first in naval history, as was the report. In assuring Long that no serious damage had been caused in the incident, Roosevelt took advantage of the event to expound on his views regarding the qualities and dispositions of the men chosen to command U.S. Navy ships.

In his report Roosevelt wrote, "Boats so delicate, which, to be handled effectively must be handled with great daring, necessarily run great risks, and their commanders must, of course, realize that a prerequisite to successfully handling them is the willingness to run such risks." He concluded, "The business of a naval officer is one which, above all others, needs daring and decision and if he must err on either side the nation can best afford to have him err on the side of too much daring rather than too much caution."

Hailed by the press as an expression of a new spirit in the Navy Department, the report was welcomed by one newspaper for its "snap and vigor," while another editor invited Roosevelt to provide a series of such papers setting out his views on what needed to be done to revitalize a navy that had been "running along in a groove for altogether too many years."

The editor need not have worried. The new assistant secretary had been busily engaged in writing almost from his first day in office.

Although the report on the status of torpedo boats had been made public, the press was not privy to other communications from Roosevelt to both McKinley and Secretary Long, each of them filled with much "snap and vigor" on the subject of Theodore Roosevelt's positions on the challenges to, and the proper use of, naval resources.

Upon the Atlantic the issues were as old as the nation and took the form of imperialist designs on the Western Hemisphere by the major European powers of Britain, France, Germany, and Spain, each with a great fleet. Of gravest concern in the Pacific was the future of the Hawaiian Islands and a growing interest in their outright annexation. This movement was viewed with alarm by the government of Japan, concerned for the fate of twenty-five thousand Japanese residents on the islands.

Noting that the Japanese had sent their cruiser *Naniwa* to Hawaii, Roosevelt, in his capacity as operational head of the navy, had advised McKinley on April 22 that in view of this event, "I would like to inform you as to the [American] vessels at Hawaii and those which could be sent there." He went on to name and discuss in detail the attributes and advantages, as well as the inadequacies, of several warships, including the cruiser *Philadelphia,* "an old boat"; the *Marion*; the *Bennington,* en route from San Francisco; the *Baltimore* and the *Charleston,* under repair at Mare Island, along with the gunboat *Concord*; and the battleship *Oregon,* which could be in Hawaii in two weeks. "She would be an overmatch for half the Japanese Navy," he boasted while warning, "although they (the Japanese) have two battleships of the same class now on the point of completion."

The Japanese navy, he ventured darkly, was an efficient fighting navy and, therefore, might pose a serious hindrance to any American attempt to annex Hawaii.

Although President Grover Cleveland's administration had exhibited no eagerness for taking over Hawaii, the idea had found not only favor but enthusiasm in leading personalities of the Republican Party and the McKinley administration, and none more so than Theodore Roosevelt. Among his friends who looked benignly on American expansionism in the Pacific and hegemony over the Western Hemisphere were Senators Henry Cabot Lodge, William E. Chandler, and Albert Beveridge; Judge William Howard Taft; Charles A. Dana, editor of the New York *Sun*; John Hay, the American ambassador to England; and Brooks Adams, the brilliant but eccentric philosopher and younger brother of writer Henry Adams.

Nathan Miller described these men as well-educated and culti-vated patricians living by an aristocratic code that assumed the supe-riority of white American men; they sought relief from the boredom of an increasingly mechanized commercialism by finding romance in the sound of far-off bugles. Referred to as "the expansionist lobby," they were also categorized by a word—*jingo*— that had been popular-ized in the English vocabulary in 1878 by a London music hall ditty composed by G. W. Hunt. Written during the Crimean War in refer-ence to the opposing British and Russian designs on the Turkish port of Constantinople, the song contained this bit of bravado:

> We don't want to fight yet by Jingo!
>   if we do
> We've got the ships, we've got the men,
>   and got the money too.

Originally a euphemism for "Jesus" or "God," *jingo* had by 1897 in America come to mean a bellicose patriot or warmonger. Theodore Roosevelt had accepted the label *jingo* unabashedly and with no apologies.

Such an attitude was nothing new to Roosevelt. In 1886 when newspapers were filled with predictions of war with Mexico, he had offered to organize a cavalry battalion from the harum-scarum cow-boys of his ranch in the Dakota territory. That July 4 he told an audience in the West that he hoped to see a day "when not a foot of American soil will be held by any European power."

In 1894 he had been among the first to call for Hawaiian annexa-tion and endorsed the building of an ocean-linking canal through Nicaragua, whether the Nicaraguans agreed or not. Speaking to the National Republican Club on May 28, 1895, he had called for a navy "that will sustain the honor of the American flag [and see] the Monroe Doctrine upheld in its entirety."

Writing on the subject of the Monroe Doctrine in *The Bachelor of Arts* in March 1896, he declared, "The United States ought not to permit any great military powers, which have no foothold on this continent, to establish such a foothold; nor should they permit any aggrandizement of those who already have possessions on the conti-nent. Every true patriot, every man of statesmanlike habit, should look forward to the day when not a single European power will hold a foot of American soil."

When Great Britain sought to settle a boundary dispute with Venezuela without considering the interests of the United States, he all but welcomed a war. "American cities may be bombarded," he said, but "we will settle the Venezuelan question in Canada. Canada will surely be conquered, and once wrested from England it would never be restored."

During a brief crisis involving the treatment of U.S. sailors by Chile, he had been teased by his wife and friends about his dream of valiantly leading a cavalry charge. They had called him "Theodore the Chilean Volunteer."

At the height of the Venezuelan crisis, he wrote to Henry Cabot Lodge on December 27, 1895, "This country needs a war." But he added, forlornly and angrily, that the "bankers, brokers and anglomaniacs generally" appeared to favor "peace at any price." In expanding on these feelings of animus toward individuals who put profit and personal interest ahead of patriotism, Roosevelt later wrote in his autobiography, "These men were not weak men, but they permitted themselves to grow shortsighted and selfish; and while many of them down at the bottom possessed the fundamental virtues, including the fighting virtues, others were purely of the glorified huckster or glorified pawnbroker type—which when developed to the exclusion of everything else makes about as poor a national type as the world has seen. This unadulterated huckster or pawnbroker type is rarely keenly sympathetic in matters of social and industrial justice, and is usually physically timid and likes to cover an unworthy fear of the most just war under high-sounding names."

Hand in hand with these men, he went on, was "the large mollycoddle vote—the people who are soft physically and morally, or who have a twist in them which makes them acidly cantankerous and unpleasant as long as they can be so with safety to their bodies."

He believed all these elements taken together formed a body of public opinion so important during the decades since the Civil War as to put a stop to any serious effort to keep the nation in a condition of military preparedness. A victim of that shortsighted view, he believed in June 1897, had been the U. S. Navy. Consequently, the theme he had chosen for his speech to the Naval War College graduating class was inspired by America's first president.

"To be prepared for war," George Washington had advised, "is the most effectual means to promote peace."

Roosevelt entitled his war college address "Washington's Forgotten Maxim."

More than sixteen years had gone by since Roosevelt's 1881 debut as a speaker in his freshman year as a lawmaker in Albany when a veteran of the legislature observed that he had appeared to speak with some difficulty, "as if he had an impediment in his speech." The delivery had been marked by moments of breathlessness that seemed to convey nervousness. But this may have been due to Roosevelt's chronic asthma. One newspaper reporter had found the quality of the young newcomer's voice to be like "a Dundreary drawl." Another declared Roosevelt the possessor of "a wealth of mouth."

The mouth was big and wide and dominated by a set of teeth so remarkable in their appearance that they and the nose glasses he wore for his acute nearsightedness were to become hallmarks of the Roosevelt image and a favorite of newspaper and magazine political cartoonists. Perhaps the best description of the teeth had been written in the first few days of Roosevelt's term as president of the New York Board of Police Commissioners. Observed while Roosevelt questioned errant cops at departmental trials, his teeth were immortalized in the *New York World* as "exceptionally white and almost as big as a colt's."

"They are broad teeth, they form a perfectly straight line," the article stated. "The lower teeth look like a row of dominoes. They do not lap over or under each other, as most teeth do, but come together evenly." The Roosevelt voice, according to the *World,* was "rasping."

In addition, Roosevelt had a habit while speaking of punctuating his remarks with one hand curled into a fist, which he pounded into the palm of the other. His face frequently reddened with excitement.

Since his first speech in the New York Assembly he had delivered countless addresses in the legislature, to scores of civic groups, and all over New York City as a candidate in his own right during the 1886 mayoral election and on behalf of the Republican slate when he was not on the ballot. He had been a much-sought-after speaker in Washington during his service on the Civil Service Commission. In the contest for president of the United States in 1896, he had barnstormed the West on behalf of McKinley, a tireless effort which had been rewarded by McKinley's appointing Roosevelt to the post that had brought him to the command of the fleet and to the podium at the Naval War College.

That the staff and class eagerly anticipated an extraordinary event is without doubt. Such was the Roosevelt reputation as an orator and colorful character that wherever he spoke there were no empty seats. The naval officers could not have expected, however, that they were about to hear Roosevelt enunciate for them and for the nation the culmination of years of thinking on the role of the United States in the world. They would hear all the principal ideas on America's greatness that were to be the bedrock of Roosevelt's political philosophy. And they would witness Roosevelt open a guidebook to America's international relations, not only for the immediate future of the Naval War College class of '97, but for the next century as well.

The writer of history began with history.

Noting that a century had passed since Washington had written his maxim, Roosevelt chided the nation for paying "lip-loyalty" to advice that "has never sunk deep in our hearts." History proved, he continued, that "no nation can hold its place in the world or can do any work really worth doing unless it stands ready to guard its rights with an armed hand. That orderly liberty which is both the foundation and the capstone of our civilization can be gained and kept only by men who are willing to fight for an ideal; who hold high the love of honor, love of faith, love of flag, and love of country."

He was confident that he did not have to spell out for his audience the challenges posed to the United States by the Hawaiian annexation question and by the threats and insults to the Monroe Doctrine in the form of British interference in Venezuela, Spanish domination of Cuba, and powerful European navies capable of stirring trouble in American waters. Rather, he dwelt on the mistakes of the past and the perils of repeating them.

"It has always been true," he said, "and in this age it is more than ever true, that it is too late to prepare for war when the time of peace has passed."

To those who would bargain he warned, "Diplomacy is utterly useless where there is no force behind it; the diplomat is the servant, not the master, of the soldier."

Had Thomas Jefferson built a powerful American fleet rather than relying on small defensive gunboats to protect the coast, said Roosevelt, the War of 1812 might have been avoided. Rather than maintain a ready defense, he continued, subsequent American leaders had permitted the navy to languish to the point that "we entered the

Civil War with captains seventy years old." Of these persons he said, "There are some *doctrinaires* whose eyes are so firmly fixed on the golden vision of universal peace that they cannot see the grim facts of real life until they stumble over them, to their own hurt, and, what is much worse, to the possible undoing of their fellows. There are some educated men in whom education merely serves to soften the fibre and to eliminate the higher, sterner qualities which tell for national greatness; and these men prate about love for mankind, or for another country, as being in some hidden way a substitute for love of their own country."

The lesson in this was evident. "We must therefore make up our minds once and for all to the fact that it is too late to make ready for war when the fight had once begun. The preparation must come before that."

Therefore, he continued, it logically followed that in confronting America's present international challenges, there must be adequate preparation for conflict and that "this preparation must take the shape of an efficient fighting Navy."

The fleet was key because he envisioned no threat from land armies. "The enemies we have to face will come from over sea; they may come from Europe, or they may come from Asia; but this generation has been forced to see that they move even faster in the oldest East. Our interests are as great in the Pacific as in the Atlantic, in the Hawaiian Islands as in the West Indies. Merely for the protection of our own shores we need a great Navy; and what is more, we need it to protect our interests in the islands from which it is possible to command our shores and to protect our commerce on high seas."

Asserting "this nation cannot stand still if it is to retain its self-respect," he asked "that the work of upbuilding the Navy, and of putting the United States where it should be among maritime powers, go forward without a break. We ask this not in the interest of war, but in the interest of peace. No nation should ever wage a war wantonly; but no nation should ever avoid it at the cost of the loss of national honor."

In closing, he said, "We ask for a great Navy, we ask for an armament fit for the nation's needs, not primarily to fight, but to avert fighting. Preparedness deters the foe, and maintains right by the show of ready might without the use of violence. Peace, like freedom, is not a gift that tarries long in the hands of cowards, or of those too feeble or too short-sighted to deserve it; and we ask to be given the means to insure that honorable peace which alone is worth having."

Had the remarks gone no farther than the auditorium in Newport, Roosevelt would have simply preached to the converted. But such was the interest of the American press that the speech was carried in full by the country's major newspapers from coast to coast. The New York *Sun* deemed it "a manly, patriotic, intelligent and convincing appeal to American sentiment in behalf of the national honor, and for the preservation of the national strength by means requisite self-defense and vigorous aggressive resistance to efforts to interfere with our progress and national dominion." Calling it a "fine address," the *Herald* of New York reported it as a speech "filled with a flow of splendid patriotism, from its opening sentence to its close, and its careful reading can scarcely fail to inspire the youth of America with the same lofty spirit of devotion to our country's honor, glory and prosperity that actuated its utterance by the speaker." In far-off Louisiana, the *New Orleans Times Picayune* found in it "the sentiments of the great majority of thinking people." Even *Harper's Weekly*, hardly a supporter of expansionism, deemed the speech "very eloquent and forcible."

That veteran Roosevelt-watcher, the *Washington Post,* which had once wondered if Roosevelt would ever find a suitable role, now exclaimed, "Well done, nobly spoken! Theodore Roosevelt, you have found your proper place at last—all hail!"

Privately, the president of the United States said to a longtime Roosevelt friend and political ally, Lemuel Quigg, "I suspect that Roosevelt is right." The only difference between the assistant secretary of the navy and himself, said William McKinley, "is that mine is the greater responsibility."

Part I

By Jingo

Chapter 1

"Theodore is too pugnacious."

Across the Atlantic Ocean on the day Roosevelt delivered his speech at the Naval War College, a close friend with similar views was taking part in a royal celebration with other diplomats assigned to the most important post in the world. Having been appointed by President McKinley to be U. S. ambassador to the Court of Saint James in London, John Hay found himself at the heart of a worldwide empire on which, the British bragged, the sun never set. In June 1897 few subjects of that realm, which stretched from England to India, had ever known any ruler but the queen who had been on the British throne for sixty years and had given her name to an era. To mark this unique milestone, a diamond jubilee had been planned to celebrate not only the longevity of Victoria as monarch but the majesty and power of the empire she ruled. The theme of jubilee week festivities, beginning June 22, 1897, was to be nothing less than the unity, magnitude, and splendor of the British Empire.

Taking his place in the crowd of diplomats to observe the opening procession, Hay watched fifty thousand troops, including contingents from more than thirty of Victoria's colonies, and eleven colonial prime ministers passing in review in grand state coaches, each with its own honor guard. Then came the queen herself, followed by an equestrian grouping of forty-two European princes. By the time the last of the soldiers in the seven-mile-long parade had marched past, there was no doubt in the mind of any onlooker of Britain's military power. The following Sunday provided the opportunity for a display of the might of the Royal Navy. At Spithead, the Admiralty proudly turned out 170 warships while making it clear to the world's diplomats that these ships represented only a portion of a fleet that leant credence to the boast that "Britannia rules the waves."

In providing reports of the jubilee for its readers, the Chicago *Record* described the martial and naval demonstration as "the most imposing outward display of the political, social and military factors of modern civilization which the world has yet witnessed."

"The point underlying all this pageantry was clear enough to the thoughtful observer," wrote David Healy in his 1970 book, *U.S. Expansionism: The Imperialist Urge in the 1890s.* "The world was still a world of empires, and the British Empire was still incomparably the largest and most imposing. All of the great powers, however, had colonial possessions and were ambitious for more; in all the world the United States now seemed the most important exception to the prevalence of national land-hunger."

Having watched this flaunting of the benefits of empire and acutely aware that the vast nation he represented possessed no colonies, John Hay wrote wistfully to President McKinley, "It is a pity we have so many men among us who do not and who cannot believe in the American people and in their glorious destiny. . . . The greatest destiny the world ever knew is ours."

In holding this view of America's manifest destiny, Hay had found a stalwart ally in Theodore Roosevelt. Two weeks before the big parade in London, Roosevelt had written to Hay, "By the way, don't let them bluff you out of the word 'American.' I don't [think] anything better has been done than your calling yourself the American Ambassador and using the word American instead of United States. It is good all through."

Concerning Hay, Roosevelt wrote in his autobiography that he was "one of the most delightful of companions, one of the most charming of all men of cultivation and action."

Twenty years older than Roosevelt (born October 8, 1838, in Salem, Indiana), Hay graduated from Brown University (1856) and entered his uncle's law firm in Springfield, Illinois, in 1859. There he met another Illinois lawyer, Abraham Lincoln, for whom he became assistant private secretary in 1861. Following the assassination of Lincoln in 1865, he served as first secretary of the American legation at Paris (1865–67), chargé d'affaires at Vienna (1867–68), and first secretary at Madrid (1868–70). During the administration of Rutherford B. Hayes, he was assistant secretary of state. Like Roosevelt, he enjoyed the friendship of Henry Cabot Lodge and shared the views of Lodge and the other expansionists who had gathered around Theo-

dore Roosevelt during Roosevelt's years in Washington with the Civil
Service Commission (1887–95).

A year after he had quit the commission to become president of
the New York Board of Police Commissioners, Roosevelt confessed
that he was experiencing regret over leaving Washington. In a letter
to his sister Anna, he said he was "so absorbed by my own special
work and its ramifications that I have time to keep very little in touch
with anything outside my own duties. I see but little of the life of the
great world; I am but little in touch with national politics."

At the time Roosevelt was embroiled in a nasty public dispute
with fellow police commissioner Andrew Parker over the running of
the department. He also felt stymied by the opposition of "an unscru-
pulous scoundrel as Comptroller," the hostility of Democrats and the
"almost equal hostility of the Republican machine," "a hostile legislature," and "a bitterly antagonistic press." He complained that the
work of the police board had "nothing of the purple in it." A Republican victory in the 1896 presidential election, he hoped, might provide
a way out of his frustrating situation.

Despite his protestation that he was out of touch, he had found
time in 1896 to have dinner with Captain Mahan to talk about naval
affairs, criticize the secretary of the navy's report on the status of the
fleet, visit and inspect the warships *Indiana* and *Montgomery,* and
read a two-volume history of modern ironclads and Lord Brassey's
Naval Annual, noting in a letter to his sister Anna's new husband,
Lieutenant Commander William Sheffield Cowles, that Brassey had
deemed "our battleships inferior to the British." He also found the
time to contribute his lengthy essay "The Monroe Doctrine" to *The
Bachelor of Arts,* published in March, declaring in the opening sentence that "the Monroe Doctrine should not be considered from any
purely academic standpoint, but as a broad, general principle of living
policy."

Describing those who "take the wrong side, that is, the anti-
American side," of the Monroe Doctrine as "too short-sighted or too
unimaginative to realize the hurt to the nation that would be caused
by the adoption of their views," he dismissed such persons as those
"who undervalue the great fighting qualities, without which no nation
can ever rise to the first rank."

Analyzing Roosevelt's pugnaciousness as evidenced in such statements and in numerous combative incidents in his life, biographer

William Henry Harbaugh wrote in *Power and Responsibility: The Life and Times of Theodore Roosevelt,* "It is difficult and probably impossible to square many of Roosevelt's statements on war with Roosevelt the moral man. Doubtless, as many students of Roosevelt's life have concluded, his aggressiveness derived in some part from his boyhood struggle against illness. It is likely, however, that the experience of his youth did more than determine the degree of his belligerence, for thousands of men of divergent psychological makeup subscribed to the same general theories." Had Roosevelt been born in a later era, Harbaugh surmised, he might have vented his primordial instincts on the athletic field. As it was, he thought of war in terms of man-to-man combat, dashing cavalry charges, and brilliant tactical maneuvers.

Ironically, the Republican nominee for president of the United States in 1896, William McKinley—about whom Roosevelt confessed feeling "very nervous" because he utterly distrusted McKinley's firmness—was a veteran of the Civil War, which had provided the sickly boy Teedie with his passion for fighting ships and idealistic visions of heroic men bearing arms out of pure patriotism. But Roosevelt's misgivings concerning McKinley's ability to hold up in a crisis, whether "a soft money craze, a gigantic labor riot, or danger of foreign conflict," paled in comparison to his loathing of McKinley's Democratic opponent. In William Jennings Bryan, Roosevelt saw a "Witches' Sabbath" whose election would spell national ruin. Consequently, he was eager to do all he could to help McKinley win the election—and possibly get himself back to Washington.

Should Roosevelt's assistance prompt McKinley to reward him with a post in the new government, Roosevelt had one in mind. But in broaching the subject he chose to use an intermediary who possessed a unique access to McKinley—Maria Longworth Storer, wife of Bellamy Storer. Invited to spend the first weekend in August at Sagamore Hill, Roosevelt's home in Oyster Bay, New York, Maria Storer looked forward to visiting the man with whom she had become acquainted during his years in the nation's capital. Herself a familiar figure in Washington, Storer had employed her and her husband's wealth by lobbying on behalf of the Roman Catholic Church. Some of that money (ten thousand dollars) had gone to William McKinley in 1893 in the form of a loan when McKinley was in possibly ruinous financial straits.

Storer found Roosevelt charming with his winning, childlike spontaneity and rapier wit coupled with a determination to do right; she was delighted that one "never knew what he would say next." And she thought his penchant for vituperation was "extremely amusing."

All these traits proved to be in full bloom at Sagamore Hill as Roosevelt discussed his woes at police headquarters and when he turned to the subject of the political future of the country in general and the McKinley candidacy in particular. Then, with that boyish spontaneity that so enchanted his guest, he suggested they go out for one of his favorite Sagamore Hill pastimes, rowboating on Oyster Bay.

As he worked the oars, he returned to the subject of the disappointments and frustrations of the police commissionership, couching his feelings in dark tones of a future in which he saw himself as an unpopular politician destined to become a "melancholy spectacle" of "an idle father" writing books that did not sell. A secure future, he suggested, might lie in his return to Washington.

"There is one thing I would like to have," he said. "But there is no chance of my getting it. McKinley will never give it to me. I should like to be assistant secretary of the navy."

After a moment of thought as the rowboat drifted and Roosevelt gazed at her hopefully, Storer replied that she was sure "something could be arranged."

Presently, as summer waned and the election campaign began in earnest, McKinley announced that he had no intention of going out to the hustings himself, but would conduct his fight for the presidency from the front porch of his house in Canton, Ohio. Instead, an army of surrogate campaigners would fan out across the nation on his behalf under the guidance of his campaign manager, Mark Hanna. A precursor of twentieth-century campaign blitzes and fueled by the fattest war chest in history to that date, it was an effort that prompted Theodore Roosevelt to gripe to friends that McKinley was being sold "as if he were a patent medicine."

This disdain notwithstanding, Roosevelt happily left behind the internecine warring of the New York City Police Board to accept an invitation from Hanna to take to the hustings himself.

After beginning with campaign speeches in New York State and in the city whose political discourses he had come to dominate as police commissioner, he took the western states by storm, prompting the *Chicago Tribune* to exclaim of Roosevelt's appearance, "In many respects it was the most remarkable political gathering of the campaign in this city." Then it was on to Michigan, where he followed

Bryan's campaign train and even found himself among the audience (unrecognized) at one of the Boy Orator of the Platte's whistle stops. Late in October he dashed across New York, New Jersey, Delaware, and Maryland before finishing his campaigning on the eve of an election he described as "the greatest crisis in our national fate, save only the Civil War."

Handily elected with a plurality of 600,000 votes, McKinley soon found himself intensely courted for a job for Roosevelt, though the courting was done by intermediaries. In a meeting with Maria Storer he listened respectfully to her cajolings that Roosevelt be named assistant secretary of the navy, only to reply, "I want peace. I am afraid your friend Theodore is too pugnacious."

The president expressed the same misgivings to Henry Cabot Lodge. After numerous appeals to McKinley, Lodge wrote to Roosevelt that "the only, absolutely the only thing I can hear averse, is that there is a fear that you will want to fight somebody at once."

The plain fact was that Theodore Roosevelt's reputation for combativeness had left McKinley feeling nervous. To prove his point, the president had only to refer to the recent unbecoming squabble between Roosevelt and Andrew Parker. Even worse, in the midst of this unfortunate struggle, with the work of reforming the police department stalled, Roosevelt had engaged in an unseemly public display with the city comptroller, Ashbel Fitch. It had come to a head in the office of Mayor William L. Strong. A debate over the propriety of using city funds to finance the undercover work of plainclothes detectives had taken an ugly turn.

"I know you are a fighter," Fitch taunted Roosevelt. "You have a great reputation in that line."

"Well, you are not a fighter," Roosevelt shot back. "You would run away from a fight. If you want to fight in this matter, I can give you all you are looking for."

"Oh come on," Fitch answered with a dismissive gesture. "I don't want to fight with you."

"I know you won't fight," Roosevelt snapped, leaning across the table separating them. "You would run away."

"I would never run away from you," retorted Fitch, a man with an earned reputation as an accomplished swordsman and duelist. "What shall it be, pistols or—"

Roosevelt bolted to his feet. "Pistols or anything else!"

At this portentous moment, according to the account in the *World,* the mayor blurted, "Gentlemen, gentlemen, I warn you right now that if this thing goes on, I shall call the police and have you both arrested."

Like most others in the United States, William McKinley was keenly aware that the life story of Theodore Roosevelt was crowded with such colorfully bellicose anecdotes.

One yarn involved Roosevelt's debut in 1881 as a member of the New York Assembly. Learning that some elders of the legislature were plotting a special sort of welcome for him, the freshman had tracked down the alleged leader of the pack, an ox-like saloon keeper, "Big John" McManus. "Look here," Roosevelt demanded, "I understand you fellows want to toss me in a blanket. Am I right?"

McManus replied challengingly, "Well, what if you are?"

Roosevelt answered, "Just this. I serve notice now that if you try anything like that I'll fight. I'll bite, kick, and do anything that my teeth, fists, and feet can do."

The blanket party never happened.

With the blossoming of Roosevelt's reputation as an up-and-coming political figure, newspaper and magazine writers became fascinated by the true story of a sickly youth—so sickly that doubts were cast upon his chances for attaining adulthood—who had now grown so formidable. With relish, the writers unearthed a pivotal anecdote involving the weak and bookish thirteen year old and his father.

"Theodore, you have the mind, but you haven't the body to succeed," said the concerned parent. "Without the help of the body, the mind cannot go as far as it should. You must make your body. It is hard drudgery to make one's body, but I know you will do it."

The youth replied, "I will."

Seven years later at Harvard, Owen Wister walked into a gymnasium that rose like a gas tank from a pie slice of ground between three streets on the yard side of Memorial Hall. The Harvard Athletic Association was holding its spring boxing meet there. Wister settled down to watch a match between W. W. Coolidge, class of '79, at 133¼ pounds, and Theodore Roosevelt, class of '80, at 135. Displaying "more coolness and skill than his opponent," according to the *Harvard Advocate,* Roosevelt won, thus qualifying him for the championship bout with C. S. Hanks, class of '79, also weighing 133¼.

From his ringside position on the gymnasium floor, Wister saw what he later described in his memoirs as a "prophetic flash of the

Roosevelt that was to come." Time had been called by the referee. Roosevelt dropped his guard, and Hanks landed a heavy blow on the nose, bloodying it.

"Loud hoots and hisses from gallery and floor were sent up," Wister recalled, "whereat Roosevelt's arm was instantly flung out to command silence, while his alert and slender figure stood quiet."

"It's all right," Roosevelt shouted to the crowd. "He didn't hear the time-keeper." With bleeding nose he crossed the ring and shook hands with Hanks.

Conceding that Hanks was "the better all through," Roosevelt lost in a bout that the *Advocate* called "a spirited contest." The *New York Times* saw the fight as "almost professional" but noted that Hanks "punished Roosevelt severely."

Boxing remained a favorite diversion for Roosevelt. He was just as enthusiastic in recommending it to others. As police commissioner he backed the use of city funds to promote boxing as a means of keeping boys and young men off the streets and away from the clutches of criminality. He urged boxing as part of the program of the Young Men's Christian Association (YMCA). Only later as governor of New York did he reluctantly feel "obliged to come to the conclusion that the prize ring had become hopelessly debased and demoralized." He signed a law putting a stop to professional boxing for money. Nonetheless, he wrote in his autobiography that "the men who take part in these fights are hard as nails, and it is not worthwhile to feel sentimental about their receiving punishment which as a matter of fact they do not mind. Of course the men who look on ought to be able to stand up with the gloves, or without them, themselves; I have scant use for the type of sportsmanship which consists merely in looking on at the feats of someone else."

Tales of Roosevelt's personal toughness also abounded in his life after Harvard and after his two terms in the New York Assembly. One of the first newspaper accounts of Roosevelt as New York's police commissioner had noted, "Under his right ear he has a long scar. It is the opinion of all the policemen who have talked to him that he got that scar fighting an Indian out West. It is also their opinion that the Indian is dead."

Although McKinley could find no evidence that Roosevelt ever hurt an Indian, or anyone else, during his time in the Dakota territory, there was no lack of stories of his personal courage amidst the hardy cowboys. Among those who could swear to Roosevelt's unwillingness to back down from a fight had been a local tough named Jake Maunders. Warned that this man had been "talking it around that he's going to kill you," Roosevelt said quietly, "Is that so?" and went to fetch his horse.

Confronting Maunders at his shack, Roosevelt announced, "I hear you want to shoot me. I came over to find out why."

Astonished and evidently impressed, Maunders blurted, "Why, Mr. Rosenfelder, that's a mistake. I never said nothing of the sort."

Also contained in the lore of Theodore Roosevelt out West was his stint as a deputy sheriff leading a posse on the trail of Redhead Finnegan's gang of thieves. Tracking them through a blizzard, Roosevelt and his party located their quarry's camp beside an ice-clogged river on April 1, 1886. As they bounded from the underbrush, guns drawn, and took the thieves by surprise, only Redhead Finnegan hesitated at the command to drop their guns. But as Roosevelt stepped forward, covering Finnegan's chest "so as to avoid overshooting," Finnegan "saw that he had no show," cursed Roosevelt, let his rifle drop into the snow, and thrust up his arms in surrender. Although thrilled and excited by the capture, Roosevelt conceded, "There is very little amusement in combining the functions of a sheriff and those of the Arctic explorer."

Although these episodes of physical bravado had enhanced Roosevelt's reputation after having been described dotingly by a large and growing segment of the press, William McKinley still worried about Roosevelt's "wealth of mouth," which its owner unleashed in an equally pugnacious manner on the subject of the gravest issues confronting the man just elected the twenty-fifth president of the United States.

Fifteen years older than Roosevelt, McKinley had been born and raised in Ohio. The son of ironmaker William McKinley and Nancy Allison, he had attended school in Poland, Ohio, and Allegheny College in Meadville, Pennsylvania. Enlisting in the 23rd Ohio, he had fought in the Civil War while Teedie Roosevelt was a toddler. Rising to the rank of captain, he had ended the war as a brevet major and returned to civilian life to study law and open a practice in Canton, Ohio, in 1867. Attracted to politics, he won election to Congress, serving in the House of Representatives from 1877 to 1883 and again from 1885 to 1891. Defeated for reelection in 1890, he returned to Ohio to win election as governor in 1892.

A man of his time, he shared the widely held view that expanding the opportunities for individual material security was the way to promote social welfare. He thus backed Republican efforts to underwrite and regulate an economy in which all citizens might succeed by their talents. While strongly in favor of protective tariffs, he did not embrace the expansionist movement that so enthused Theodore Roosevelt and his coterie of like-minded friends, such as Lodge, Mahan, and Hay, who believed they had found a champion for their cause in Roosevelt.

Although Roosevelt considered the placid, gentlemanly, even courtly McKinley "an upright and honorable man, of very considerable ability and good record as a soldier and in Congress," he privately expressed, as noted earlier, his apprehension that unless McKinley were well backed, "I should feel rather uneasy about him in a serious crisis."

As Republicans met in convention in St. Louis in June 1896, Roosevelt's preference for the presidential nomination was Thomas B. Reed, Speaker of the House of Representatives. Regarding McKinley, he wrote his sister Anna that he felt "nervous" that the man "whose firmness I utterly distrust, will be nominated, and this . . . I much regret."

But McKinley had been nominated and gone on to be elected, a victory that owed much to Roosevelt's campaigning. Yet as he heard implorings for a reward to Roosevelt in the form of the navy post, McKinley felt a nagging anxiety that Roosevelt, if in a position to directly command naval operations, might spell the sort of trouble the president-elect hoped to avoid: war.

It seemed that everyone who had anything to write or say on the subject of Theodore Roosevelt invoked such manly adjectives as *robust, strenuous, active, vigorous,* and the one that McKinley himself voiced with alarm, *pugnacious.*

At long last, yielding to the pressure on Roosevelt's behalf, the president-elect said to Lodge, rather anxiously, "I hope he has no preconceived plans which he would wish to drive through the moment he got in."

Lodge confidently replied that McKinley "need not give himself the slightest uneasiness on that score."

Chapter 2

Too Little Instead of Too Much

On March 4, 1897, William McKinley became the twenty-fifth president of the United States. A month and a day later, Henry Cabot Lodge telegraphed to Sagamore Hill that the nomination of Roosevelt to be assistant secretary of the navy was to be sent to the Senate the next day. A delighted Roosevelt wired back that "Sinbad had evidently landed the old man of the sea." Three days later the Senate voted its consent.

Exultant to be going back to Washington and onto a national stage, and relieved to be escaping the frustrations of the Mulberry Street police headquarters, Roosevelt's happy preparations were dimmed by the realization that he would not be taking his family with him immediately. His wife, Edith, was pregnant and would have to remain at Sagamore Hill, as would their sons Theodore, Kermit, and Archibald and their daughter Ethel. Roosevelt's oldest offspring, Alice Lee, would remain as well; she had been born to his first wife, Alice, who had died a few days after giving birth to her in 1884.

Until Edith and the children were able to join him in the capital, Roosevelt would be a guest at 1765 Massachusetts Avenue, the spacious home of his friend, chief ally, and mentor, Henry Cabot Lodge. Eight years Roosevelt's senior, Lodge was also a person of both letters and politics. Before election to Congress from the Lynn-Nahant District of Massachusetts, he had been editor of the *North American Review* and author of biographies of George Washington, Daniel Webster, Alexander Hamilton, and other American greats. He had taught history at Harvard. In 1897 he was junior senator from Massachusetts and a power in the Republican Party. He and Roosevelt had

become close friends in 1884 as they joined forces to block (unsuccess-
fully) the nomination of James G. Blaine for president .

Known to his intimates as "Cabot," Lodge and his vivacious wife,
Nannie, had become the locus of Washington's social life. An invitation to one of their salons meant sharing a pleasant afternoon with
persons of politics, wealth, and letters, including Rudyard Kipling,
William Dean Howells, Charles Bonaparte, Henry Adams, or his
brother Brooks. Another frequent guest was John Hay, who referred
to this assemblage as the Pleasant Gang.

To another friend, Henry White, Roosevelt wrote that he was having "a delightful time" staying in the Lodge residence, then went on
to express amusement over a recent article in the London *Times* containing "a wail over my supposed jingoism." He railed, "I wish to
Heaven we were more jingo about Cuba and Hawaii! The trouble with
our nation is that we incline to fall into mere animal sloth and ease,
and tend to venture too little instead of too much."

These views were shared by all the members of the Pleasant
Gang. Gathered in the Lodge residence, they spoke of America's new
manifest destiny, defined by Roosevelt as "not only the extension of
American influence and power, [but] the extension of liberty and order, and the bringing by gigantic strides of the day when peace shall
come to the whole earth." As discussed, these ideas had been central
to Alfred Thayer Mahan's book on the influence of sea power upon
history, in which he extrapolated that the United States could become
a force in the world only through the creation of a mighty navy.
"Whether they will or not," Mahan had written, "Americans must now
begin to look outward."

No more outward-looking group could be found in Washington
than the Pleasant Gang. In *The Spanish War: An American Epic—
1898,* G. J. A. O'Toole found this group sharing the attitudes of the
Northeastern establishment. "In spirit they stood midway between
London and Chicago, viewing with equal disdain the decadence of the
Old World and the vigorous greed of the nouveau riche of the Midwest." Although Roosevelt's carefully tailored suit, his precise enun-
ciation, and his upper-class nasalization that echoed the Harvard
Quad might have misled the casual observer into classifying him as
another of these wordy salonists, O'Toole recorded that people "better
acquainted with the thirty-eight-year-old aristocrat knew him to be
as much a man of action as of words, a practicing advocate of the

strenuous life, and someone not content merely to write history but resolved to make it as well."

Among the most fascinating of this gang of outward-lookers was forty-seven-year-old Brooks Adams. He was also a Harvard man, and like Roosevelt and Lodge he had been a member of the exclusive Porcelain Club. Having left the practice of law fifteen years earlier to devote himself to the study of history, he was the author of two books: *The Emancipation of Massachusetts* and *The Law of Civilization and Decay*.

In the latter, Adams had asserted that mankind had progressed through the accumulation and concentration of wealth and that the early stages of this development were marked by a certain predominant type of human being, "the Imaginative Man," typified by the soldier and the artist. Later came "the Economic Man," whose devotion to industry, trade, and capital had brought in an age of greed.

Looking at the America of an age already being called "gilded," Roosevelt found a nation controlled by examples of Adams's Economic Man, individuals who counted business and commercial success above national honor and manliness. In a review of the book for *The Forum*, Roosevelt wrote, "It certainly is extraordinary that just at this time there seems to be a gradual failure of vitality in the qualities, whatever they may be that make men fight well."

Fascinated with Brooks Adams, Roosevelt frequently left his office in the Navy Department to stroll across Pennsylvania Avenue and through Lafayette Park to lunch with him at the massive four-story red-brick Romanesque home of Henry Adams, who was traveling at the time in Europe. On many occasions the two men were joined by Lodge for spirited discussions and debates. Had he not been sent to England as American ambassador to the Court of Saint James, a neighbor of the Adamses, John Hay, might have dropped in as well.

When not taking midday repast with Brooks Adams, Roosevelt found convivial conversation at the Metropolitan Club among sympathetic senators, members of the House of Representatives, army and navy officers, journalists, authors, lawyers, and scientists. To those who were not able to lunch or dine with him while he devoured his favorite dish, double lamb chops, he wrote letters.

Joseph Bucklin Bishop, a journalist, friend of Roosevelt's, and editor of a collection of his letters, wrote that these particular letters show "Roosevelt was endowed, in a really marvelous degree, with the gift of vision his correspondence indubitably shows. He saw clearly what men would do because he had accurate knowledge of and calm judgment upon what men had done. He saw clearly into the motives and actions of men and nations because he had mastered their history and could gauge their conduct in the future by that past. He had read human history, not for the purpose of strengthening his prejudices, but of informing his mind, and from fullness of mind and matured conviction he spoke."

Among these initial letters from the Navy Department none was as illuminating as one to Mahan dated May 3, 1897. It began with a caveat that would become familiar to his correspondents: "This letter must, of course, be considered as entirely confidential."

Noting that because of his position he was obligated to "merely [carry] out the policy of the Secretary and the President" regarding caution in the matters of annexing Hawaii and pressuring Spanish Cuba, Roosevelt hastened to record that if he had his way "we would annex those islands [Hawaii] tomorrow. If that is impossible, I would establish a protectorate over them." In addition, he continued in the lengthy letter, "I believe we should build the Nicaraguan canal at once, and in the meantime that we should build a dozen new battleships, half of them on the Pacific Coast; and these battleships should have a large coal capacity and a consequent increased radius of action. I am fully alive to the danger from Japan."

Turning his attention to the Atlantic, he saw "big problems" in the West Indies. "Until we definitely turn Spain out of those islands (and if I had my way it would be done tomorrow), we will always be menaced by trouble there. We should acquire the Danish Islands, and by turning Spain out should serve notice that no strong European power, and especially Germany, should be allowed to gain a foothold by supplanting some weak European power."

Regarding England, Roosevelt held to his previous view that in any conflict with the British, Canada would fall "hostage for her good behavior."

Returning to the Hawaiian question, he informed Mahan that they appeared to have an ally in the secretary of the navy, John D. Long. "He believes we should take the islands, and I have just been preparing some memoranda for him to use at the Cabinet meeting tomorrow," he wrote, adding, "I have been pressing upon the Secretary, and through him on the President, that we ought to act now without delay, before Japan gets her two battleships which are now ready for delivery to her in England. With Hawaii once in our hands most of the danger of friction with Japan would disappear. The Secretary also believes in building the Nicaraguan canal as a military measure, although I don't know that he is as decided on this point as you and I are."

To Cecil Spring Rice, an engaging young British diplomat who had served as best man when Roosevelt married Edith Carow in London, he wrote, "My chief, Secretary Long, is a perfect dear."

Nineteen years Roosevelt's senior, John D. Long had been governor of Massachusetts and a member of Congress. He had brought to Washington the gentlemanly, conservative caution of a New Englander. In appearance (plump, white-haired) and manner (soft-spoken and slow-gaited, due to corn-troubled feet) he was the opposite of the bombastic Roosevelt. Steady and of a judicial temperament, he shared Roosevelt's love of books, although his chief literary works to date had been a translation of the *Aeneid* and a volume of after-dinner speeches. Short but with broad shoulders and a large head, he was noted for arriving early at the office, with a green bag stuffed with documents and papers. Despite hailing from the rich maritime culture of the Northeast, he had no interest in the technical intricacies that fascinated the number-two administrator in the Navy Department. Speak to Long about dry docks, gun turrets, blueprint specifications, or the frailty of torpedo boats, and his eyes glazed with boredom.

Regarding the assistant secretary's obvious relish for the details of running the navy, Long allowed, "What is the need of my making a dropsical tub of any lobe of my brain when I have right at hand a man possessed with more knowledge than I could acquire?" Following his first meeting with Roosevelt, he noted in his diary, "Best man for the job."

This opinion was embraced by most of the capital press corps, best exemplified by the correspondent for the *Chicago Times-Herald,* who wrote that nearly everybody in Washington was glad that Roosevelt was back. He was ensconced in the ornately Victorian edifice immediately west of the White House (then called the President's House or the Executive Mansion) in a wedding-cake-like building containing the Departments of State, War, and Navy. Occupying the east wing, the latter was decorated with magnificent models of fighting ships, portraits of naval heroes, and vivid paintings of historic sea battles.

A third-floor library contained more than twenty-five thousand volumes. Its windows and those of Roosevelt's office afforded a splendid vantage of the white-painted walls of the Executive Mansion.

To find an appropriate desk for himself, Roosevelt descended to the basement to retrieve a massive mahogany piece splendidly adorned with carvings of monitors and other naval motifs. The desk had been used by another of his Civil War heroes, Gustavus Fox, who had been President Abraham Lincoln's assistant secretary of the navy. Seated behind this fitting accoutrement, Roosevelt launched into his work.

Secretary Long found in him a man who "worked indefatigably, frequently incorporating his views in memoranda which he would place every morning on my desk."

On April 22 Roosevelt authored the long letter to McKinley, mentioned earlier, that outlined his analysis of American naval preparedness in Hawaii and precisely what ships could be available to counter any hostile move by the Japanese. Four days later he sent the president the benefit of his thinking on why it seemed ill-advised to send a battleship to the Mediterranean to protect American interests in the face of a conflict between Greece and Turkey, "unless we intend to make a demonstration in force, in which case we should send certainly three or four armored vessels, and not one." If any battleships were to be dispatched, he recommended the *Iowa,* but only in an emergency. "We should keep the battleships on our own coast," he argued, "and in readiness for action should complications arise in Cuba." (Ultimately, the ships that sailed to show the flag were the *San Francisco,* the *Raleigh,* and the *Bancroft,* none a battleship.)

Almost immediately it became clear that Roosevelt would not be confined to a desk, however magnificent and historic it might be. There was the torpedo boat accident to be investigated and a report to be written. Then he had in mind a visit to Newport News to survey the building of the battleships *Kentucky* and *Kearsarge.* These ships' double turrets were of considerable concern to him. He did not like them on the grounds that they made it necessary to train both light- and heavy-caliber guns on the same target.

As June 2 neared, the author of *The Naval War of 1812* had his Naval War College speech to write. Though it was received with accolades in the press and stoically by McKinley, as described earlier, the text of the speech was read by Secretary Long with dismay, and he lost no time in telling him so. Two days after the speech, Roosevelt wrote to Captain Mahan, "He didn't like the address I made to the War College the other day."

However, the news of Long's displeasure was relegated to the next-to-the-last paragraph of Roosevelt's letter to Mahan. Of more immediate concern to Roosevelt was the fact that Long had proven to be "only lukewarm about building up our Navy, at any rate as regards battleships."

"This is, to me, a matter of the most profound concern," Roosevelt continued. "I feel that you ought to write to him—not immediately, but sometime not far in the future—at some length, explaining to him the vital need of more battleships now, and the vital need of continuity in our naval policy. Make the plea that this is a measure of peace and not of war. I cannot but think your words would carry weight with him."

Roosevelt's reason for asking that Mahan not write immediately was that Long was about to leave town. Because summer would mean stifling heat and humidity, not to mention swarms of mosquitos rising from the swamps that surrounded the nation's capital, the secretary had planned a season-long vacation in the cooler climes of New England. He left Roosevelt to swelter under the derisive title of hot-weather secretary.

Among places where Roosevelt could seek respite from the heat was the Metropolitan Club. It was here, early in June, that the Roosevelt circle widened to include Commodore George Dewey, the president of the Naval Board of Inspection and Survey, and Leonard Wood, an army man and attending surgeon to the president.

In terms of their impact upon the history of the United States, few meetings rise to the significance of Roosevelt's introductions to these two men. These meetings rank in importance with the Prussian-born General von Steuben presenting himself to George Washington at Valley Forge and offering his expertise in training soldiers, and Abraham Lincoln's first encounter with General Ulysses S. Grant. From the moment these men shook hands, the course of history and their own destinies changed.

That any momentous achievement still lay before Dewey seemed unlikely. At the age of sixty he faced retirement from the navy in three years, bringing to an end more than three decades of service with the fleet. Small, wiry, suntanned, and immaculate in a uniform whose trouser creases were described as "well-defined as his views on naval warfare," he was born on the day after Christmas, 1837, in

Montpelier, Vermont. He had studied at Norwich University and graduated from the U.S. Naval Academy in 1858, just in time to see action in the Civil War. As executive officer of the *Mississippi,* he had been part of Admiral David Farragut's fleet at New Orleans in 1862 and Port Hudson the next year, then saw action blockading Confederate ports. His postwar duties had included commanding the *Narragansett* for a survey of the Gulf of California. Promoted to captain in 1884, he was named chief of the navy's Bureau of Equipment and Recruiting in 1889. He had shown extraordinary resourcefulness in a crisis over Chile in 1891, resulting in the appointment to his present duty in 1895 and promotion to the rank of commodore in 1896. In him, Roosevelt had found someone who had lived Teedie Roosevelt's dream of ships, ships, ships, and fighting ships.

Also a New Englander, Leonard Wood had trained in medicine and had chosen to be a doctor in the military. Tall and fair with the lithe physique of a man who thrived on athletics, he was almost exactly two years younger than Roosevelt. Born October 9, 1860, in Winchester, New Hampshire, he earned his medical degree at Roosevelt's alma mater four years after Roosevelt had graduated. Now, paths that had not crossed in Cambridge met at the Metropolitan Club.

Their contemporary at Harvard, Owen Wister, would not meet Leonard Wood until several years later. Wister found him inclined to be silent and grave. He wrote, "I never saw him throw his head back and roar with laughter, as Roosevelt and most of the others did on occasion." Instead, Wister discerned "some sort of latent splendor about him, something massive, and capable, and impressive, that brought such words as Rome, and Proconsul, to mind."

For Roosevelt, Wood was the embodiment of boyhood dreams of heroics on distant fields of honor. Having served briefly as house surgeon at Boston City Hospital and after a short time in private practice, Wood had received in 1885 an interim appointment as a contract surgeon in the army. Posted in Arizona, he was commissioned assistant surgeon with the rank of first lieutenant in 1886. Three years later, for his role in the capture of the Apache leader Geronimo, he was promoted to captain assistant surgeon and awarded the Congressional Medal of Honor. The position of physician and aide to the president had been given him by Grover Cleveland in 1892 and renewed by McKinley. Discerning a man of resolution, wit, and fertility of mind, Roosevelt took to Wood immediately. Then, to his further delight, he discovered that there was nothing Leonard Wood enjoyed more than a brisk, invigorating morning walk in Rock Creek Park. Not long after their meeting, Roosevelt wrote to Henry Cabot Lodge about one of these outings, "He walked me off my legs."

Rock Creek Park also played a part in the blossoming relationship between Roosevelt and Commodore Dewey, although their mutual exposures to fresh air and sun were limited by Dewey's age and his preference for discussing the future role of the Navy in international affairs while horseback riding.

Roosevelt's early June was not taken up entirely with his fascinating new associates and the fate of the navy, however. The intrepid author of books and writer of letters took time on June 10 to correspond with his publishing firm, G. P. Putnam's Sons, on the subject of the publisher's desire to bring out a new collection of Roosevelt's essays. Roosevelt expressed doubts. "I have not got enough essays of a purely political character, using the word 'political' in its narrowest sense, to make a volume of size sufficient to warrant its publication," he wrote, adding, "There are a number of things which I have written that are not worthy of republication, and of those that are, there are not enough to divide. Now, if you think it unwise to publish the volume of essays in the way I have indicated, I want you to say so frankly, and without the least hesitation. It would not be to your advantage, or for mine, to have them brought out if it wasn't going to be worthwhile to bring them out."

The issue was resolved. Putnam's published *American Ideals* that year. Dedicated to Henry Cabot Lodge, it contained Roosevelt's article on the Monroe Doctrine and the text of his speech to the Naval War College, as well as an 1894 essay for *The Forum* entitled "True Americanism." The latter essay concluded with the words, "We Americans can only do our allotted task well if we face it steadily and bravely, seeing but not fearing the dangers. Above all we must stand shoulder to shoulder, not asking as to the ancestry or creed of our comrades, but only demanding they be in very truth Americans, and that we all work together, heart, hand and head, for the honor and the greatness of our common country."

The day after his letter to Putnam's, Theodore Roosevelt sent off a cheery missive to another Roosevelt, young Franklin, then a student at Groton. He welcomed his cousin to visit Sagamore Hill "on either the 2d or 3d of July, for as long as you can stay," and listed ferry and train schedules between Manhattan and Oyster Bay for Franklin's convenience.

In June 1897 Franklin Delano Roosevelt was fifteen years of age. As described by Nathan Miller, biographer of both Roosevelts (*F.D.R., An Intimate History* and *Theodore Roosevelt, A Life),* Franklin was "slender and handsome with his hair parted in the middle like two wings over his high forehead." Carrying himself with a jaunty self-assurance, he also had much in common with Theodore. He had an interest in nature. Twice a week he took boxing lessons from an instructor who came up from Boston, and he, too, had lost a bout in a school tourney. Drawn to the sea and ships, he had listened to the same tales Theodore had heard of relatives who had served aboard warships during the Civil War. He harbored dreams of attending the Naval Academy and having a career in the navy. Franklin also had read works by Captain Alfred Thayer Mahan and had become a disciple.

Five days after the note to Franklin, Theodore Roosevelt addressed a missive to his brother-in-law William Sheffield Cowles, saying that he felt he was "getting a little more familiar with the ground, and know somewhat 'where I am at.'" He described his function as "purely advisory" but added with satisfaction that "now and then I carry weight."

Whether Roosevelt's views would carry weight on the issue of the annexation of Hawaii remained to be seen. At a meeting with McKinley on June 8 he had urged "immediate action." He assured, "If we take Hawaii now, we shall avoid trouble with Japan."

Eight days later McKinley approved an annexation treaty and sent it to the Senate for ratification. The next day the secretary of the navy left Washington for two weeks vacation in New England (a longer hiatus was planned for later), leaving an exuberant Roosevelt in charge of the Navy Department and "very much pleased about the Hawaiian business."

On June 18 he wrote Long, "I hope you are enjoying yourself and will not return until you wish to. I have made arrangements to go away the 2d of July, and stay ten days or thereabouts . . . but my plans can be changed anytime."

The "ten days or thereabouts" were to be spent at Sagamore Hill with Edith, the children, and his cousin Franklin. But before leaving there were navy tasks to be done. High on his list of priorities was cutting down on departmental paperwork, especially that which in his view was "overloading the torpedo boats." Writing to Long on June 23, he declared his intention to implement, unless Long objected, his plans for reducing the burden. The letter then went on to inform the secretary that the navy had obtained "secret information as to the submarine torpedoes used on the new Japanese war vessels."

"We also have information that the Japs are feeling decidedly ugly about Hawaii," he further confided, "but I am very sure that their feelings will not take any tangible form."

But of greatest concern in the waning days of June was the finalizing of the Navy Department's revised contingency plan for war. Reviewing its suggested strategies, Roosevelt was pleased. In nearly every aspect the plan coincided with his expansionist designs in both the Pacific and Atlantic.

Chapter 3

Like Riding a
High-Mettled Horse

On the first of July Theodore Roosevelt left his war plans behind for the place he loved above all others. In a letter to his sister Anna he spoke admiringly of the white marble city on the Potomac, but "nothing could be lovelier," he said, than the home he had built for himself and his family at Oyster Bay.

"At Sagamore Hill," Roosevelt wrote in his autobiography, "we love a great many things—birds and trees and books, and all things beautiful, and horses and rifles and children and hard work and the joy of life."

When he arrived at the big house on a hill overlooking Long Island Sound, he found Edith and "sixteen small Roosevelts" in the form of his own children and their cousins, including Franklin. For the vacationing student from Groton, the summer proved to be a turning point. Throughout the rest of his life he deliberately modeled his career on that of "Cousin Theodore." Considering him the greatest man he ever knew, he followed in Theodore's footsteps from Harvard to Columbia University Law School, the New York legislature, the Navy Department as assistant secretary, the governor's mansion in New York, and the White House. He even emulated Theodore's preference in eyeglasses. Along the way he also married one of cousin Theodore's favorite nieces. The shy and gawky daughter of Roosevelt's late brother, Elliott, Eleanor Roosevelt was, in Edith's sympathetic eyes, a poor, plain little soul whose mouth and prominent teeth seemed to have "no future."

Although this Sagamore Hill respite proved as delightful as always, it came to an end on July 11 with the arrival of a navy torpedo boat. It docked long enough for Roosevelt to join its crew for a dash to the navy torpedo boat station at Goat Island in Newport. Impressed by the speed and maneuverability of the fragile little craft, he found the experience thrilling: "Like riding a high-mettled horse."

Following this second visit to Newport in a little over a month, he headed westward for an inspection of the Great Lakes Naval Militia installations in Mackinac and Detroit (Michigan), Chicago (Illinois), and Sandusky (Ohio). Organized along the lines of state army militias and partly funded by the federal government, these naval organizations existed in fourteen states and counted 3,339 men in their ranks. Officers consisted mainly of graduates of the Naval Academy, some of whom had received training at the Naval War College and the Naval Torpedo School. An act of Congress on August 3, 1894, had authorized the secretary of the navy to lend to each state's naval militia one of the navy's inactive vessels, along with uniforms, charts, books, and navigational instruments to promote drilling and instruction. In addition, an act of 1891 had granted a subsidy to privately owned ships (including foreign-built vessels registered in the United States) for carrying the mails, provided these ships would be made available to the navy in time of war. By 1896 the "auxiliary navy" consisted of twenty-nine vessels, the largest of which were the *New York, Paris, St. Louis,* and *St. Paul.*

At the Sandusky naval militia base, Roosevelt scornfully dismissed a formal protest from the Japanese government over McKinley's action in annexing Hawaii. He pounded a fist into a palm and thundered, "The United States is not in a position which requires her to ask Japan, or any other foreign power, what territory it shall or shall not acquire."

Barely recovered from his shock and displeasure over the assistant secretary's bombast at the Naval War College, the secretary of the navy was aghast. A few days after the Sandusky speech, a scolded Roosevelt wrote to Henry Cabot Lodge that Long "nearly threw a fit [as] he gave me as heavy a wigging as his invariable courtesy and kindness would permit."

Placated by Roosevelt's apologies and assured that Roosevelt would not repeat his transgression, Long left Washington for the cool tranquility of Massachusetts. He intended to spend the remainder of his summer vacation at his farm at Hingham Harbor.

Although Roosevelt had promised he would not speak out publicly on aspects of foreign policy without asking for permission from Long, he had given no such assurances regarding anything he might put into writing. On August 2, in a letter to Captain B. H. McCalla, he wrote (prophesying events twenty years later), "I entirely agree with you that Germany is the power with which we may very possibly have ultimately to come into hostile contact. How I wish our people would wake up to the need for a big navy."

Nine days later, Germany was again the topic in a letter to Cecil Spring Rice, then with the British delegation in Berlin. "As an American I should advocate—as a matter of fact I do advocate—keeping our navy at a pitch that will enable us to interfere promptly if Germany ventures to touch a foot of American soil. I would not go into the abstract rights or wrongs of it; I would simply say that we did not intend to have Germans on the continent, excepting as immigrants, whose children would become Americans of one sort or another, and if Germany intended to extend her empire here she would have to whip us first."

Even more interesting than Roosevelt's apparent prescience regarding war with Germany was a prediction about Russia in the same letter. If that nation chose to develop "purely on her own line and to resist the growth of liberalism," he foresaw "a red terror which will make the French Revolution pale."

Still expounding his interpretation of foreign affairs, he wrote to General James H. Wilson on August 23: "We cannot rival England as a naval power . . . but I do think we ought to stand ahead of Germany."

On the nineteenth, Roosevelt informed Bellamy Storer, "The Secretary is away and I am having immense fun running the Navy."

Indeed, during July and August, in the absence of Long (as well as that of McKinley, who also had fled the stifling weather for a vacation), the hot-weather secretary did more with his time than dictate letters. He found himself not only in direct command of fleets that roamed the seas but in charge of managing a vast and complex civilian bureaucracy that seemed to be floating on an ocean of paperwork. Arrayed beneath him in the organizational chart of the Department of the Navy were the naval bureaus and the men in charge of them: Yards and Docks (Mordecai T. Endicott), Equipment (F. E. Chadwick), Ordnance (Charles O'Neil), Construction and Repair (Philip Hichborn), Steam Engineering (G. W. Melville), Supplies and Accounts (Edwin Stewart), and Navigation (A. S. Crowninshield). The latter bureau—by far the largest—included Personnel and Fleet

Operations, whose ships and crews were divided into five stations: North Atlantic, South Atlantic, European, Asiatic, and Pacific.

The heartbeat of the North Atlantic Squadron was four first-class battleships: the *Indiana, Massachusetts, Oregon,* and *Iowa.* Smaller and not as heavily armed were the second-class *Texas* and *Maine.* Both had been authorized by Congress in the year in which Theodore Roosevelt had returned from ranching in Dakota to make an unsuccessful run for mayor of New York, and the year his friend Henry Cabot Lodge was first elected to Congress.

While the *Texas* had been constructed according to traditional European plans, the *Maine* had been a project of the navy's Bureau of Construction and Repair. The final design had called for a ship so long (324 feet) that the ways on which she was to be built had to be lengthened. This work had been carried out at the navy yard in Brooklyn.

While there is no record to show that the ship was ever visited by Roosevelt during this period of construction, it is hard to imagine someone so fascinated by warships not to have paid a visit to one so magnificent and easy to reach from his home in Oyster Bay. Or he might have left his town house in Manhattan on an evening or warm Sunday afternoon in the spring to stroll across John Roebling's Brooklyn Bridge, another marvel of the age, for an inspection.

Nothing like these warships had existed in the naval battles of 1812. *The Naval War of 1812* had been filled with wooden ships driven by canvas sails. The *Maine* and other fighting ships of the U.S. Navy under Roosevelt's command in August 1897 were armed and armored with the finest of American-made steel.

Chapter 4

Beauty and Majesty

There is no record of what Theodore Roosevelt said at the Cramp Shipyard in Philadelphia in the summer of 1897 when he first laid eyes on the U.S. Navy's newest battleship. A masterpiece of state-of-the-art warship design, the eleven-thousand-ton *Iowa,* with batteries of twelve-inch guns, was deemed equal to any battleship in the British, German, Japanese, and Spanish navies.

What is known is that he "broke the record in asking questions" of the men who had designed and built the warship. During that bombardment of queries he surprised the shipbuilder, Charles H. Cramp, who commented on his "evident theoretical knowledge of the construction of ships of war down to the details of bolts and rivets."

That Roosevelt and those who conducted him on his inspection felt free to call the *Iowa* a *battleship* represented a victory of semantic maneuvering in a strategic struggle to outfit the U.S. Navy with a fleet capable of commanding a respect commensurate with the power and prestige of a great seafaring nation.

Since 1872 the French had been routinely building iron and steel warships. In 1876 the British had a pair of all-steel fighting vessels under construction. Development in the size, range, and accuracy of armament had marked succeeding years. This meant that the major European powers had fleets fully capable of casting intimidating shadows across the Atlantic to the Americas.

Although the first of a new generation of formidably armored warships had been introduced on both sides of the Civil War, the United States had failed to recognize that no nation could be a great world power without an ocean-spanning navy with a backbone of first-class battleships. Without them, the Monroe Doctrine would not be taken seriously by colony-acquiring nations with expressed desires to expand into the Western Hemisphere.

Although the navy possessed what Roosevelt and others called "coast defense battle-ships," such ships were not capable of long-distance operations. These cruisers were classified as second-class battleships. Because the *Iowa* was a true battleship with long-range operating capabilities, the possibility of protests from "this lingering remnant of public opinion that clung to the coast defense theory" were anticipated in what Roosevelt called "a beautiful fashion." The *Iowa* and others to follow her into the fleet were called "seagoing coast defense battle-ships." For Roosevelt this was an oxymoron with which he was delighted; the fact that the name was a contradiction in terms was of "very small consequence to the fact that we did thereby get real battle-ships."

This passionate belief in a central role for the mightiest of warships had been amply demonstrated soon after he had taken office. Shortly after his inspection of the torpedo boat mishap, he had traveled down the coast to have a look at two battleships, the *Kentucky* and *Kearsarge,* being completed in the naval shipyard at Newport News, Virginia.

As mentioned, Roosevelt was concerned with the placement of the guns of the secondary battery. These eight-inch guns had been located atop the thirteen-inch rifles of the main battery, primarily as a weight-saving measure. In writing an appropriations bill, the Congress had limited the tonnage of such ships (an example of the sort of short-sightedness that Roosevelt found appalling). Although constrained by the requirement, the navy's ship designers sought to include armament equal to that carried by any likely foreign enemy. Because it meant that both batteries were forced to fire in the same direction, the double-deck arrangement was bitterly criticized by many naval officers.

Roosevelt agreed. On May 28 he wrote to Commander Richard Henry Dana, husband of an old family friend, Fanny Smith Dana, that he hoped to have the double turrets on the *Kentucky* and *Kearsarge* removed. In the short run, he was unsuccessful. The Navy Department continued the double dispositioning in battleships until the building of the *Louisiana* in 1904, well into the first term of President Theodore Roosevelt.

Positioning of guns was one of Roosevelt's topics in a June 22, 1897, letter to the chair of the House Naval Committee, Charles Addison Boutelle. This complaint involved a law that dictated placing a battery of rapid-fire guns on the old cruiser *Hartford*. Roosevelt argued that such a weapon on the *Hartford* was "of no earthly use" and that it ought to be put on the *Philadelphia* or *San Francisco,* "where it will be of real service."

This letter also expressed the assistant secretary's opinion that it was a pity "that we should lose from the Navy the names of famous old ships and of the great sea officers of the past." He wished "some provision could be made by law to enable us to name any future battleships and big cruisers after our ships which have been victorious in the past. Names like the *Wasp, Hornet,* etc., would be very appropriate for the torpedo boats, and would commemorate the most gallant little sloops that ever sailed or fought on the high seas; and I should like to see our big fighting ships commemorate the skill and prowess not only of great admirals like Farragut, but of captains like Decatur, Hull, Perry and Macdonough."

Ironically, the names *Wasp* and *Hornet* were to achieve fame again, but not as torpedo boats. Both played significant roles in World War II against the foe Roosevelt had worried about in 1897—Japan. The *Wasp* and *Hornet,* however, were a type of warship no one in Theodore Roosevelt's time could have anticipated: the aircraft carrier.

In another irony of American naval history, one of these flat-top ships—which had been designed to replace Roosevelt's favorite type of warship, the battleship—bore the name *Theodore Roosevelt.* Battleships did not fade away gently, however. In 1991, Operation Desert Storm opened with the firing of a cruise missile that found its target in Baghdad, Iraq. The missile was launched from the deck of the battleship *Wisconsin.* Four years later it was not uselessness but economics that brought the battleship era to an end. Because the costs of maintaining such warships proved too great, they were decommissioned, and in 1995 a plan was announced to dispose of them, either for scrap or to become museums.

The naming of battleships for states was not formalized until Theodore Roosevelt's worshipful cousin, Franklin, did so as president of the United States in 1938. At that time, in anticipation of World War II, four were built: the *Wisconsin,* the *Missouri,* the *New Jersey,* and the new *Iowa,* the first to be started (in 1938) and the one that lent its name to the entire class.

Forty-one years earlier, in August 1897, Theodore Roosevelt had traveled up from Washington to Charles Cramp's navy shipyard to board the first *Iowa.* The following month he again went down to the Virginia Capes to witness the *Iowa*'s shakedown cruise and to observe the first target practice for its mighty guns. Always a keen appreciator of the value of friendly relations with the press, he invited three journalists to accompany him, including the best-known illustrator in the nation, who also happened to be a friend who shared Roosevelt's enthusiasm for the American West.

Frederic Remington was first linked to Roosevelt when he had been engaged by *Century* magazine to provide illustrations to accompany Roosevelt's series of articles on the West, later published as a book (*Ranch Life and the Hunting Trail*). Born on October 4, 1861, in Canton, New York, Remington had attended the Yale School of Fine Arts (1878–80). After five years in the West, he had returned with a portfolio of sketches and paintings. An exhibit at the National Academy in 1886 had secured his reputation as the country's foremost portrayer of the life and people of the frontier. In 1895 he took up sculpture. Working in bronze and continuing to depict western themes, he produced *The Bronco Buster,* a spectacular rendering of a cowboy attempting to tame a horse.

On September 7, 1897, miles eastward of Hampton Roads, Virginia, Remington stood next to Roosevelt on the deck of the *Iowa* as the graceful warship cut through a calm sea. Scattered like seagulls around the *Iowa* lay six other ships, all painted white, of the North Atlantic Squadron. With an artist's eyes, Remington studied the smooth but sun-flaked green water, his ears protected against the thunderous blasts he had been warned to expect when the ship's eight- and twelve-inch guns opened up, and then he spotted the target. It was but a speck on the horizon. When the ship's surgeon had handed out earplugs, he had also explained the best way to withstand the tremendous shocks to the body that would accompany each salvo: "Open your mouth, stand on your toes, and let your frame hang loosely."

A naval cadet marked the closing of the distance between the advancing ship and the target with a shout of "two thousand seven hundred yards!"

Squinting through nose glasses at a wooden float that would be the object of the gunners in their turrets, Roosevelt stood beside the *Iowa*'s skipper, Captain William T. Sampson. At age fifty-seven (born in Palmyra, New York, in 1840), he was the embodiment of Roosevelt's romantic image of the seafaring warrior. A graduate of the Naval Academy, he had been aboard ships for forty years.

Now he held the bridge of one of the world's mightiest warships, bearing down and training its enormous guns on a tiny dot twenty-six hundred yards away.

Had Sampson and Roosevelt shared such a moment with sailors of the bygone era of wooden warships, the deck on which they stood would have swarmed with valiant young heroes readying their cannons and waiting for the order to fire: thirty-two-gun frigates with guns in rows of thirteen above, twelve below, and seven twenty-four-pound cannonades above; or thirty-eight-gun frigates with their broadside guns in rows of fourteen and ten; or the massive forty-four-gun frigate *United States,* with thirteen long twenty-four-pound cannonades below and a dozen forty-two-pounders above. In the naval war of 1812 those who had manned guns had advanced so close to their adversaries that they were able to see their faces.

Not so for the gunners of Sampson's *Iowa,* snug in steel turrets with weaponry so powerful and with such a long-range capability that the crew might see the enemy only as a tiny silhouette at the rim of the sea. Aboard the *Iowa,* boasted her builder, almost nothing required the touch of a human hand, save "the opening and closing of throttles and pressing electric buttons."

"Two thousand five hundred yards!"

More than a mile and a fifth away, the target bobbed peacefully as *Iowa*'s eight-inch second battery opened fire with a deafening, bone-jarring, hull-shaking, deck-shuddering thunderclap. Tongues of orange flame and roiling plumes of yellowish gray smoke shot from the muzzles.

Short by fifty feet, the shells kicked up harmless geysers.

An instant later, the main battery let loose with a salvo that rocked the *Iowa* as easily as if she were a mere toy boat in a bathtub. The concussion was so powerful that it stove in a lifeboat, shook several watertight doors loose from their hinges, and tossed into the air two of the civilian spectators who had not heeded the surgeon's advice to let their bodies go slack.

Peering through smoke-fogged eyeglasses, Roosevelt waited for the smoke and water around the target to settle and clear. When they did, he found not a trace of the tiny target. Had it been a ship of the British, French, German, Japanese, or Spanish navy, it would have been on its way to the ocean floor.

Eight days later the experience remained on Roosevelt's mind as he sent off a letter to his friend Remington, who had returned to the West. Always the romantic in all things—and ever the politician looking for a supporter for a cause—he wrote, "I wish I were with you out among the sagebrush, the great brittle cottonwoods, and the sharply-channeled, barren buttes; but I am very glad at any rate to have had you along with the squadron; and I can't help looking upon you as any ally from henceforth on in trying to make the American people see the beauty and the majesty of our ships and the heroic quality which lurks somewhere in all those who man and handle them."

The next day there was the same poetry in a letter to Boutelle:

> Just a line to report progress. I spent three most delightful days with the squadron off Hampton Roads. Oh, Lord! if only the people who are ignorant about our Navy could see these great warships in all their majesty and beauty, and realize how well they are handled, and how well fitted to uphold the honor of America, I don't think we would encounter such opposition in building up the Navy to its proper standard.
>
> Everything is getting along well, and very quietly. The torpedo-boat flotilla will be ready October 1st. There are innumerable things about which I wish to talk to you, and which I can hardly put down at length in a letter, so I will have to wait until you come on [back from vacation].

Two days after writing this letter, and despite having taken some journalists with him to witness the *Iowa*'s gunnery tests, he sent off a missive to Lieutenant William Wirt Kimball, author of the navy's contingency plan for war with Spain, to warn him about the press. He began, "Now a word, confidentially," and went on:

> The correspondent of the *Journal* here told me he was going to be allowed to go with your squadron. I think you ought to be very careful about having any representative of either the *World* or the *Journal* aboard. They both, but particularly the *Journal,* try in every way to discredit the Navy by fake stories. They make their correspondents write such stories, and they alter them to suit themselves. What they want is something sensational. They would not care a bit for the report of a successful trip. What would interest them would be a make-believe story of a breakdown, of a description of imaginary mis-conduct. If I were you I would be very careful what newspaper men I allowed aboard. It is an excellent thing to take out several for two or three hours with the flotilla . . . when you have the boats behaving pretty well; but on a longer cruise I would only take a man of whom I was absolutely sure, and who was connected either with the Associated Press or with some thoroughly reputable newspaper; most certainly not a *Journal* or *World* man.

Fresh in Roosevelt's mind as he sent this advice to Kimball were experiences with these two New York newspapers during his two years as police commissioner. Frequently critical and quite nettlesome, these dailies constituted, in Roosevelt's view, the very worst aspects of the sensationalistic style of the era, called *yellow journalism.*

In an article for the *Atlantic Monthly,* "Administering the New York Police Force," published shortly after he left Mulberry Street for the Navy Department, Roosevelt asserted, "Of all the forces that tend for evil in a great city like New York, probably none are so potent as the sensational papers. Until one has had experience with them it is difficult to realize the reckless indifference to truth or decency displayed by papers such as the two that have the largest circulation in New York City."

These impassioned beliefs did not wane. In 1912, after his years as president, he wrote, "Yellow journalism deifies the cult of the mendacious, the sensational, and the inane, and, throughout its wide but vapid field, does as much to vulgarize and degrade the popular taste, to weaken the popular character, and to dull the edge of the popular conscience, as any influence under which the country can suffer. These men sneer at the very idea of paying heed to the dictates of a sound morality, as one of their number had cynically put it, they are concerned merely with selling the public whatever the public will buy—a theory of conduct which would justify the existence of every keeper of an opium den, of every foul creature who ministers to the vices of mankind."

Joseph Pulitzer, a leading exponent of yellow journalism and the owner of the *World,* had made it clear to his readers that he and his newspaper hated jingoism. His chief rival in the New York newspaper circulation wars of the 1890s was William Randolph Hearst, owner of the *Journal.* Hearst was a committed jingoist, but his paper had found nothing else to admire in Theodore Roosevelt. At the zenith of Police Commissioner Roosevelt's unpopular enforcement of laws closing saloons on Sundays, the *Journal* had parodied the popular song "Sidewalks of New York" to regale the paper's beer-quaffing readership with "East Side, West Side, all around the town, yesterday went King Roosevelt I, ruler of New York and patron saint of dry Sundays."

Rare among newspaper editors was the New York *Sun*'s Charles A. Dana, who not only shared Roosevelt's jingoistic outlook but lent him advice and support.

Despite his strongly negative views on the quality of journalism practiced at the time, Roosevelt deeply appreciated the importance of the press, especially to an ambitious politician. In the first hour after being sworn in as president of the Board of Police Commissioners in 1895, he had appointed himself official spokesperson for the police department. During the first few months of his term, his name had been in the headlines so often that a placard carried in a parade protesting the closing of saloons on Sunday asked, "How many times did you see Roosevelt's name in the papers today?"

He had often reaped the benefits of alliances with newspaper reporters. This was especially true of his connections with Jacob A. Riis, police reporter for Dana's *Sun,* and Lincoln Steffens, a reporter who began his career as a Riis protégé and went on to journalistic immortality as a muckraker during the first half of the next century. Also counted as friends throughout Theodore Roosevelt's political life were Joseph Bucklin Bishop, who would ultimately publish *Theodore Roosevelt and His Time, as Shown in His Letters;* Stephen Crane, who worked for New York newspapers while authoring his landmark novel *The Red Badge of Courage*; Richard Harding Davis, despite the fact he worked for the *Journal;* and Frederic Remington, another occasional Hearst employee and Roosevelt's recent guest on the *Iowa.*

While Roosevelt began September on the battleship, Secretary Long remained on vacation and on the receiving end of letters from his assistant. Along with keeping the secretary informed of activities in the department, the author of the letters offered assurances that because things were going along so well there was no hurry about Long returning to the capital. One letter suggested, "You must be tired, and you ought to have an entire rest." As to answering the letters, Long need not be "bothered at all."

Regarding Roosevelt's activities, the *Sun* had noted enthusiastically on August 23, "The liveliest spot in Washington at present is the Navy Department. The decks are cleared for action. Acting Secretary Roosevelt, in the absence of Governor Long, has the whole Navy bordering on a war footing. It remains only to sand down the decks and pipe to quarters for action."

A week after Roosevelt's three-day cruise aboard the *Iowa,* President McKinley was back in Washington and inviting Roosevelt to accompany him for an afternoon carriage ride. Delighted to do so, Roosevelt found himself basking not only in the warmth of a sunny September 14 but in a surprising admission from McKinley. Regarding the speech in Sandusky for which Long had "wigged" him, Roosevelt heard McKinley concede that the assistant secretary had been right in stating that the United States did not require the approval of Japan or anyone else regarding the annexation of Hawaii, nor in any other foreign policy matter. He then congratulated Roosevelt on his management of the Navy Department over the preceding seven weeks.

Pleased and emboldened as the carriage rattled slowly on, Roosevelt took advantage of McKinley's affability to bring up the issue of Cuba. Thoughtfully, the president allowed for the possibility of trouble.

Roosevelt blurted that if war did come, he intended to enlist in the army the moment hostilities began.

McKinley wondered what Mrs. Roosevelt and Henry Cabot Lodge might have to say about that.

Roosevelt retorted that both "would regret it, but this was one case where I would consult neither."

With a laugh, McKinley promised that "if war by any chance arose," he would do all he could to guarantee that Roosevelt "should have the opportunity to serve."

In reporting to Lodge on this excursion with McKinley, he wrote that he took the president's expressions of approval with a grain of salt. "Of course the President is a bit of a jollier," he reminded Senator Lodge, "but I think his words did represent a substratum of satisfaction."

McKinley certainly remained interested in Roosevelt's views. He invited him to dinner at the Executive Mansion the following Friday and for another carriage ride the next afternoon.

Eager to seize the opportunity to support his positions, Roosevelt took along a paper, described in a letter to Lodge on September 23, that showed "exactly where all our ships are and [an outline of] what I thought ought to be done if things looked menacing about Spain."

Arguing for "the necessity of taking an immediate and prompt initiative, if we wished to avoid the chance of some serious trouble," he ignored the official Navy Department war plan and sketched his own. He proposed a two-stage naval offensive that would begin with a squadron of cruisers followed by a fleet of his beloved battleships operating out of Key West. These ships would be ordered to Cuban waters within forty-eight hours of a formal declaration of war with Spain.

Regarding Spain's Pacific colony, the Philippines, he proposed that "our Asiatic Squadron should blockade, and if possible take Manila."

Seven days after this face-to-face briefing, Roosevelt sat at his splendidly nautical desk to draft yet another letter to Secretary Long. Running several pages, it provided details of Roosevelt's views on the position of the United States at that moment and an impassioned argument intended to bolster Long's hesitancy on the issue of vastly strengthening the nation's readiness for war by means of greatly increasing the navy's might.

Letters to Long had customarily begun with "My dear Mr. Secretary." The salutation of this one was a respectful "Sir."

As if he feared that his vacationing boss's interest in the lengthy letter might falter, Roosevelt stuffed the opening sentence with a breathlessly encapsulated review of recent American history, an overview of the foreign powers who might prove to be troublesome, and an earnest plea on behalf of the Monroe Doctrine, plus a bit of prognostication (proven correct in the long-run).

Presumably seated comfortably in the shade of his porch, Long read:

> The steady growth of our country in wealth and population, and its extension by acquisition of noncontiguous territory in Alaska, and at the same time the steady growth of the old naval powers of the world, and the appearance of new ones, such as Germany and Japan, with which it is possible that one day we may have to be brought into contact, make me feel that I should respectfully, and with all possible earnestness, urge the advisability of the Navy Department doing all it can to further a steady and rapid upbuilding of our Navy.

Assaying the great navies of the world, Roosevelt saw no possibility of competing with Queen Victoria's Royal Navy, and nothing desirable in rivaling the French. The likelihood of a hostile contact with "Russia's three-fold sea front" and Italy's "peculiar position" were dismissed as "the last degree improbable." But Japan was "steadily becoming a great naval power in the Pacific, where her fleet already surpasses ours in strength; and Germany shows a tendency to stretch out for colonial possessions which may at any moment cause a conflict with us." Therefore, it was essential that the Pacific Fleet be kept constantly above the Japanese Fleet, and that U.S. naval strength as a whole be kept superior to that of the Germans.

He continued, "It does not seem to me that we can afford to invite responsibility and shirk the burden that we incur; we cannot justify ourselves for retaining Alaska and annexing Hawaii unless we provide a Navy sufficient to prevent all chance of either being taken by a hostile power; still less have we any right to assert the Monroe Doctrine in the American hemisphere unless we are ready to make good our assertion with warships."

Echoing the main points of the Naval War College and Sandusky speeches that had riled Long, he preached, "A great navy does not make for war, but for peace. It is the cheapest kind of insurance."

This insurance could be bought for nothing less than six new battleships, two to be stationed on the Pacific coast and four on the Atlantic; six large cruisers with heavy armament; seventy-five torpedo boats (one-third of them for the Pacific); a new dry dock on the Pacific coast and three on the eastern seaboard; the replacement of slow-fire guns on all battleships and cruisers; smokeless powder in all ordnance (which would increase firepower and the rapidity of firing); and the stockpiling of two million pounds of gunpowder "at once."

Roosevelt concluded, "We are now in a situation to build up a navy commensurate with our needs, provided the work is carried on continuously, for the era of experiment has passed, and we possess designs suitable for our own use, with types of vessels equal to those of any other power." If they delayed or interrupted this work, he warned, "we should be exposing the country to the possibility of the bitterest humiliation."

The letter never mentioned Spain and Cuba by name, but both were there between the lines.

Exactly how serious Roosevelt was in finding an active role for himself should there be a war over Cuba was spelled out in a mid-September letter to "an old friend," Colonel Francis Vinton Greene, Seventy-first Regiment, New York:

> There is always a possibility, however remote, that we will have a war with Spain, and now that the cool weather is approaching that would probably mean not merely a naval war, but a considerable expeditionary force. I suppose you would be going, would you not? I shall certainly go in some capacity. What I should like to do if it were possible would be to go under you. I suppose we should have to raise a regiment, with you as Colonel, and with me as Lieutenant Colonel.

My military experience is strictly limited; I was a captain in the National Guard for three years; nevertheless I know that under a man like yourself I could do first-class work, and I would have what assistance the administration could give in getting up the regiment, etc. Would this suit you should the need arise? I don't suppose there is any chance of the need arising, and very possibly you have totally different arrangements in mind, but I want to take time by the forelock so as to have my plans all laid and be able to act at once in case there is trouble.

As Washington's stifling summer slipped into autumn, trouble proved neither long in the offing nor far away.

Part II

The Noble Elk

Chapter 5

The Wolfhound

After a summer of letters brimming with Theodore Roosevelt's assurances that all was well in Washington—letters that had bolstered John D. Long's inclination to tarry in Massachusetts—the secretary of the navy roused himself to declare his intention of returning to his desk on September 28. But before doing so, he dismissed a recent *Boston Herald* story asserting in a mocking tone that Roosevelt coveted Long's job. (Roosevelt denied this vehemently in yet another letter.) Apparently undisturbed, Long told dinner companions at the Massachusetts Club in Boston not to worry about relations between him and his hot-weather secretary.

He said, "His enthusiasm and my conservatism make a good combination." He added, jocularly, "It is a liberal education to work with him."

What Long did not know as he headed back to the capital was that Roosevelt was about to give him a lesson in the art of politics rooted in personal relationships. The illumination would come in the form of a decision that Long would have to render regarding the appointment of the commander in chief of the Asiatic Squadron. For Roosevelt, nothing on the secretary's agenda, with the possible exception of an approval of his plan for adding battleships to the fleet, was of more moment. In Roosevelt's opinion there was only one man worthy of the post.

"In a crisis," he would write, "the man worth his salt is the man who meets the needs of the situation in whatever way is necessary." Such a man was his newly found friend and companion at the Metropolitan Club, Commodore George Dewey. The veteran officer had recently demonstrated his mettle during some trouble with Chile.

Relating the incident in his autobiography, Roosevelt wrote, "Dewey was off the Argentine, and was told to get ready to move to the other coast of South America. If the move became necessary, he would have to have coal, and yet if he did not make the move, the coal would not be needed. In such a case a man afraid of responsibility always acts rigidly by the regulations and communicates with the Department at home to get authority for everything he does; and therefore he usually accomplishes nothing whatever, but is able to satisfy all individuals with red-tape minds by triumphantly pointing out his compliance with regulations."

Dewey proved to be no such commander. He bought coal and was ready to move at once if the need arose. When the crisis ended without orders to Dewey to move, there was a chance that he might be reprimanded for his unauthorized actions, for, in Roosevelt's words, "our people are like almost all other peoples in requiring responsible officers under such conditions to decide at their own personal peril."

Noting that "the people higher up ultimately stood by Dewey," Roosevelt wrote that the decisiveness that Dewey had shown "made me feel that here was a man who could be relied upon to prepare in advance, and to act promptly, fearlessly, and on his own responsibility when the emergency arose."

In anticipating the actions of the Asiatic Squadron in a war with Spain, he pictured Dewey slipping "like a wolf-hound from a leash," and "striking instantly and with telling effect."

To Roosevelt's horror and dismay, on the day before Secretary Long's return to duty he discovered that another candidate "was being pushed by certain politicians who I knew had influence with the Navy Department and with the President." This alarming development came to his notice when he opened a letter addressed to Long from Senator William E. Chandler.

Chandler recommended the appointment of Commodore John A. Howell. Although he held seniority over Dewey, Howell was, in the view of Roosevelt, "irresolute" and "extremely afraid of responsibility." These traits were the opposite of those needed in a man who in the event of a war with Spain might have to wrench the Philippines from the grip of the Spanish fleet half a world away.

Recognizing that Senator Chandler's views would carry great weight with Long and McKinley, Roosevelt sent him a note stating that before he committed himself "definitely to Commodore Howell I wish very much you would let me have a chance to talk to you."

When the appeal proved fruitless, Roosevelt cast aside his hope that Dewey would get the appointment "without appealing to any politician at all." Convinced that the "essential thing was to get him the appointment," he summoned Dewey to his office and asked, "Do you know any Senators?"

Dewey replied that he knew Redfield Proctor.

The name was music to Roosevelt's ears. He knew that the senator from Vermont was close to McKinley, "very ardent for the war, and desirous to have it fought in the most efficient fashion."

According to Roosevelt's autobiography, he merely "*suggested* to Dewey" (emphasis added) that he enlist Proctor's services. In concluding a discussion of the episode, Roosevelt simply noted that it "was accordingly done" and proved to be "a fortunate hour for the Nation."

Promptly calling on McKinley, Senator Proctor strongly urged the appointment of Dewey. Whether he had linked the appeal to the name of the president's amiable companion during a pair of recent carriage rides is not recorded. It is known that McKinley acted swiftly. He dictated a memorandum requesting that Dewey be appointed. It awaited Secretary Long on the very day he returned from his prolonged hot-weather hiatus. The Chandler letter landed on his desk somewhat later.

In his autobiography, Roosevelt explained his willingness to ask Dewey to appeal to a politician: "For a naval officer to bring pressure to get himself a soft and easy place is unpardonable; but a large leniency should be observed toward the man who uses influence only to get himself a place in the picture near the flashing of guns."

The memoir does not touch on either the unpardonability of or leniency toward an assistant secretary of the navy who intercepts a letter to his superior and then prevents its recommendation from becoming a reality. Nor does it explain how Chandler's letter was delayed in getting to Long's desk from the one with the carvings of warships, behind which sat Theodore Roosevelt.

What mattered to Roosevelt at the close of September 1897 was that the commander of the fleet in Asia was his man.

Chapter 6

The Limelight

After six months as Senator Henry Cabot Lodge's houseguest on Massachusetts Avenue, Theodore Roosevelt looked for a house to rent for him and his family. He found one at 1810 N Street. Opposite the British embassy, it was suitable for a man of his station, for pregnant Edith, and for a flock of energetic children. They settled into it in mid-October amid furnishings he described as having been garnered "largely from the wreck of Edith's forefather's houses sixty years back, with an occasional relic of my own family thrown in—all of the mesozoic or horse-hair furniture stage." Two weeks after moving into this "very nice house," he and the family celebrated his thirty-ninth birthday.

Owen Wister, who had known him for more than twenty years, observed that the 135-pound collegiate boxer he had seen in the Harvard gymnasium "was putting on weight and impressiveness with the passing of years, and the jaw was acquiring a grimness which his experience of life made inevitable; and beneath the laughter and the courage of his blue eyes, a wistfulness had begun to lurk which I had never seen in college; but the warmth, the eagerness, the boisterous boyish recounting of some anecdote, the explosive expression of some opinion about a person, a thing, or a state of things—these were unchanged."

Neither had his energy waned. In addition to hearing him on the subject of his work in the Navy Department, Edith and his many friends found themselves listening to his plans for adding four more volumes to the already monumental *The Winning of the West* and an idea for an article on what he called "the Mongol Terror," detailing the "domination of the Tartar tribes over half of Europe during the Thirteenth and Fourteenth Centuries." There always seemed to be a letter that needed writing. And there was politics.

A letter in that category went to Seth Low, formerly the mayor of Brooklyn, who was running for mayor of the newly created city of greater New York that was to be brought into existence by the consolidation on January 1, 1898, of Manhattan, Brooklyn, Staten Island, Queens, and the Bronx. In the election for the first mayor of this metropolis, scheduled for November 1897, Low had the backing of a faction of the Republican Party that could not bring itself to support attorney Benjamin Tracy, the choice of Thomas Platt. Known as "the Easy Boss," Platt had been a foe of Roosevelt's passion for government reform.

"I only wish I could be on the stump with you," Roosevelt wrote to Low, "for I have hardly ever felt more interested in anyone's success." He added that all he "could do on the quiet has been done." But the next day while visiting Oyster Bay he wrote to Henry Cabot Lodge to express his view that Lodge "did very wisely" in refusing "to mix in this ugly contest."

When the voters had their say, the unified Democrats, led by the Tammany Hall machine of Boss Richard Crocker, won, installing in city hall an obscure judge and party regular, Robert A. Van Wyck, who took office with the cry, "To hell with reform."

Other Roosevelt missives included one to Frederic Remington, who was taken to task for depicting badgers "too long and thin."

As he arrived at his desk each morning, Secretary Long could count on finding a fresh communication. Taking note of this prolific output in his memoir, Long complained, "His typewriters had no rest. He, like most of us, lacks the rare knack of brevity."

Recognizing that Roosevelt was "especially stimulating to the younger officers, who gathered about him and made his office as busy as a hive," Long decided to direct the Roosevelt "ardor" to an investigation of a chronic problem with morale. He named Roosevelt president of a panel of inquiry. The Naval Personnel Board, consisting of Roosevelt and nine naval officers, was directed to "consider the matter of reorganization of the personnel of the navy," write a report with recommendations, and provide the language for a bill to be sent to Congress.

This assignment would allow Roosevelt to attack a situation he had already criticized, the navy's system for promoting officers. The problem was described by Charles Oscar Paullin in his *History of Naval Administration, 1775–1911,* published in 1968 by the U.S. Naval Institute at Annapolis, as both chronic and acute:

There was not a corps in the navy that did not believe that it suffered some hardship. The especial grievance of the line officers was the infrequency of promotions. Some of the lieutenants had spent more than 20 years in their grade, and a few officers were still lieutenants who had entered the navy as midshipmen during or immediately after the Civil War. Several lieutenants were between 40 and 50 years of age. This long service in the lower ranks worked an injustice to the officers, and was detrimental to the navy since it unfitted the officers for command ranks. Men who had spent the best years of their lives in subordinate stations occupied often with trifling and routine tasks, were not likely to have the executive habit, initiative, decision and resourcefulness, when having passed the meridian of life they became captains, commodores and rear admirals. Moreover, the existing system rushed the officers through upper grades so rapidly that they were unable to acquire but little experience in them.

With the same zeal he had exhibited as president of the Board of Police Commissioners in tackling similar problems two years earlier, Roosevelt convened the Naval Personnel Board in the first week of November. Among the board's five line officers (those who actually served on ships) were the skipper of the *Iowa,* Captain William T. Sampson, and Captain A. S. Crowninshield, head of the Bureau of Navigation. Among the four staff officers, the principal representatives at the table were G. W. Melville, in charge of the Bureau of Steam Engineering, and Chief Engineer Charles W. Rae.

In keeping with a belief that merit ought to be the primary reason for promotion (as he had insisted on when revamping the New York police force), Roosevelt vigorously condemned the existing system of promotion by seniority. He argued that it made the "promotion of an officer dependent not upon the zealous performance of his duties but upon the possession of a good stomach and of an easy nature; while a positive premium is put upon the man who never ventures to take a risk, and who therefore never does anything great."

Despite the additional work imposed upon him by the personnel policy review, the assistant secretary found time on November 19 for a letter to Lieutenant Kimball on the subject of Cuba. The letter was written, as he described it, "with a frankness which our timid friends would call brutal":

I would regard a war with Spain from two viewpoints: First, the advisability on the ground of both humanity and self-interest of interfering on behalf of the Cubans, and of taking one more step toward the complete freeing of America from European domination; second, the benefit done to our people by giving them something to think of which isn't material gain, and especially the benefit done our military forces by trying both the Army and Navy in actual practice. I should be very sorry not to see us make the experiment of trying to land, and therefore to feed and clothe, an expeditionary force, if only for the sake of learning from our blunders. I should hope that the force would have some fighting to do. It would be a great lesson, and we would profit much by it.

Significantly, neither this letter nor others of a similar nature considered the lives that might be lost in pursuit of his romantic vision of a military adventure as a learning experience and a way to tone the flabby morals of the American people. Death did not figure into the equation. Indeed, in 1902 he still held that position, writing that he was not "in the least sensitive about killing any number of men if there is an adequate reason."

Even more illuminating is the fact that he wrote the admittedly brutal letter to Kimball only a few hours after celebrating a birth. Quentin Roosevelt's arrival, "quite unexpectedly," had required his father to hop onto his bicycle to summon a doctor and nurse "just . . . in time." He then kept alive the tradition of Roosevelt men being educated at Groton by notifying the school of the boy's existence and registering him in the appropriate future class. Informing his sister Anna about Quentin's birth, he reported, "We are very glad and much relieved" and "Edith is doing well." He then left for the Navy Department and his day's work, including the sabre-rattling letter to Kimball.

The letter could have been sent to anyone in his intimate circle of sympathizers. Exactly how important these men were to him at the time was demonstrated on the very first page of the book he would write at the end of the war he was so avidly seeking in November of 1897. "Naturally, when one is intensely interested in a certain cause," he declared in *The Rough Riders,* "the tendency is to associate particularly with those who take the same view."

One did not have to agree with him to be his friend, however. He had many who felt very differently and "looked upon the possibility of war with sincere horror." But in Roosevelt's mind, members of Congress who did not agree with his views on expansionism and a strong defense in the form of a powerful navy "were content to follow the worst of all possible courses, that is, to pass resolutions which made war more likely and yet to decline to take measures which would enable us to meet the war if it did come." Exceptions to the anti-war thinking in the House of Representatives existed primarily in those who had come from the West, where pro-war feelings ran strongly.

Allies were to be found, of course, in the jingoistic members of the Senate, including Commodore Dewey's friend Redfield Proctor, Cushman Davis, John Morgan, William E. Chandler (his backing of Commodore Howell for the Asiatic Squadron notwithstanding), and the stalwart Henry Cabot Lodge, whom Roosevelt canonized in his autobiography as one who "has ever stood foremost among those who uphold with farsighted fearlessness and strict justice to others our national honor and interest."

The trouble with senators, members of the House, and even naval officers was that they all came and went. But there was one friend who was always around. In the president's surgeon, Dr. Leonard Wood, Roosevelt had discovered a man of "kindred tastes and kindred principles." Furthermore, there were Wood's admirable military adventures in the West, serving in "inconceivably harassing campaigns against Apaches, where he had displayed such courage that he won that most coveted of distinctions—the Medal of Honor."

Perhaps Wood's most winning trait, as mentioned, was his zest for the kind of vigorous exercise that appealed to Roosevelt, especially long summertime walks through the beautiful broken country that surrounded Washington. In winter the two friends varied these hikes by kicking a football in an empty lot. Should there be snow, they tried out a couple of pairs of skis that had been sent to Roosevelt by a Canadian friend. On their way to and back from their walks or other exercises, they engaged in an activity that Roosevelt favored even more than athletics and letter writing. They talked.

Invariably, the subject turned to the possibility of war with Spain. Both felt strongly that it would be as righteous as it would be advantageous to the honor and interests of the nation. Should the war come, both men were determined to take an active part.

In his autobiography Roosevelt recalled, "He was as anxious as I was that if there were war we should both have our part in it. I had always felt that if there were a serious war I wished to be in a position to explain to my children why I did take part in it, and not why I did not take part in it. Moreover, I had very deeply felt that it was our duty to free Cuba, and I had publicly expressed this feeling; and when a man takes such a position, he ought to be willing to make his words good by his deeds unless there is some strong reason to the contrary. He should pay with his body."

Another member of the Roosevelt band of allies, although removed from Washington, was Owen Wister. Their means of communication had to be letters. On December 10, 1897, Roosevelt expressed a desire to read Wister's second book about the West, *Lin McLean,* but complained, "I have been so busy recently that I haven't read anything, of any kind or sort." If this claim had been true when written, he evidently found time in the next three days to open Wister's work. "I have now read all your book," he said on December 13, pointing out that he had found "a couple of points which I shall criticize when we meet."

In describing this period in his memoir of his friendship with Roosevelt, Wister referred to Cuba as "a noise" that could not be ignored because it "was just at our doors." Regarding President McKinley's "step by step" facing of "the unfamiliar possibility of a war," Wister welcomed the presence of Roosevelt as "an uneasy thorn in the side of the Administration."

On the frequent criticism of his friend as a publicity-hungry seeker of the limelight, Wister wrote, "He was his own limelight, and could not help it: a creature charged with such a voltage as his, became the central presence at once."

On September 19 the *Boston Sunday Globe* had acknowledged that Roosevelt was by far the most entertaining performer in "the great theater of our national life." Whatever he felt about this journalistic notice did not find its way into a letter. As to his name being mentioned in connection with the highest office in the land, he had become accustomed to such musings in the press and among politicians. Predictions that he might one day find his way to what Henry Cabot Lodge once termed "a larger kingdom" had been voiced throughout his public career.

Yet on at least one occasion Roosevelt had railed against that kind of talk. The suspicion that he had set his sights on being president of the United States had been thrown directly in his face by one of his best friends and staunchest allies. In the summer of 1895 Jacob Riis of the New York *Sun* (along with Riis's journalistic ally and protégé, Lincoln Steffens of the *Post*) had barged into Roosevelt's office in the Mulberry Street headquarters of the New York Police Department to demand, "Are you working to become President?"

Leaping to his feet and running around his desk, Roosevelt roared, "Don't you dare ask me that. Don't you put such ideas into my head."

Shocked at the outburst, the reporters cowered and gaped in amazement. Calmed down, Roosevelt went on to explain, "Never, never, you must never either of you ever remind a man at work in a political job that he may be President. It almost always kills him politically. He loses his nerve; he can't do his work; he gives up the very traits that are making him a possibility." Continuing with his face screwed up into a knot, as Steffens remembered the moment, he conceded, "I must be wanting to be President. Every young man does. But I won't let myself think of it; I must not, because if I do, I will begin to work for it. I'll be careful, calculating, cautious in word and act, and so I'll beat myself."

If thoughts of being president wafted through his mind in the autumn of 1897, he could not find encouragement in the article in the *Boston Sunday Globe*. It had warned that it would not be at all prudent of voters to permit an entertaining performer in the theater of national life to get into the presidency. The newspaper feared that a President Theodore Roosevelt would produce national insomnia.

But it was not the limelight of present or future political honors that concerned him as the glowering gray skies of December signaled the rapid approach of the deadline he had set for himself to complete his study of the navy's personnel problems. He had chosen to transmit the eight-thousand-page document to Secretary Long on December 9.

Having done so, Roosevelt was free to give an appreciative bow to a man who had honored him in a way that a political career never could. He was C. Hart Merriam. A mammalogist, he claimed in the *Proceedings of the Biological Society of Washington* (the state) to have found a new species of Olympic Mountain elk. Recognizing Roosevelt as a lifelong naturalist, Merriam decided that it would be "fitting that the noblest deer in America should perpetuate the name of one who, in the midst of a busy public career, has found time to study our larger mammals in their native haunts and has written the best accounts we have ever had of their habits and chase."

He named his discovery *Cervus Roosevelt*.

Roosevelt responded, "No compliment could be paid me that I would appreciate as much as this—in the first place, because of the fact itself, and in the next place because it comes from you. To have the noblest game animal of America named after me by the foremost of living mammalogists is something that really makes me prouder than I can well say."

Chapter 7

A Process of Evolution

Washington, December 11, 1897

My Dear Captain Mahan:

I agree with all you say as to what will be the result if we fail to take Hawaii. It will show that we either have lost, or else wholly lack, the masterful instinct which alone can make a race great. I feel so deeply about it I hardly dare express myself in full. The terrible part is to see the men of education who take the lead in trying to make us prove traitors to our race.

Faithfully yours,
Theodore Roosevelt

In jotting down these thoughts for Captain Alfred Thayer Mahan, Roosevelt addressed a man whose life's foundations were in many ways like his own, although Mahan had not been born into a family with wealth. In childhood both had been voracious readers of stories and books about ships and naval lore. Both had grown up to write history and reap acclaim for their efforts. Each had a strong father: Dennis Hart Mahan had been a professor of civil and military engineering and the dean of faculty at the U.S. Military Academy; Roosevelt's namesake was the scion of a family that had helped found the Dutch settlement of New Amsterdam and had made a modest personal fortune in business. Both fathers had imbued their sons with manliness and self-reliance; ambition; patriotism; a belief in the importance of education in the social, political, economic, and cultural tenets of Anglo-American civilization; and Christian faith and values.

There, however, the similarities ended. Roosevelt had become the person of action as well as words, the sunburned adventurer and advocate of the strenuous life, the gregarious and popular figure of New York and Washington social circles, and the magnet for the young officers who represented the future that Roosevelt envisioned for the U.S. Navy. In Mahan there was nothing at all so swashbuckling and charming. By all accounts he was exceedingly vain and self-assured (to the point of arrogance), contentious, humorless, and without close personal friends. Whereas Roosevelt had been thrilled by his experiences aboard torpedo boats and when the *Iowa's* great guns thundered, Mahan despised everything about being aboard ship and was deathly afraid of the sea itself.

Yet this fifty-seven-year-old ex-sailor who got seasick and in his forty years in the navy never participated in a battle at sea had emerged in retirement as the nation's best-known naval figure. With the publication of *The Influence of Sea Power upon History,* he had introduced Americans to new ways of looking at their country's future position in world affairs and the strategic role of a powerful navy in attaining and maintaining that position. But no reader of the book proved more significant than the one who endorsed its lessons and theories and carried them with him into an office from which they might be implemented. In Mahan, Roosevelt had discerned "a man steeped through and through in the peculiar knowledge and wisdom of the great naval expert who was also by instinct and training a statesman to whom the past and the present in all international matters of profound importance were open books whose inmost meaning he had mastered."

Mahan's analysis of the proper place of the United States in the world and his advocacy of an assertive foreign policy were not based solely on his interpretation of the role of navies throughout history. They also rested upon the tenets of a philosophical view of the world known as social Darwinism.

In applying the evolutionary theories that Charles Darwin had advanced in *Origin of Species* and *The Descent of Man,* the social Darwinists argued that various peoples were at different stages in the process of evolution. Because some were far more advanced than others, it went without saying that white Europeans, and their American cousins, stood at the top of the evolutionary ladder. They therefore had a moral duty to protect their interests and lead their inferiors toward higher civilization. In Mahan's thinking, "The first law of states, as of men, is self-preservation."

If such preservation had to be achieved by national expansion and force of arms, Mahan asserted, naval history and the evolution of states had proved that war was an effective coercive instrument placed in human hands by the Creator to enable God-fearing and God-loving peoples to defend that which was good, just, and righteous and to oppose that which was evil, unjust, and wrong.

The application of these beliefs convinced Mahan that the United States was fated to come to terms with an increasing presence of the Japanese navy in the Pacific. To thwart expansion by Japan, he advocated an American defense perimeter anchored in the Hawaiian Islands. He viewed as inevitable a military conflict between the United States and Japan, and he went so far as to forecast that it would begin with a Japanese attack.

Just as Mahan shared Roosevelt's understanding of modern history and an appreciation of the role of naval power in affecting it, Brooks Adams, in his 1895 book *The Law of Civilization and Decay,* afforded a view of the tides of history that alerted Roosevelt to the importance of Asia in world development. Citing the density of population in the countries of the Far East, combined with the centralizing methods of trade and industry, Adams predicted that China and Japan would emerge as significant world powers. As a result, he said, the determination of the direction of world affairs would inevitably pass from Europe and America to the Orient.

In interpreting the influence of Adams's book, David H. Burton observed in his biography of Roosevelt, "While not accepting the Adams thesis at face value, Roosevelt was alerted to the supreme importance of Asia in world development. He became convinced at this time that if the greatness of the United States was to be sustained, it must have a substantial role to play in Far Eastern affairs. . . . Without a great navy, complete with bases to support its farflung operations, no American influence would be possible in that part of the world."

Thus, social Darwinism provided a further rationale for the movement to annex Hawaii. Doing so would declare American determination to block Japanese expansion in the Pacific. Having set this course, Washington could not escape the certainty that any conflict with Spain over Cuba would require the nullification of the Spanish armada based in the Philippines. Therefore, it was with satisfaction that on October 21, 1897, Roosevelt read the following memorandum from Secretary Long to Commodore Dewey:

> On November 30th, 1897, you will regard yourself detached from duty as president of the Board of Inspection and Survey, Navy Department, Washington, D.C., and from such other duty as may have been assigned to you. You will proceed to San Francisco, Cal., and thence to Yokohoma, Japan, taking passage in the steamer of the Pacific Mail Steamship Company, sailing from San Francisco on December 7th next. Upon your arrival at Yokohoma you will report to Rear Admiral Frederick V. McNair, U.S.N., the commander-in-chief of the Asiatic Station, aboard the U.S.F.S. Olympia, for duty as commander-in-chief of that station, as the relief of that officer.

Before departing, Dewey had been guest of honor at a farewell salute given by friends and leading officers of the navy at the Metropolitan Club on Saturday, November 26. Over an after-dinner cigar he turned to the navy captain next to him and said, "My chance has come. And I owe it largely to Theodore Roosevelt. Why he took such an interest in my application, I don't know. There were three applicants, you know, and my claim was not the best. The Assistant Secretary overcame all opposition. And, now, I go."

Writing in *McClure's Magazine* of October 1899, Roosevelt recalled:

> the high professional reputation [Dewey] enjoyed, and the character he had established for willingness to accept responsibility, for sound judgment and for entire fearlessness. Probably the best way (although no way is infallible) to tell the worth of a naval commander as yet untried in war is to get at the estimate in which he is held by the best fighting men who would have to serve under him. In the summer of 1897 there were, in Washington, captains and commanders . . . who were already known for the dash and skill with which they handled the ships, the excellence of their gun practice, the good discipline of crews, and an eager desire to win honorable renown. All these men were a unit in their faith in Commodore Dewey, in their desire to serve under him, should the chance arise, and in their unquestioning belief that he was the man to meet an emergency in a way that would do credit to the flag.

In Roosevelt's estimation, Dewey represented exactly the kind of officer whose career had been hindered by the outmoded system of personnel management that Long had asked him to study and help reform. He told Long, "We should consider well the question of personnel. If neglected, all other efforts to perfect the Navy will be as nothing in the end. We must do away with every cause of weakness and disorganization."

If Roosevelt's experiences as a member of the Civil Service Commission and president of the New York Board of Police Commissioners had demonstrated anything about his character, it was his insistence on efficiency. Appalled by the lack of it in the naval services at a moment in the nation's history that he saw as pivotal, he told Long, "In view of how much there is at stake, the nation should omit no effort, and be deterred by no ordinary expense, in promoting the highest state of efficiency in personnel of the Navy."

Roosevelt felt that the true reforms should begin by eliminating the division of naval personnel into two traditional classifications: engineers and those who did everything else on a ship, including the actual fighting. Although this arrangement had been practical in the past, in an age when technology advanced so rapidly every officer on a modern war vessel had to be an engineer. He pointed out, "Everything on such a vessel goes by machinery, and every officer, whether dealing with the turrets or the engine room, has to do engineer's work." As a result, there was no longer a reason for having a separate body of engineers. "What we need is one homogeneous body, all of whose members are trained for the efficient performance of the duties of the modern line officer. The midshipmen will be grounded in all these duties at Annapolis, and will be perfected likewise in all of them by actual work after graduation. We are not making a revolution; we are merely recognizing and giving shape to an evolution, which has come slowly but surely and naturally, and we propose to organize the Navy along the lines indicated by the course of the evolution itself."

For this evolutionary process to succeed, two other changes in policy were required: (1) the unclogging of the old process of promotion through a weeding out of those in the upper ranks who were deemed "least fit to meet the heavy requirements of modern naval duty"; and (2) the guaranteeing that "enlisted men aboard ship shall be given the same reward of pension and retirement enjoyed by their brethren who fight ashore."

Roosevelt the naval historian and visionary now had to give way to Roosevelt the practical politician. While the bill that would go to Capitol Hill to implement these changes was "so obviously in the interest of the whole service" that it seemed to him "unlikely that there will be serious objection to what it proposes to do," he warned that there might be objections on one point. Manpower reform would cost money. If the recommendations were approved, there would be a resulting rise in payroll of $600,000 a year.

Furthermore, an increase in budget was anticipated for target practice. Strenuously arguing that the current yearly sum of $600,000 for gunnery training was insufficient, Roosevelt wrote:

> There is no use in having the best ships and the best guns if these ships are not to be handled in the best way and the guns served with the utmost accuracy. Much depends upon building our ships and guns, but even more depends upon using them aright after they have been built. We can hardly pay too high a price for the highest performance of duty afloat, and the best use of the material—that is, the most perfect training of the personnel—can only be obtained by the expenditure of money. The men must be drilled, and drilled, and drilled again; the ships must be maneuvered in squadron month in and month out; the practice with the great guns at targets must go on without ceasing.

In this lengthy report to Secretary Long, the voice that came through was not that of an assistant secretary of the navy pleading for funds, but of Theodore Roosevelt the accomplished author and, certainly, the romantic boy with a head aswim in the glories of warring ships. He wrote:

> All that is done—the building of the ships, the training of the men, the education of the officers, and the continued struggle to perfect armor and instruments for war, for which millions upon millions are being yearly spent by all the non-effete nations of the world—is for one purpose. All efforts focus on the one crucial period, the hour of battle, where, once started, the one mind—that of the captain alone—decides whether the vast machinery of the battle ship responds well or ill is demanded by all the weary years of preparation. It will be an hour of high tension, when the man in the fighting tower must not fail his country, and it is our duty to see that the man placed there is so chosen and so trained that he can stand the grave test to which he will be subjected. We owe it to him that he should be properly paid. We owe it to the nation that he shall be chosen by the exercise of the best intelligence and not merely by seniority.

As Roosevelt forwarded his report to Long on December 9—it would then be sent to Congress for whatever action that body deemed appropriate—the man whom Roosevelt had vaulted past others was making his way across the Pacific Ocean. The voyage aboard the Pacific mail steamer *Gaelic* from San Francisco to Yokohoma took seventeen days (with the calendar set back a day as the ship crossed 180 degrees longitude). He arrived on Christmas, and on the next day, his sixtieth birthday, Commodore Dewey left for the port of Nagasaki to take command of the Asiatic Squadron.

Upon taking charge, he would command from the bridge of the flagship of the squadron. The largest and most powerful ship of the Pacific Fleet, the *Olympia* was a protected cruiser of 5,870 tons, mounting four eight-inch guns in twin turrets, ten five-inch guns in casements, and an assortment of small rapid-fire weapons. Undoubtedly, Roosevelt would have preferred his man in the Orient to have been on the bridge of the type of warship recommended by Roosevelt's own mentor. Wars at sea could be settled, and command of the seas established, asserted Alfred Thayer Mahan, only by concentrated fleets of battleships that could maneuver so as to bring a greater part of their firepower and personnel to bear against the foe in a decisive "Big Battle."

Unfortunately, Roosevelt's hopes of realizing his and Mahan's dream of a mighty fleet of battleships, expressed in Roosevelt's plea to the secretary of the navy to seek authorization from Congress to build six new ones, proved unavailing. Long had asked Congress for one. Until that vessel joined the fleet, the navy had the first-class battleships *Massachusetts, Iowa, Indiana,* and *Oregon,* and the second-class *Texas* and *Maine.*

The latter had been launched into New York's East River on November 18, 1890, but had required five years of fitting before being declared ready for service on September 17, 1895. In configuration she was a naval-design hybrid. She was steam-powered but had been given two masts like those of old sailing ships. But for some reason no canvas had been provided, rendering the masts useless. (An early design had included three masts.) Interested in what that student of and writer about warships thought of the design, the *Maine*'s first skipper, Charles Dwight Sigsbee, wrote Roosevelt a letter expressing his own opinion that sails were an anachronism. He wanted to know if the assistant secretary concurred.

Roosevelt replied, "We must face the fact that sails have gone just as three centuries ago oars went."

A letter also came from the *Maine*'s executive officer, forty-nine-year-old Lieutenant Commander Richard Wainwright. Known to Roosevelt and admired for his work on the navy's war plan while serving as the navy department's chief intelligence officer, he included a request for a photograph. Roosevelt replied, "As you are unwise enough to want a picture of mine, I send it." He then "wished there was a chance that the *Maine* was going to be used against some foreign power."

He would take Spain "if nothing better offered."

Part III

No Place for Mercy

Chapter 8

A Gem of an Island

"Everything is green as April in Andalusia."

So observed Christopher Columbus as he gazed from the bow of the *Santa Maria* one morning in October 1492.

The singing of birds was such that it seemed as if one would never desire to depart. Flocks of garishly hued parrots obscured the sun. Beyond the blue sea's snowy breakers and palm-fringed beaches stood lush trees of a thousand species. Behind them in the distance rose the sun-and-cloud kissed sierra. Was this paradise, which seemed to float between the sea and the sky, China or Japan?

When he knew it was neither, Columbus chose to claim it for Spain and honor the prince of Castile by naming it *Isla Juana*. Later it would be known as *Fernandina*. Still later, *Santiago*. Finally, it was called by the name given it by its natives. To the Tainos, it was *Colba*. The Spanish tongue twisted that into *Cuba*.

On the northwest coast lay one of the finest deep-water harbors in the world. The Tainos' name for it was *Avan*. The Spanish christened it *Havana*. Three centuries following Columbus, another visitor declared the port "the boulevard of the New World." In 1762 it fell, briefly, into the hands of the British. However, Cuba remained indisputably the Spanish "Pearl of the Antilles." Despite the attempts to overthrow Spanish rule in the Western Hemisphere by the early-nineteenth-century revolutionary leaders Francisco de Miranda, Miguel Hidalgo, Agustín de Iturbide, Bernardo O'Higgins, José de San Martín, and Simón Bolívar, Cuba and the smaller nearby island of Puerto Rico remained Spain's "Ever-Faithful Isles."

Meanwhile, not far to the west, citizens of the nation that had not been ever-faithful to their mother country, having staged the first successful anticolonial war in history, soon enunciated a policy that championed and pledged to defend the independence of the peoples in all territories of Columbus's New World. On December 2, 1824, President James Monroe included in his annual message to Congress a four-point doctrine that would forever bear his name. It asserted that (1) the continents of America were no longer to be considered as subjects for future colonization by European powers; (2) there existed in the Americas a political system that was essentially different and separate from that in Europe; (3) the United States would consider dangerous to its peace and safety any attempt on the part of European powers to extend their system anywhere in the Western Hemisphere; and (4) the United States would not interfere with existing colonies.

Two decades later, President James K. Polk "interfered" in Cuba by offering to buy the island from Spain for $100 million. It would have been quite a purchase. In the almost four centuries since Columbus first laid eyes on it, Cuba had proved to be infinitely more precious than a mere pearl. Although Spanish hearts had been broken by the discovery that the island held no gold, the land had provided riches in the form of sugar cane, tobacco, and other agricultural products, as well as minerals such as copper and nickel. And there were enormous profits to be made in the trade that passed through the seaports of Havana and Santiago.

So alluring was the idea of American annexation that Spain's curt refusal to accept Polk's offer prompted an illegal attempt to seize the island through a privately financed expedition organized by a Venezuelan adventurer, Narciso López, and Colonel William L. Crittenden, a member of a prominent Kentucky family. The scheme had the backing of such Southern luminaries as John C. Calhoun and Jefferson Davis, who liked the idea of dividing Cuba into five slave-owning states. Planned for 1849, this bold grab was thwarted by Polk's successor, President Zachary Taylor.

Emboldened by Taylor's death the next year, the plotters tried once more, only to find little enthusiasm for the idea among Cubans. Undaunted, López and Crittenden tried again in 1851 and failed miserably.

During the next decade, the idea of annexing Cuba remained alive, though fruitless, then went dormant during the Civil War. In the years that followed, it was little more than a subject for interesting and lively debate in the Washington drawing rooms of expansionists and jingoes, like the one on Massachusetts Avenue belonging to Henry Cabot Lodge.

Others who talked of freeing Cuba—though not of making it into one or several states in the American Union—were Cuban exiles. Based in large part in New York City, they organized rallies at which firebrands called for the freeing of Cuba by force. Observed a dubious *New York Times:* "The most alarming Cuban revolutions have occurred in New York for many years—in speeches."

The most notable of the orators was José Martí. A poet, he had published an anti-Spain newspaper, *La Patria Libre,* and had served six years at hard labor in a rock quarry in Cuba and Spain as punishment. In travels across the United States from his home on the New York waterfront, he sought to rally other Cuban exiles to contribute money to finance gunrunning and the infiltration of revolutionaries into Cuba by means of smuggling operations known as *filibustering.*

Then dawned February 28, 1895. News despatches from Havana reported that on the twenty-fourth an insurrection had broken out. Denying there had been a revolt, the Spanish minister in Washington said the trouble involved "bandits." Assurances came from the Spanish authorities in Cuba that the "rioters" either had been dispersed or were begging for clemency. In fact, Martí and others had tried to land three boats of insurgents at different sites. However, something had gone wrong. Boats were impounded. Two insurgents were taken into custody. The only ones to make it ashore had been a small force led by General Antonio Maceo. Landing in the eastern province of Oriente, they were ultimately joined by a party led by Martí and seventy-two-year-old General Máximo Gómez.

On March 31 the revolutionaries set out through the mountains and jungles, marching westward. In time they would be met by a combination of Spanish regulars and Cuban loyalist troops led by Spain's most illustrious military hero, General Arsenio Martínez de Campos, in a series of indecisive fights. During one of these clashes the rebels lost their most inspirational leader. On May 20, near the little town of Dos Rios, José Martí took a Spanish bullet through the heart. Knocked from his white horse, he was dead before he hit the ground. When the news reached the United States, Cuban-exile propagandists with an appreciation of the American appetite for heroes instantly hailed Martí as a martyr in the cause of Cuban liberation. Meanwhile, Máximo Gómez's guerrillas fought on.

As the first anniversary of the campaign approached, the increasingly frustrated and worried Spanish government leader, Premier

Antonio Cánovas del Castillo, received an astonishingly frank message from his military commander in Cuba.

"Even the timid will soon follow the orders of the insurrectionary chiefs," wrote General Campos on June 1, 1896. The only means to prevent this, he suggested, would be to "reconcentrate the families of the countryside in the towns." To do so, much force would be needed. The misery and hunger would be terrible. "Summary executions and similar acts" would be required.

"Perhaps it will come to this," he concluded, "but only as a last resort." He then informed Cánovas, "I think I lack the qualities to carry through such a policy."

However, the general had someone in mind who could do so. He suggested General Valeriano Weyler. "Among our present generals, only Weyler has the necessary capacity for such a policy."

Premier Cánovas heeded the advice and appointed as Cuba's next governor-general Valeriano Weyler y Nicolau.

Born in Majorca in 1838, Weyler was of German ancestry and had a spartan outlook on living. He prided himself on sleeping on a thin, hard mattress and surviving on a menu of sardines and bread. Having served as military attaché in Washington during the American Civil War, he claimed to have learned his first lessons in all-out warfare from General William Tecumseh Sherman's march through Georgia.

"Mercy has no place in war," he declared. "I care not what is said about me. I am not a politician. I am Weyler."

Asking, "How do they want me to wage war?" he answered his own question with a sarcastic query. "With bishops' pastorals and presents of sweets and money?"

He arrived in Cuba on February 10, 1896, and immediately issued a series of *bandos* (decrees). All Cubans living in the countryside in the rebel-infested provinces of Oriente and Camaguey were to be relocated into fortified towns within eight days. If they had cattle, the animals were to be confiscated. No food could be taken with them. Their houses were to be put to the torch. Not a thing was to be left standing that might be of aid and comfort to the guerrillas. Once these goals had been achieved in the two provinces, the *reconcentrado* orders were extended across the island, thus introducing to history the concentration camp, four decades before it was employed on a monumental scale in Weyler's native Germany under Adolf Hitler's Nazis.

As reports of this campaign trickled northward from Havana to New York, William Randolph Hearst, the owner of the New York *Journal,* recognized the ingredients of a circulation-boosting story. Crowning Valeriano Weyler "the most cruel and bloodthirsty general in the world" and naming him Butcher Weyler, Hearst's *Journal* on February 23, 1896, ranted, "Weyler, the brute, the devastator of haciendas, and the outrager of women . . . [is] pitiless, cold, an exterminator of men. . . . There is nothing to prevent his carnal, animal brain from running riot with itself in inventing tortures and infamies of bloody debauchery."

Then, to set out for *Journal* readers all the grisly details of exactly what was happening on that island but ninety miles from the United States, Hearst sent two of Theodore Roosevelt's friends.

Frederic Remington's job was to provide pictures.

Richard Harding Davis was to provide the words.

Chapter 9

Writers and Artists

The plan was for Davis and Remington to link up with the rebels and their leader, General Gómez.

Having tried and failed to get ashore surreptitiously, they made up their minds, in Remington's words, to forget about trying to gain entry through "the coal cellar window" and approach via the front door. Using bogus passports and other documents, they booked passage on the steamer *Olivette,* landed in Havana without difficulty on January 9, 1897, and checked into the Hotel Inglaterra on the ocean-front promenade known as the *Prado*.

Their forged travel papers had been made out of what Remington called "some sort of custom-house blanks" by a friend of Davis's in Key West. Thoroughly impressed by his journalistic companion's enterprise and daring, he named him Richard-the-Lion-Harding Davis.

Born in Philadelphia on April 18, 1864, Davis had had the benefit of an excellent education at the Philadelphia Episcopal Academy, Swarthmore College preparatory department, and Lehigh University, where he exhibited journalistic interests by editing the *Lehigh Burr,* a passion for drama by founding the dramatic society, and athletic ability in helping to establish football at the college. Enrolled in a Latin-scientific course of study, he left without a degree in June 1885 to attend Johns Hopkins University as a special undergraduate student. A year later he began working for the *Philadelphia Record*. He switched to the *Philadelphia Press* in 1889 and then moved to New York and the *Evening Sun*.

Temperamentally eager for adventure, he had by 1897 traveled in the West and Southwest, toured Europe, gone down to Central America and Venezuela, reported on the coronation of Czar Nicholas II, and in 1886 visited mines near Santiago de Cuba. In 1894 he had missed covering the Sino-Japanese War because he was too impatient to spend three weeks on trains and ships to reach the fighting. He believed that being a war correspondent was the highest form of journalism because it provided an opportunity to observe "men under the stress of all the great emotions."

Davis had gotten to know Theodore Roosevelt in New York and had accompanied Police Commissioner Roosevelt on at least one of his famous "midnight rambles," during which the incognito head of the police force scoured city streets looking for cops who were not doing their duty. Like Roosevelt, he had a romantic vision of men in battle being "inspired by noble courage, pity, the spirit of self-sacrifice, loyalty, and pride of race and country."

Safely arrived in Havana in January 1897, he and Remington arranged through the good offices of the American consul general, white-haired and portly Fitzhugh Lee (famed for his exploits in the Civil War), to be permitted an interview with General Weyler. As Remington sketched him in profile, he observed a surprisingly small man. He later drew a word picture: "A black apparition—black eyes, black hair, black beard—dark, exceedingly dark complexion; a plain black attire, black shoes, black tie, and soiled collar and not a relief from the aspect of darkness anywhere on his person."

When Remington managed to locate and render drawings of a group of *reconcentrados*, he saw "scarred Cubans with their arms bound stiffly behind them being marched" to their confinement. In the caption to one of the drawings, he said, "The blood curdles in my veins as I think of the atrocity, of the cruelty, practiced on these helpless victims."

Disgusted, angry, and convinced that under such a tyranny the rebels could not prevail, and desperately wishing to get out of Cuba, he sent a telegram to Hearst:

EVERYTHING IS QUIET. THERE IS NO TROUBLE HERE.
THERE IS NO WAR. I WISH TO RETURN

Hearst shot back:

PLEASE REMAIN. YOU FURNISH THE PICTURES AND
I'LL FURNISH THE WAR

Although this cable is arguably the most famous message ever sent in the history of American journalism, New York newspaper historian Hy B. Turner, in his study of journalism greats, *When Giants Ruled: The Story of Park Row,* wrote that Hearst had later told his son, William Randolph Jr., that he had never sent such a cable. Whether he did or not, those eleven words capture the essence of the dominant personality behind the style of newspapering that burst upon the scene in the 1890s.

Yellow journalism got its sobriquet from the first comic strip. Drawn by R. F. Outcault, "The Yellow Kid" presented the adventures of an engaging slum urchin. He had first appeared in Joseph Pulitzer's *World.* Then Hearst hired an artist of his own, George Luks, to provide a Yellow Kid for the amusement of *Journal* readers. Exactly who considered these competing cartoons as emblematic of the fierce competition between two newspaper giants and coined the phrase *yellow journalism* to identify their sensationalistic style is not known.

How William Randolph Hearst came to be the most famous exponent of this style is, however, well known, although the story is substantially different from the one told by Orson Welles in his film *Citizen Kane,* which many critics believe is a portrait of Hearst. In the movie, Charles Foster Kane uses an inheritance to buy a decrepit New York City newspaper; William Randolph Hearst had attained a failing San Francisco paper, the *Examiner,* as a gift from his father.

To the surprise of Senator George Hearst, his son transformed the paper into a moneymaker. The senior Hearst died in 1891. When "Willie" Hearst decided to turn his talents to running a paper in New York City, his widowed mother, who had inherited $17 million from her husband, sold her seven-sixteenths interest in the Anaconda Copper Mining Company and gave him $7.5 million. Barely denting this fortune, he paid $180,000 to purchase the *New York Morning Journal.* He arrived in New York in 1895, in the colorful phraseology of James Melvin Lee's *History of American Journalism,* "with all the discreet secrecy of a wooden-legged burglar having a fit on a tin roof."

The seller of the *Morning Journal* was John R. McLean, who had gotten it for $1 million from Albert Pulitzer, the younger brother of the newspaper pioneer who soon became Hearst's chief target.

Born in Hungary in 1847, Joseph Pulitzer had left his homeland for the United States after being rejected as a volunteer by both the Austrian and French armies in 1864. He found no qualms about his fitness, however, when he volunteered for the Union army. Having served under General Philip Sheridan in the Civil War, he settled in St. Louis and into journalism as a reporter for a German-language paper published by Carl Shurz. In spite of jokes about his heavy accent, he was an excellent journalist and, in 1878, scraped together twenty-five hundred dollars to buy the *St. Louis Dispatch* at auction. Subsequently acquiring the *St. Louis Post,* he combined the two papers into one and created a sensationalistic style featuring crusades for public reform. He garnered enough profits to purchase the New York *World* for $346,000 from Wall Street financier Jay Gould in 1883. Although frail health and eventual blindness forced him to give up direct control of his newspapers, he remained the undisputed monarch of New York journalism until the arrival of Hearst.

The opening shot of Hearst's attack on the heart of newspapering, Park Row, was to continue to sell issues of the *Journal* for a penny. He then launched a raid on Pulitzer's staff of veteran journalists. He waved around his money in an attempt to woo the brilliant young editor of Pulitzer's *Sunday World,* but Morrill Goddard refused to go unless Hearst also hired the entire *World* staff. He told Hearst, "I need my writers and artists!" Not to be denied, Hearst coaxed them all to come to the *Journal.*

Thus began a vicious circulation war that would reach a fever pitch over Cuba. In one of Hearst's first signed editorials he asserted that newspapers had the power to declare war. Although Pulitzer exhibited an initial reluctance to rattle sabres, he could not ignore the fact that Hearst's bellicosity resulted in increased circulation for the *Journal.* Finally, the old man decided that he rather liked "the idea of war—not a big one—but one that will arouse interest and give me the chance to gauge the reflex of our circulation figures."

Because of the difficulty of obtaining facts from Spanish officials in Havana, who were understandably suspicious of American journalists, reporters for both the *Journal* and the *World,* as well as for other New York newspapers (including Charles A. Dana's *Sun*), relied on a source much closer to their Park Row offices. This was a little band of Cuban exiles known as the *Junta.* Chatting with reporters in their office, they fed them an endless supply of information nuggets, or what the reporters called "peanuts." The trouble with the so-called Peanut Club was that little of the information they were fed was likely to be true.

In *Citizen Hearst,* the definitive biography of the owner of the *Journal,* W. A. Swanberg wrote of this Cuban chicanery and American gullibility: "For two years, while the rebellion gained momentum, the New York newspapers published accounts of battles that never occurred, while remaining ignorant of real battles. They narrated a succession of Spanish atrocities entirely unauthenticated. They dealt in the feeblest of rumor."

For this reason, when Remington cabled that there was no war, William Randolph Hearst could confidently assure the artist that if he were to remain in Cuba, the war would be provided.

Remington ignored the order to stay and packed his bags to go home on the next boat out.

Richard Harding Davis remained. In a letter dated January 15, 1897, he disagreed with Remington. He told his mother, "There is a war here and no mistake."

Sailing out of Havana, Remington looked back, raised a fist, shook it, and shouted, "I won't come again except with United States soldiers."

Chapter 10

A Flurry in Havana

Frederic Remington's vow and the desires of the potentates of yellow journalism notwithstanding, the man who had taken the oath as President of the United States on March 4, 1897, had no intention of sending American troops to Cuba. William McKinley favored diplomacy.

Like his predecessor, Grover Cleveland, McKinley urged Spain to end the war. He suggested that this could be done if Spain were to make "proposals of settlement honorable to herself and just to her Cuban colony." He had a kind of Cuban autonomy in mind. In expectation of success, he named as minister to Spain Stewart L. Woodford and sent him off to San Sebastian to see what he could do to win concessions and avoid war.

Yet as McKinley pursued his pacifist policy, he could not escape the urgings of his assistant secretary of the navy to recall the admonition of George Washington that had been the theme of Roosevelt's speech at the Naval War College: The best way to ensure peace was to prepare for war. McKinley had listened in his polite and pleasantly enigmatic way, kept an eye on what was going on in Cuba, pressed the Spaniards to reach a diplomatic resolution, and did nothing to keep Roosevelt from readying the navy for action.

Meanwhile, McKinley's minister to Spain was at work. At the age of sixty-two, Stewart L. Woodford, greeted as "General," had been a Civil War commander, member of Congress, and lieutenant governor of New York. Having departed on his mission in mid-July, he had stopped in London to measure European interest in the crisis between Spain and the United States over Cuba. He found little. But while in England he received the shocking news that the official he planned to meet in Spain, Premier Cánovas, had been assassinated. Until a permanent replacement could be named, he would negotiate with the foreign minister, Carlos O'Donnell.

They sat down together at five o'clock on September 13, 1897, and met for three hours. Listening attentively and politely, O'Donnell heard a familiar refrain. American patience had run out. The Cuban problem must be settled very soon. Most importantly, the United States would expect "before the first of November next, assurance as would satisfy the United States that early and certain peace be promptly secured, and that otherwise the United States must consider itself free to take such steps as its government should deem necessary to procure the result, with due regard to our interests and the general tranquility."

O'Donnell seemed interested. However, he was soon replaced as Spain's negotiator by a new premier. Práxedes Mateo Sagasta came into office with his own formula for peace. It began with a startling action. On October 6 he announced the recall of General Valeriano Weyler, to be replaced with the more moderate General Ramón Blanco y Enenas. Blanco arrived in Havana twenty-four days later, the same day that Weyler boarded the mail steamer *Montserrat* for Spain.

As the Butcher departed, Blanco could hardly ignore or miss the significance of Weyler's send-off. Scores of Spanish-born loyalists (*peninsulares*) turned out to cheer him and condemn Spain for removing him. When he arrived in Barcelona a few days later, he was greeted by even more angry Spaniards.

Encouraged by the replacement of the embodiment of all that Americans found repulsive about Spanish rule in Cuba, President McKinley sent his first annual message to the Congress. Delivered on December 6, it treated the Cuban dilemma at great length. Rejecting a policy of Cuban independence backed by American intervention, he held that Spain should be afforded full opportunity to pacify Cuba "in the near future."

But within days of the message, Fitzhugh Lee signaled from Havana a report of increasing anti-American sentiment that might take the form of violence against American citizens and property in Cuba. He proposed the stationing of an American warship at Havana. In response, on December 10, the *Maine* cleared Norfolk, Virginia, not en route to Havana, but to Key West. She dropped anchor there on December 15.

Meanwhile, the Spanish government seemed willing to cooperate with McKinley. Having no interest in a war with the United States, the queen regent, Maria Christina, and her newly designated premier, Sagasta, signaled a change in policy. They offered to grant Cubans home rule.

Despite the conciliatory atmosphere in Spain and the patience in the United States, the rebels showed no intention of laying down their arms. Sensing a victory, they called for nothing less than an independent Cuba.

The reaction of loyalists was fury at being betrayed. Venting their anger on Wednesday, January 12, 1898, they rioted in Havana. A correspondent for the Washington *Star,* Charles M. Pepper, informed his readers that

> there was a lull during the midday, but in the afternoon, the mob rallied. It made little demonstration, and was content with throwing stones and breaking windows . . . . It was known that the authorities had been unravelling several supposed conspiracies, and that at all the recent bull-fights extraordinary precautions had been taken to prevent an outbreak. In Spain the popular uprisings usually begin at the bull ring.

Rampaging through streets whose terrified merchants had shuttered their shops, the mob chanted, "Long live Weyler! Down with autonomy."

In the American consulate, Fitzhugh Lee, who was worried about the safety of Americans, again requested a show of force from the *Maine.* Aboard the ship at Key West, Captain Sigsbee received a message containing the words "two dollars." This was code. It meant that he was to make ready for Cuban waters. Should a second message come containing another code phrase, one of the ship's guns was to be fired as a signal to summon officers and crew back to the ship.

The next morning, Roosevelt was in Secretary Long's office. Of the meeting, Long confided to his diary that Roosevelt "began in his usual emphatic and dead-in-earnest manner. After referring sensibly to two or three matters of business, he told me that, in case of war with Spain, he intends to abandon everything and go to the front. He bores me with his plans of naval and military movements, and the necessity of having some scheme of attack arranged for instant execution in case of an emergency. By tomorrow morning, he will have got half a dozen heads of bureau together and have spoiled twenty pages of good writing paper, and lain awake half the night."

As for Roosevelt's expectations regarding the events in Cuba, he used a small sheet of writing paper to advise frequent correspondent Lieutenant Kimball in a letter dated December 17: "I doubt if those Spaniards can really pacify Cuba, and if the insurrection goes on much longer I don't see how we can help interfering."

A letter also went to General Tillinghast of the New York National Guard: "I don't believe that this flurry in Havana will bring about a war; still it may, and in accordance with my promise I write to you. If there is a war I, of course, intend to go. I believe I can get a commission as a major or lieutenant colonel in one of the regiments, but I want your help and the Governor's. I think you know that I would not discredit the commission, and that I would do my duty."

Covering all the bases, he appealed to one of the New York National Guard's commanders, Colonel Francis V. Greene: "In view of this morning's news from Havana it seems possible, although not probable, that we may have trouble with Spain. If so, I must ask you to let me know as soon as possible if I can go in as one of your majors. I am going to go somehow."

But in a very nice house on N Street a situation had developed that threatened to scuttle the assistant secretary of the navy's dreams of reaping the glories of battle.

Chapter 11

A Waste of Time

Edith Roosevelt lay deathly ill. For four weeks her temperature stood at 101 degrees. Although she had a complete recovery after the birth of Quentin in November, Theodore Roosevelt could not forget that he had lost his first wife, Alice, after the birth of their daughter. On that most fateful of days, he lost not only Alice but his mother. Now, since the turn of the year, Edith had suffered acute neuralgic pains and sciatica. For a time he feared she had typhoid fever. To make her as comfortable as possible, quiet had been imposed by sending the small children away to relatives. When fourteen-year-old Alice proved to be too much for her busy father to handle and young Ted began to suffer from nervous exhaustion, they were sent to Aunt Anna. So concerned was their father about their mother's condition that he canceled one of his favorite events, the annual dinner of the Boone and Crockett Club, of which he was a founder, in New York City. The only respite from these domestic worries was work.

On January 14, 1898, he sent Secretary Long a memorandum (running five pages in book typeface) covering the galaxy of his thinking on the state of the country's affairs with Spain. Allowing that at present the troubles in Cuba seemed less acute, he warned of "serious consequences," especially for the navy, "upon which would be visited the national indignation . . . if we should drift into a war with Spain and suddenly find ourselves obliged to begin it without preparation, instead of having at least a month's warning, during which we could actively prepare to strike. Some preparation can and should be taken now, on the mere chance of having to strike. In addition to this, when the blow had been determined upon we should defer delivering it until we have had at least three weeks or a month in which to make ready. The saving in life, money, and reputation by such a course will be very great."

Certain things needed be done at once if there were any reasonable chance of trouble with Spain within six months. For instance, the disposition of the fleet on foreign stations had to be radically altered without delay. Small cruisers and gunboats that had been sent off "to various ports of the world with a total disregard" of the fact that they would be useless in the event of a war over Cuba needed to be recalled for use in a possible blockade. Or they might be employed to ferret out "scores of small Spanish cruisers and gunboats which form practically the entire Spanish naval force around the Island."

With a breadth and depth of knowledge that had to have impressed Secretary Long, the memo listed all the ships that were or would be available for action, as well as their locations, capabilities, and shortcomings.

Roosevelt pleaded for immediate orders to the commanders of ships in European waters to sail for home, lest with the outbreak of war they be "shut up in a European port" or "run the risk of capture" by the Spanish.

Looking across the Pacific, he found that Commodore Dewey had ample sea power "to warrant his making a demonstration against the Philippines, because he could overmaster the Spanish squadron around those islands." Still, the margin of superiority was so small that it might be wise that three, possibly four, ships be added to his command. This could be done, he said, without jeopardizing Hawaii.

The most urgent need, he wrote, was ammunition. The shortage was so acute that he saw no likelihood of sustaining a bombardment of Havana. Instead, he recommended engaging the enemy fleet at every point around Cuba and along the coast of Spain itself. If a flying squadron of powerful ships of speed and great coal capacity were sent to the Spanish coast, "we can give the Spaniards all they want to do at home, and will gain the inestimable moral advantage of the aggressive."

After listing the ships he preferred to be sent to accomplish this mission, Roosevelt proceeded to outline the tactics they ought to follow, including going "straight up through Gibraltar by night" to destroy the shipping in Barcelona.

He also declared a need for more men.

He concluded by warning, "If we drift into it, if we do not prepare in advance, and suddenly we have to go into hostilities without taking the necessary steps beforehand, we may have to encounter one or two bitter humiliations, and we shall certainly be forced to spend the first three or four most important weeks in not striking, but in making those preparations to strike which we should have made long before."

Three days after presenting these proposals, Roosevelt answered a letter from a friend in Germany, Herman Speck von Sternberg, who had been a companion during many of Roosevelt's vigorous walks. He reported his delight in having found "a great companion in the shape of one of our Army Surgeons . . . a splendid fellow . . . for a scramble up Rock Creek." Amenities aside, he wrote, "Between ourselves I have been hoping and working ardently to bring about our interference in Cuba."

Meanwhile, persuaded by Roosevelt's "impetuosity and almost fierceness" in the memorandum, Long chose a limited action. He ordered the *Cincinnati* and several other cruisers back from the South Atlantic and into the azure, warm waters closer to Cuba. The Atlantic Squadron, including the *Iowa,* got signals to undertake "winter exercises" by moving into Key West.

As to the mighty battleship already on station there, Long went beyond Roosevelt's recommendations by proposing to President McKinley that there might be some benefit to the peace process if the *Maine* were sent to Havana as an act of "friendly courtesy."

In keeping with diplomatic protocol, McKinley inquired of Spain's minister, Enrique Dupuy de Lôme, whether his government might be amenable to such a cordial visit.

Like Theodore Roosevelt, Enrique Dupuy de Lôme could be arrogant and blunt. He was also as shrewd. And he wrote letters to friends and trusted associates that at times could be just as intemperate, judgmental, and dangerous as those letters of Roosevelt's that began with a plea for confidentiality. Just such a missive had gone out in mid-December, addressed to José Canalejas, the influential editor of the Madrid newspaper, *El Heraldo.* However, it went to New York City because Canalejas was there for informal negotiations with members of the Junta on the proposal from the Spanish government for Cuban autonomy.

As to that idea, Dupuy de Lôme said in his letter that any talks with the insurgents were "a waste of time."

He thereupon dipped his pen into poison to characterize the president of the United States: "Besides the natural and inevitable coarseness with which he repeats all that the press and public opinion in Spain have said of Weyler, it shows once more that McKinley is weak and catering to the rabble and, in addition, a hack politician who desires to leave the door open to himself and to stand well with the jingoes of his party."

A little over a month later, on January 20, a McKinley initiative brought the author of this letter to the State Department at ten o'clock in the morning. Arriving promptly, he met with the assistant secretary of state, William R. Day, substituting for the ailing secretary, John Sherman. In the politest of diplomatic terms, Day advised the minister that the president of the United States was preparing to revive a policy that had been abandoned by the previous administration of Grover Cleveland: sending American ships on friendly visits to Cuban ports.

Enrique Dupuy de Lôme replied that his government would have to consider such a development as an unfriendly act. Why be rash? The policy of autonomy was working. Peace was within reach. By the first of May it could be in hand. Why run the risk of spoiling everything? Would it be wise to chance a break in relations between the two countries by sending a warship?

Day asked if the autonomy policy were really effective. He noted that Governor-General Blanco had appeared to be unable to control his own army. How could the United States government count on him to safeguard the lives and property of Americans?

With the issue unresolved, Dupuy de Lôme left the State Department in a gloomy mood. Four days later he was again summoned to Day's office. This time he heard that the decision to send a warship had been made. Since the United States and Spain were at peace, Day asked, how could Spain object?

The Spanish minister conceded the point and left the office gloomier than before. Not long after, Day cabled Fitzhugh Lee in Havana: "It is the purpose of this Government to resume friendly visits in Cuban ports. In that view the *Maine* will call at port of Havana in a day or two. Please arrange for a friendly interchange of calls with authorities."

In Havana an anxious Fitzhugh Lee urgently pleaded for a delay in sending the battleship "to give last excitement more time to disappear." But on the morning of January 25, 1898, the oddly configured battleship with its steam engines and twin masts for sail dropped anchor in Havana's harbor. When no demonstrations by Cuban loyalists materialized, Lee sighed with relief and cabled the State Department: "Peace and quiet reign."

The night before the *Maine*'s appearance in Cuba, John Davis Long had noted for posterity in his diary, "It is a purely friendly matter. There is, of course, the danger that the arrival of the ship may precipitate some crisis or riot; but there is far less danger of this than if the ship went in any other way. I hope, with all my heart, that everything will turn out all right."

In New York, William Randolph Hearst's *Journal* joyfully headlined:

OUR FLAG IN HAVANA AT LAST

Moored at Buoy 4 in the port that a few centuries earlier had been called the boulevard of the New World, the *Maine* was the center of attention. Peaceful but curious throngs peered out at her from four hundred yards away on the Machina Wharf. When the skipper, Captain Sigsbee, in full dress with cocked hat and gold epaulets, went ashore to report to Consul General Fitzhugh Lee and then pay a courtesy call on the Spanish admiral Vincente Manterola, he met no protests from people on the streets, save for one moment when a "stolid and sullen" group closed around him. By the end of the week a constant flow of visitors was being welcomed aboard the battleship. With the situation regarded as peaceful, American sailors, wearing civilian clothes, were soon given leave to go ashore.

On Sunday, Sigsbee decided to assay "the true feeling of the people of Havana toward the *Maine*." Taking several officers with him, he joined Fitzhugh Lee and went to the Plaza de Toros for the bullfights. On the way he was handed a broadside that Lee translated:

SPANIARDS!
LONG LIVE SPAIN WITH HONOR

What are you doing that you allow yourselves to be insulted in this way? Do you not see what they have done to us in withdrawing our brave and beloved Weyler, who at this very time would have finished with this unworthy, rebellious rabble who are trampling on our flag and on our honor?

Continuing to translate, Lee read:

And, finally, these Yankee pigs who meddle in our affairs, humiliating us to the last degree, and for a still greater taunt, order to us a man-of-war of their rotten squadron. . . . Spaniards! The moment of action has arrived. Do not go to sleep! Let us teach these vile traitors that we have not yet lost our pride. . . . Death to the Americans!

Lee dismissed the broadside with a laugh. He had seen many like it. It was meaningless. They continued on their way to the Plaza de Toros. Although the party stayed until the last of six bulls had been killed, Sigsbee did not enjoy the experience. He wrote:

> The Spanish bull-fight should be considered as a savage spectacle passed down from generation to generation from a remote period when human nature was far more cruel than at present. . . . During the progress of the last bull-fight that I attended, several poor, docile horses were killed under circumstances that were shocking to the American mind. In a box near that which my friends and I occupied, a little girl of ten or twelve years of age sat apparently unmoved while a horse was prostrate and dying in prolonged agony near the middle of the ring.

The commander of the *Maine* had expressed similarly strong views against the brutalizing of men in American prizefights.

As Sigsbee mingled with Cubans at bullfights and on the streets of Havana, halfway around the world where the American flag flew above the *Olympia* at anchor in Yokohoma Bay, Commodore Dewey received a cable from the Navy Department. Dated January 27, 1898, it ordered him to hold in service anyone in the Asiatic Squadron whose enlistment was due to expire.

American sailors in the Land of the Rising Sun who went on leave ashore probably felt as though they were stepping into the Gilbert and Sullivan operetta *The Mikado*. But for their commander in chief, the emperor of Japan was not a figment of the imagination of a pair of English songwriters. In full uniform, resplendent with ribbons and medals, flanked by aides, court chamberlains, and gentlemen-in-waiting, the god incarnate of the Japanese received the American visitor in the white uniform of the navy with great cordiality.

A practiced and eloquent diarist with a respect for history, Dewey memorialized the occasion by contrasting his visit with the visit of Commodore Matthew Perry, who had forced open Japan's doors to the West four and a half decades earlier. He wrote:

> The one [Perry], regarded with an apprehensive consternation only rivalled in degree by the cataclysmic changes in beliefs, customs and national policy of which he was the precursor, the other [meaning himself], welcomed with all the amenities of civilization; the one [Perry], after vexatious delays, allowed to meet the representatives of an invisible and impotent Mikado, the other received openly by an

Emperor who was that anomaly in the Far East—a constitutional monarch; the one [Perry], landing in a country hidden in Oriental isolation, the other, debarking in a thriving port open to the commerce of the world and being transported to Tokyo by railway. The world has seen great changes in its time, but none more radical than the extraordinary *bouleversement* of all the practices and preconceived ideas of Japan such as followed the memorable visit of Commodore Perry.

In beginning the process of drawing Japan out of isolation and into the modern world, complete with a formidable navy, what had Perry achieved? In the view of Alfred Thayer Mahan and his student, Theodore Roosevelt, the *bouleversement* of Japan had sown the seeds of inevitable conflict with the United States for dominance across the Pacific.

For the present, however, Roosevelt discerned no immediate likelihood of such a clash. He had detected no indication that the Japanese intended anything more worrisome regarding the annexation of Hawaii than disapproving rhetoric. Consequently, the assistant secretary of the navy and his man in the Far Pacific felt free to disperse ships of the Asiatic Squadron in a manner that would allow their most effective use, in case of a war over Cuba, against Spanish interests in the Pacific. In the thinking of Commodore Dewey, the ideal place for his squadron, should war come, was not in Japanese waters but across the China Sea in the port nearest to the Philippines. Therefore, on February 9, on his own volition and while the *Olympia* was taking on a full store of ordnance from the munitions supply ship *Concord*, he made ready to sail from Yokohoma on the eleventh. His destination would be Hong Kong.

In America on the morning of February 9, readers of William Randolph Hearst's *Journal* read with even more than customary astonishment the following headline:

THE WORST INSULT TO THE UNITED STATES IN ITS HISTORY

The accompanying story contained Dupuy de Lôme's December letter to Don José Canalejas, with its intemperate language regarding President McKinley. There was also a cartoon showing Uncle Sam giving the thumb to a cowering de Lôme, with a one-word caption: "Git." But in the true Hearstian tradition of yellow journalism, there was also a poem:

Get out, I say, get out before I start a fight.
Just pack your few possessions and take a boat for home.
I would not like my boot to use—but—oh—get out De Lôme.

The newspaper called for immediate American intervention in Cuba, demanding, "The flag of Cuba Libre ought to float over the Morro Castle within the week."

That same morning, in the big wedding-cake-like building that managed to contain most of the offices of the executive branch of the U.S. government, Assistant Secretary of State Day welcomed two unexpected callers from New York. They were Horatio Reubens, legal adviser to the Junta, and John J. McCook, a New York lawyer whose pro-Cuban-freedom sympathies had kept William McKinley from appointing him attorney general. They had called on Day to show him the actual letter that, somehow, had made its way into the hands of the canny propagandists of the Junta.

Dubious of the letter's authenticity, Day called in Second Assistant Secretary of State Alvee Adee. After careful study of the signature, Adee said it certainly looked genuine. Still not assured, Day summoned Dupuy de Lôme.

Not only was the letter his, the diplomat told Day, but he had already cabled his resignation to Madrid.

At a reception that evening Theodore Roosevelt could not contain his desire for immediate action in Cuba. Cornering Senator Mark Hanna and others, he urged them to work for a declaration of war. In his carriage going home, a disgruntled and embarrassed Hanna told his wife he was glad Roosevelt had not been made assistant secretary of state and grumbled, "We'd be fighting half the world."

But Roosevelt's purpose was not to humiliate Spain. A few days later, on February 14, he wrote to New York businessman Francis Cruger Moore:

"I do not believe in any entangling alliance, but neither do I believe in any entangling antipathies. Nothing is worse for a country than to shape its policy with the desire of either gratifying or irritating another country, the latter quite as much as the former."

Leaving his office that evening, he felt that Spain's humiliation was certain; indeed, it was more certain without war than with it, for the Spanish could not keep the island permanently. They minded yielding to the Cubans more than to any demands made by the United States. While the United States had important commercial concerns regarding Cuba—especially sugar and tobacco—it was more interested from the standpoint of humanity. Cuba was at the very doorstep of the United States. It was a dreadful thing to sit supinely and watch the country's death agony. It was a duty, even more from the standpoint of national honor than of a national interest, to stop the devastation and destruction. For these reasons, Roosevelt believed a war was both necessary and just.

He had done everything in his power to bring it about.

Yet in the big white house so visible from Roosevelt's office sat a president of the United States who always had been against war and, despite all that had happened and the implorings of friends, political allies, and much of the press, evidenced no inclination to alter his conviction that he could win peace in Cuba with no cost in American blood.

If appeals to duty, honor, country, Christian humanitarianism, and even the insult of the Spanish minister in Washington had not stirred McKinley's ire, would—*could*—anything?

In contemplating this question that vexed his friend Theodore, Henry Cabot Lodge had been able to offer only a hopeful prognostication.

He said, "There may be an explosion any day in Cuba which would settle many things."

Part IV

A Name to Remember

Chapter 12

"Lord God, help us!"

On the same day that Commodore Dewey set his destination for Hong Kong and Hearst's *Journal* published Dupuy de Lôme's fateful and misguided letter, a small, frail, seventy-six-year-old woman who suffered from acute bronchitis gazed across the harbor from the deck of the cruiser *Montgomery* toward a "shining thing" that was the battleship *Maine*. Minutes later she landed in Havana.

The founder of the American Red Cross during the Civil War, Clara Barton had come to Cuba to see what she could do to help alleviate the suffering of innocent victims of the war, including *reconcentrados*. Numbering thousands, these miserable homeless and hungry people, most of them women and children, littered the streets of Havana and other towns of the island and filled every hospital to overflowing. But she was hardly a Johnny-come-lately to the plight of the people of Cuba under Spanish rule. Fourteen years earlier, in an 1874 letter to a friend, she had denounced Spain's rule in all of its colonies as tyrannical. "And Cuba, you know," she wrote, "has an insurgent army of so-called rebels fighting for their freedom. If she [Cuba] ever gets free, she must come to the United States, as she is too small to stand alone."

In 1897 Barton was painfully aware of the newspaper reports of the atrocities attributed to General Weyler and his successor. She had read the description of the island as a place "wrapped in the stillness of death" in the report of attorney William Calhoun after his fact-finding visit to Cuba at the request of McKinley. Outraged, she had gone to see the president in July of 1897 and had come away with an authorization for the Red Cross to handle volunteer relief for the Cuban people. She immediately formed a committee in New York "to ask money and material of the people at large to be shipped to Cuba for the relief of the *reconcentrados*."

Six months later, in the towns she visited before arriving in Havana on February 9, she had found conditions so horrible that she said the massacre of Armenians by Turks in 1892, which she had witnessed, was "merciful in comparison." Going directly to the hospital nearest the Havana waterfront, she found piles of waiting coffins by the door. Inside, living skeletons were beyond hope. Babies with hunger-distended bellies clung to the milkless breasts of dying mothers.

Alternately demanding and begging officials to do something, Barton was answered with the sympathetic words and shrugs of people who were overwhelmed and paralyzed. She found them "perplexed on both sides; first by the Spanish soldiery, [who were] liable to attack [relief workers], likewise the Cuban guerrillas, who were equally as dangerous." Doing what was possible, she organized food distribution centers in Havana and in as many nearby towns as she was permitted to visit.

Four days after arriving in Havana she allowed herself a respite. She accepted an invitation from Captain Sigsbee to come to the *Maine* for lunch with him and his officers. She found the sailors who met her with the captain's gig to wisk her out to Buoy 4 "strong, ruddy and bright." While she told Sigsbee, Lieutenant Commander Wainwright, and other officers of her work, she could not help but compare "the lunch at those polished tables, the glittering china and cut glass," with the abysmal conditions of the war victims whom she had come to Cuba to help.

Lying near the *Maine* was another warship, Spain's cruiser *Alfonso XII*, and the Ward Line passenger steamer *City of Washington*. Together the three ships seemed a pretty sight to the correspondent of the New York *Herald*, who viewed the ships from the same hotel that had been chosen by Frederic Remington and Richard Harding Davis the year before, the Inglaterra. A veteran of ten years in the U.S. Navy before becoming navy editor of the *New York Times* in 1892, Walter Scott Meriwether had been enticed into the employment of James Gordon Bennett Jr. in 1895 to cover naval affairs for the *Herald*. Settling into a third-floor room in the hotel shortly before the arrival of the *Maine,* he had joined John Caldwell (the man he was relieving in Havana), Freeman Halstead (a Canadian), George Bronson Rea, and their Mexican translator, Feliupe Ruiz.

Also filing stories about the new arrival in the harbor was Sylvester Scovel of Pulitzer's *World*. He had spent several months in documenting atrocities. One of his dispatches had noted mutilations of rebel bodies "so beastly, so indecent, no Apache could have conceived anything equal to it." He informed *World* readers that Spain's "settled purpose" in Cuba was the extermination of the Cuban people "under the cloak of civilized warfare." He had heartily welcomed the presence of the *Maine.*

Missing from these representatives of the American press was Richard Harding Davis. Although he had remained in Cuba long after the departure of Remington, his reporting had prompted a tempting offer by the London *Times* to cover the Greco-Turkish war. He found the Greek soldiers in a holiday mood. "After Cuba," he said, "it is like a picnic. It is all the difference between intruding in a club of gentlemen or walking in on the scene of a murder." One day in Athens he had run into another former New Yorker, Stephen Crane, whom he had first met in London.

Back in London, and after hearing that the *Maine* had been sent to Havana, Davis had hesitated to accept an assignment from the *Pall Mall Gazette* to cover Lord Kitchener's campaign in the Sudan. He explained that it looked "as though we are getting near a ruction with Spain, and I want to be there in time to kick a Spanish officer to death."

Had Davis been in Havana on February 15, he could not have been more succinct or accurate than Meriwether's cable to the *Herald* on the Cuban situation on that rainy day: "*Tranquillo.*"

Out in the harbor aboard the *Maine,* a bugler noted the end of that tranquil day with Taps. The notes drifted over the placid water to the civilian steamer, *City of Washington,* commanded by Captain Frank Stevens. One of her passengers, Sigmund Rothschild, paused on deck to listen to the music. But Frederick C. Teasdale, captain of the nearby British bark *Deva,* was quite accustomed to such naval formalities and went about writing his daily log.

Aboard the *Maine* as the last plaintive notes of the bugle call signified "lights out," most of his crew's 328 enlisted men were already in bunks and hammocks. But a handful of officers who thought that a quarter to nine was too early to turn in were in the wardroom near the aft gun turret. The battleship's chaplain, Father John P. Chidwick, lay in his bunk reading a copy of George Bronson Rea's recent book, *Facts and Fakes about Cuba.* Rather sympathetic to the Spanish side, it took to task a number of Rea's newspaper colleagues for sensationalism and outright fabrications in their reporting.

As the *Maine* settled into stillness, the streets, hotels, and cafés overlooking the harbor were still active. The rain had ended. Rea,

Sylvester Scovel, his wife, and a few other night owls of the press corps sipped coffee and chatted in one of the colorful cafés. Strolling the *Prado,* Meriwether dodged masked and costumed revelers on their way to pre-Lenten festivities and enjoyed the greenery and palms. Yet he appreciated that this was deceptive. Behind the gay masks and under the hospitality there was a breathless and expectant tension that he had felt as a boy on the Fourth of July when he touched a lighted match to the short fuse of a firecracker. Earlier in the day he had glanced at a wall on a side street and found some crude graffiti that showed a strutting, grinning Uncle Sam, blissfully unaware that a figure representing Spain had tucked a banana peel under his foot.

With a veranda affording a view of the wide harbor and the big white American warship, Clara Barton's house was quiet as she and her assistant planned their next day's activities on behalf of the victims of the war. At that moment the gracious officer who had hosted the lunch in her honor aboard the *Maine,* Captain Charles Sigsbee, completed his official writing and picked up his pen again to write to his wife. Three weeks had passed since his ship had put in at Havana with some apprehension. But he and his crew had been given every courtesy. Now he had orders to hoist anchor and proceed to New Orleans and show the Stars and Stripes at Mardi Gras. He felt glad that the so-called courtesy visit was about to end. Putting down the pen again, he opened a humidor, helped himself to one of Cuba's fine cigars, lit it, took a pleasant puff, and left his quarters to proceed up to the poop deck.

The great ship faced west by north, her ten-inch bow guns in the direction of the city. The deck officer, Lieutenant John J. Blandin, gave the skipper a snappy salute and continued with the organization of the quarter watch. The muggy air was misty, but stars could be seen in the black night sky, and the surface of the harbor winked with reflections of the lights of the festive city and nearby ships.

At high tide the *Maine* would lie in about thirty-six feet of water. She drew twenty-two, leaving fourteen feet between harbor floor and the hull. The tide was ebbing as Blandin sounded three bells.

Across the harbor, Captain Teasdale of the *Deva,* moored at the Regla Wharf, did not have to look at the clock in his cabin to know the time. Three bells meant it was 9:30 P.M. Seated at his desk ten minutes later, he felt his ship shudder. Fearing another ship had collided with the *Deva,* he raced topside. Barging out onto the deck, he felt another jolt. Turning with horror, he watched a huge rising column of smoke. The air over the harbor was full of flying debris. The sky flared with a light like a display of holiday fireworks at a seaside resort.

On the deck of the *City of Washington,* Sigmund Rothschild heard a tremendous explosion and felt himself lifted out of his deck chair. Looking toward the sound, he saw the bow of the *Maine* rise a little out of the water. A split second later, the center of the ship turned into a roiling mass of fire. Suddenly, bits and pieces of the devastated warship cascaded to the deck of the steamer.

From the water near the *Maine* someone screamed, "Help! Lord God, help us!"

Chapter 13

Red Glare, Black Water

Groping out of the dark of the ship and onto the deck, gasping in the thick smoke, Private William Anthony, U.S. Marine Corps, found himself face to face with the skipper of the *Maine*. Not knowing what else to say, he blurted, "The explosion took place at nine-forty, sir."

No one had to tell either man that a ship listing so far to port with her main deck awash was well on her way to sinking. The forward portion of the ship was already submerged. Making his way to the poop deck, Sigsbee found Lieutenant Commander Wainwright and several other officers. As he leaned over the starboard rail and looked amidships, Sigsbee saw flames. To prevent further disaster, he snapped an order to flood the forward ammunition magazine. No need to, he was told; it was already under the water. Nor did Sigsbee have to worry about the after magazines. At the rate the ship was settling to the bottom, they, too, would soon be submerged.

As the water rose, it pushed air through doors and hatches, creating an eerie, whistling moan. From the water on all sides of the ship rose cries for help.

Sigsbee shouted, "Away all boats." But only two of the three lifeboats could be reached. Quickly manned and lowered, they became part of a small flotilla of rescue boats from the *City of Washington* and the Spanish cruiser *Alfonso XII*. Racing out from shore were other vessels, including one commandeered by the chief of police. It was dangerous work. Flames amidships of the *Maine* were setting off small-arms ammunition and triggering a bombardment of six-pound shells.

Having scrambled on the police chief's boat, George Bronson Rea looked ahead and found great masses of twisted and bent iron plates and beams in the heart of the smoke-blackened white warship. The bow had disappeared. The anachronistic foremast and the smokestacks had toppled.

Also racing toward the ship, Sylvester Scovel saw the superstructure looming up, partly colored by the red glare of flames reflecting off the black water. His report would state, "At first it appeared as if her bow was totally demolished. Then the mass of beams and braces was seen . . . blown forward by the awful rending."

With nothing more to be done on the poop deck of his ship, and assured that all the wounded that could be found had been rescued from the harbor, Captain Sigsbee ordered everyone into boats. The last off, he climbed into the gig that had carried Clara Barton out to the ship for a pleasant lunch. He ordered the little boat to make for the *City of Washington*.

Between thirty and forty of the sailors who had been plucked from the harbor had been rushed to the San Ambrosio hospital. Already there to assist in tending them, Clara Barton found the men "crushed by the timbers, cut by iron, scorched by fire, and blown sometimes high in the air, sometimes down through the red hot furnace room and out into the water, senseless, to be picked up by some boat and gotten ashore. The wounds were all over them—heads and faces terribly cut, internal wounds, arms, legs, feet and hands burned to the live flesh."

As she moved among them to take down names and addresses, she paused to draw back the bandages from the face of one. He asked, "Isn't that Miss Barton?"

"Yes."

"I thought it must be. I knew you were here [in Havana], and thought you would come to us. I am so thankful for us all."

She continued taking names, "till twelve had been spoken to," each with an expression "of grateful thanks, spoken under such conditions," that the experience finally proved too emotionally difficult for her.

"I passed the pencil to another hand," she recalled, "and stepped aside."

At the Havana City Hospital, it was Walter Scott Meriwether who moved among the wounded. He reported:

> Most of the victims were either dead or dying and only one was able to talk coherently. All he knew was that he was asleep in his hammock when he was hurled high in the air by a terrific explosion, had struck the water, and someone had rescued him. . . . Men that I took by the hand and with the best voice I could command spoke

cheerful words to are this morning dead or will be helpless cripples the rest of their lives. . . . In adjoining cots were a sailor with his face half blown away and another with both legs so badly fractured that he must lose them.

At the end of the ward was a lusty Marine crying, "For God's sake, let me die."

With all possible tenderness and care the Spanish doctors were dressing the face of a fireman. "There is something in my eyes," he said. "Wait and let me open them."

Both eyes were gone.

Aboard the *City of Washington,* Captain Sigsbee was seeing to the wounded who had been picked up by the steamer's lifeboats. A hospital had been rigged in the liner's dining salon. Satisfied that his men were receiving proper attention, he returned to the deck and gazed forlornly across the harbor. The *Maine* still burned. Ammunition continued to explode. Turning away, he went into Captain Frank Stevens's cabin, sat at his desk, and on a sheet of Ward Line stationery wrote a cable to the secretary of the navy:

Maine blown up in Havana harbor at nine forty to-night and destroyed. Many wounded and doubtless more killed or drowned. Wounded and others aboard Spanish man-of-war and Ward line steamer. Send Light House Tenders from Key West for crew and few pieces of equipment above water. No one has clothing other than that upon him. Public opinion should be suspended until further report.

The last request would prove to be a vain hope.

Chapter 14

If . . .

Sylvester Scovel had pulled a slick trick at the telegraph office. Using a stolen cable blank, he managed to get a bulletin through to Joseph Pulitzer's *World:*

> Havana, February 15—At a quarter of ten o'clock this evening a terrible explosion took place aboard the United States battleship *Maine* in Havana harbor. Many were killed and wounded. . . . As yet the cause of the explosion is not apparent. The wounded sailors of the *Maine* are unable to explain it.

But even before Scovel's message, another had gone out, sent by a Cuban who had been employed as a spy by U.S. naval intelligence. His cable had gone to the naval station at Key West and was received by Lieutenant Albert Gleaves, commander of torpedo boat *Cushing.* Highly skeptical, Gleaves carried the message to the senior officer at Key West, the skipper of the *Fern.* He was Lieutenant Commander William S. Cowles, who happened to be the husband of Roosevelt's sister Anna.

As Cowles and other officers pondered the validity of the agent's cable, the telegraph came alive again, clicking out the confirmation in the form of Sigsbee's report of the explosion, to be relayed from Key West to the Navy Department. It reached the capital a little before one o'clock in the morning, February 16.

The night had been blustery and cold, but not too severe to keep Secretary Long and his wife, Helen, from going out to a ball. They had returned to Long's suite in the Portland Hotel at 1:30. When a courier arrived with Sigsbee's cable, the secretary of the navy was already asleep. Roused by his wife, he read words that seemed "almost impossible to believe," then jotted a note to Captain Francis W. Dickins, the acting chief of the Bureau of Navigation. The note summoned Dickins to the hotel.

Arriving around three o' clock, he conferred with Long and went out again, this time heading for the Executive Mansion. A night guard let him in and ushered him to a large room next to the presidential bedroom. When McKinley appeared in a dressing gown, Dickins apologized for the late hour (early, actually; dawn was a pink hint in the sky) and handed him Sigsbee's cable.

McKinley muttered, "The *Maine* blown up! The *Maine* blown up!" He ordered Dickins to let him know of further developments.

Presently, with the sky brightening on that Tuesday morning, Theodore Roosevelt followed his practice of being up early. Careful not to disturb Edith, who remained gravely ill with an ailment no one seemed able to diagnose, he had a breakfast of hard-boiled eggs, rolls, and coffee and departed for the office.

By that hour every newspaper had caught up with Pulitzer's *World*. None did so with quite the verve as the one that belonged to William Randolph Hearst. Like Secretary Long, the owner of the New York *Journal* had been out for the night. But he had not followed his habit of dropping in at the paper. Instead, he had gone directly from his evening's diversions to his apartment in the Worth House hotel. Upon his arrival he was told by his valet, "There's a telephone from the office. They say it's important news."

Hearst returned the call immediately. "What's the important news?"

"The battleship *Maine* has been blown up in Havana harbor."

"Good heavens, what have you done with the story?"

"We have put it on the first page, of course."

"Have you put anything else on the front page?"

"Only the other big news."

"There is not any other big news. You spread the story all over the front page. This means war."

Roosevelt agreed. In his autobiography he wrote that preventing it "would have been impossible." Not since the assassination of President James A. Garfield in 1881 had Americans been so distressed and angry. All he had to do to measure the depth of public feeling was look through his office window at the silent, mournful crowds gathered on Pennsylvania Avenue. Had he inquired of them, he would have learned that few accepted any explanation for what had happened other than that the Spanish had been behind it. Certainly, the yellow press voiced no doubts.

Yet, Theodore Roosevelt was not so certain. Letters written on February 16 were of two minds. One to Secretary Long began, "In view of the *accident*" . . . (emphasis added). The second, to fellow Harvard graduate Benjamin Harrison Diblee, stated that he believed the *Maine* "was sunk by an act of dirty treachery on the part of the Spaniards," adding the caveat, "though we shall never find out definitely." Officially, it would go down as an accident.

"Being a Jingo," he said, "I will say, to relieve my feelings, that I would give anything if President McKinley would order the fleet to Havana tomorrow. This Cuban business ought to stop."

But the president of the United States, who had seen warfare firsthand, told intimates, "I have been through one war. I have seen the dead piled up, and I do not want to see another." He saw his duty as plain: "We must learn the truth and endeavor, if possible, to fix the responsibility. The country can afford to withhold its judgment and not strike an avenging blow until the truth is known."

This counsel to keep cool had little effect. War fever swept the country. Mass meetings in Buffalo, New York, demanded a declaration of war on Spain. Students at Richard Harding Davis's old collegiate stomping grounds, Lehigh, began drilling and parading while carrying banners proclaiming "To Hell with Spain."

In villages, towns, and cities from coast to coast, sentiment was the same, a good deal of it inflamed by newspaper headlines, such as the banner on page one of Hearst's *Journal* two days after the disaster:

THE WARSHIP MAINE WAS SPLIT IN TWO BY
AN ENEMY'S SECRET INFERNAL MACHINE

Accompanying it was a seven-column drawing of the ship anchored over mines. Wires stretched to a Spanish fort on shore. Readers were informed that Captain Sigsbee "practically declares that his ship was blown up by a mine or torpedo," though Sigsbee had said nothing of the kind.

Successive days brought the following headlines:

THE WHOLE COUNTRY THRILLS
WITH THE WAR FEVER
[February 18]

HOW THE MAINE ACTUALLY LOOKS AS IT LIES,
WRECKED BY SPANISH TREACHERY, IN HAVANA BAY
[February 20, with drawing]

HAVANA POPULACE INSULTS THE MEMORY
OF THE MAINE VICTIMS
[February 21]

THE MAINE WAS DESTROYED BY TREACHERY
[February 23]

During this drumbeat of demand for punishing Spain, McKinley remained resolutely against precipitous action. He did not propose "to be swept off my feet by the catastrophe."

An exasperated Roosevelt was quoted by Hearst's *Journal* as saying in an interview that the president of the United States had "no more backbone than a chocolate eclair." With great glee the paper also claimed that Roosevelt had said, "It is cheering to find a newspaper of the great influence and circulation of the *Journal* tell the facts as they exist and ignore the suggestions of various kinds that emanate from sources that cannot be described as patriotic or loyal to the flag of this country."

Roosevelt denied the words, calling the *Journal*'s claim of having interviewed him "an invention from beginning to end."

Although some of the phrases certainly could have been attributed to Roosevelt, it is unlikely that he would talk with a Hearst reporter, and so candidly, given his long-held animosity toward the *Journal*. And it seems highly improbable that he would wish to boost Hearst's ego by praising the *Journal* for its "great influence and circulation."

Of far greater concern and interest to Roosevelt in the aftermath of the disaster was how to deal with it, not only in regard to whether war was the appropriate response, but in terms of practicalities. In another lengthy memorandum to test the eyesight and patience of his immediate superior, he recommended to Long that steps be taken to raise the *Maine*. He also cautioned against sending another of the country's precious battleships in harm's way by ordering one to Havana. The "moral effect" would be the same in the form of "any cruiser flying the American flag."

With cold calculation he wrote on February 16, "If there is a need for a battleship at all there will be need for every battleship we pos-

sess; and the loss of a cruiser is small compared to the loss of a battleship."

Ever the historian, Roosevelt filled the memo with what-might-
have-beens:

> *If* we had gone to war with Spain a year ago we should have had
> seven armored ships against three; and there would be no chance of
> any serious loss to the American Navy. . . .
> *If* ever some such incident as the de Lôme affair, or this destruc-
> tion of the *Maine,* war should suddenly arise. . . .
> . . . advice which, *if* followed by Congress, would have [ensured us]
> at the present moment, a Navy which would have forbid any danger
> of trouble with either Spain or Japan.

He then looked to the future—hopefully. He told Long that

> *if* you recommend, in view of what has happened, the increase of the
> Navy to the size we should have . . . the skirts of the Department will
> then be cleared; and it is certain that until the Department takes the
> lead, the Congress will not only refuse to grant ships, but will hold
> itself justified in its refusal.

He warned that

> the margin of difference between our force and [Spain's] has become
> so small that by the sinking of the *Maine* it has been turned in
> [Spain's] favor so far as the units represented by the seagoing armor-
> clads on the Atlantic are concerned.

Two days later, on February 18, he wrote at length on a type of
vessel second only to battleships in his affection—the torpedo boat.
He asked for no less than one hundred new ones.

Again, Roosevelt could not resist a lecture on naval history, with
a particular eye toward the fate of the *Maine:*

> If Great Britain had stopped maneuvering her squadrons after the
> sinking of the *Captain,* the *Vanguard* or the *Victoria;* if Germany had
> abandoned any effort to upbuild her navy after the sinking of the
> *Kurfurst;* if the Russians had ceased to build ships when the *Gangout*
> sank; if the French had given up on torpedo boats when they found
> that two-thirds of those in commission in the Mediterranean were
> disabled by accidents; then each and all of these nations would have
> shown that they were unfit any longer to stand as great powers, that

they lacked the nerve to face the ordinary punishment which must be encountered by every nation in traveling the road to greatness.

Exactly the same judgment will be deservedly passed upon us if for these reasons, or for any other reasons, we refuse to go with the upbuilding of our navy, whether our refusal takes the form of stopping work on dry docks, battleships or torpedo boats.

The next day, both in person and by letter, he took advantage of the situation to plead with Long to reverse his decision on building only one new battleship. "I earnestly wish you could see your way clear now, without waiting a day," he asserted, "to send a special message [to the Congress], stating in view of the disaster to the *Maine,* and perhaps in view of the possible needs of this country, instead of recommending one battleship, you ask that two, or better still, four battleships be authorized immediately."

Meanwhile, burials had been the order of the day in Havana. On Thursday, February 17, a procession of nineteen hearses had left the Governor-General's Palace in Havana and made its slow course through crowded streets. A military honor guard led the cortege carrying Consul General Fitzhugh Lee, Captain Sigsbee, a party of American naval officers, Spanish officials, and Father Chidwick to Colon Cemetery in the city's suburbs. Following the ceremonies for the nineteen dead (none of them identified), Sigsbee learned that forty more had been recovered from the harbor, but that most of the dead remained in the wreckage. Divers were promptly ordered to begin attempting to retrieve them the next day.

Like every American at home, Sigsbee pondered the cause of the explosion. He knew, as Sylvester Scovel had told readers of the *World,* that the cause could not be known until the hull was inspected by divers. Scovel's story on the day of the funerals noted, "If their investigation shows that the indentation of the hull is inward, the conclusion that the magazine was exploded by a bomb or torpedo placed beneath the vessel is inevitable. If the indentation is outward, it will be indicated that the first explosion was in the magazine."

In surveying naval officers, the Washington *Star* found that most thought there had been an accident. They pointed to the fact that one of the *Maine*'s coal bunkers was near the forward magazine. The coal was bituminous, and this soft coal was notorious for spontaneous combustion. Fires had broken out on a dozen U.S. ships, including the battleship *New York* and cruiser *Cincinnati.* However, the chief of the

Navy's Bureau of Equipment, Rear Admiral Royal B. Bradford, insisted that the coal on the *Maine* had been of good quality.

Evidently, Sigsbee did not suspect the coal. On the day that the *Journal* ran its fanciful drawing of mines under the hull of the ship, he had telegraphed Secretary Long, "Probably the *Maine* was destroyed by a mine, perhaps by accident." He referred to a widely held suspicion that the harbor had been mined as a defensive measure. "I surmise that her berth [the mine's] was planted previous to her [the *Maine*'s] arrival." If so, the *Maine* might have hit a mine accidentally. Only divers could answer such questions.

They arrived on the third day after the explosion, on the North Atlantic Squadron's coastal steamer *Bache*. But when they attempted to reach the wreck, they found their way blocked by a cordon of Spanish patrol boats. They were informed that American divers could not go down without a Spanish diver. When Sigsbee went to the site, he also was turned away. Accompanied by Fitzhugh Lee, he hurried to lodge a protest with Governor-General Blanco. They insisted that because the *Maine* had been welcomed to Cuba as a friendly visitor, under international law the ship was in the same category as the American consulate: She was considered American territory. Blanco replied that the issue also involved Spanish law and Spain's honor. He proposed a joint Spanish-American investigation of the sinking.

The assistant secretary of the navy was outraged. Expressing deep suspicion of Spain, he "earnestly" urged Secretary Long to "advise the President against our conducting any examination in conjunction with the Spaniards as to the *Maine*'s disaster." He saw no chance that the American public would stand for it. He wrote, "There is of course a very large body of public opinion to the effect that we some time ago reached the limit of forebearance in our conduct toward the Spaniards, and this public opinion is already very restless, and might easily be persuaded to turn hostile to the [McKinley] administration."

Roosevelt also expressed his doubt that even with Spanish help the cause could ever be determined.

During the stalemate over American divers going down to see the *Maine,* the Spanish government assured that it would not stand in the way of recovering bodies inside the wreck, provided divers made no attempt to investigate the cause of the explosion. The grim and grisly task began promptly. Day after day, they descended into the dark water and the twisted black hulk, while above them, against the clear blue skies, the Stars and Stripes fluttered at half-mast.

Another American flag flew at half-mast in respect of the dead of the *Maine,* but this one was made of paper. The day before the sinking, it had been at the top of one of the masts of a wooden model of the *Maine* on display in the Navy Department. With word of the disaster in Havana, the model's glass casing had been temporarily removed to allow the paper flag to be lowered to half-mast.

Chapter 15

Everything That Will Float

On the day before the funerals in Havana, Secretary Long let it be known that the investigation into the sinking would be strictly an American undertaking. Should the Spanish wish to carry out an independent probe, the United States would, of course, cooperate. By cable to Key West, he directed Admiral William Sicard to choose a panel of naval officers to conduct the probe. Sicard named Captain William Sampson of the *Iowa;* Captain French E. Chadwick, skipper of the *New York* and a seasoned intelligence officer; and Lieutenant Commander William Potter, an officer of technical experience and solid judgment. The judge advocate was to be Lieutenant Commander Adolph Marix. They were directed to "diligently and thoroughly inquire into all the circumstances of the loss" and whether or not it had been "in any respect due to fault or negligence on the part of the officers or members of the crew." It was to convene in Havana. It did so on the morning of February 21, 1898.

In Spain General Valeriano "the Butcher" Weyler had no doubt. He blamed the blast on the victims. The deaths of the 260 sailors had been the result of "the indolence of the crew." The Spanish government desperately hoped to prove this. Minister of Colonies Segismundo Moret told Governor-General Blanco to find facts to show "the *Maine* catastrophe cannot be attributed to us."

One Spanish naval officer in Cartagena needed no report of an investigating committee to tell him what happened. Admiral Pascual Cervera told the Minister of Marine that the explosion "occurred under circumstances which leave no doubts of its being due to the vessel herself." What worried Cervera was that one of Spain's finest ships, the magnificent black-hulled cruiser *Vizcaya,* was due in New York on February 18. Like the *Maine*'s visit to Havana, the *Vizcaya*'s visit was to be considered a courtesy call. Cervera worried that angry Americans would seek revenge by attacking the ship.

This concern was fueled by alarmist headlines and taunting editorials in the *Journal*. One front page warned:

SPANISH WARSHIP APPROACHING

In addition, the paper had invited readers to play a game that matched the U.S. battleship *Texas* against the *Vizcaya*. The object of the game was to sink the Spanish ship.

So real was Spain's anxiety over the safety of the vessel that she was not berthed, as had been planned, on the Manhattan waterfront, but in Staten Island. Her captain then cut the visit short and departed for Havana, leaving the readers of Pulitzer's *World* to never know if it were true, as the newspaper had warned, that if her guns were fired from the battery at the tip of Manhattan Island, the shells would "explode on the Harlem River and in the suburbs of Brooklyn."

While the *Vizcaya* had nestled in the relative security of Staten Island, Theodore Roosevelt addressed a reply to a letter from a Mr. J. Edward Myers, who had expressed his feeling that the navy ought to be ashamed of itself in the matter of the destruction of the *Maine*. Roosevelt shot back that Mr. Myers "had better wait until the official inquiry is made. It will be full and ample."

To Myers's suggestion that the country did not need a navy, the historian gritted his formidable teeth and snapped: "This shows on your part precisely the spirit shown by those men who, after the battle of Bull Run, desired to abandon the war and allow the Rebellion to succeed. When men get frightened by the loss of a single ship, and wish to seize this as an excuse for abandoning the effort to build a navy (and this no matter what may be the reason for the disaster), they show they belong to that class which would abandon war at the first check, from sheer lack of courage, resolution and farsightedness."

Two days later he was in a melancholy mood. Writing to his brother-in-law, William Cowles, in Havana, he called the situation "such a sad affair."

On February 25 another letter went to General Tillinghast of the New York National Guard:

You must treat this letter as strictly confidential. I have nothing official to go on, but it does seem to me that the conditions are sufficiently threatening to warrant your beginning to look at your resources, and to enter into correspondence with the War Department as to what men they would expect from you, whether you should send regiments of the National Guard or new regiments of volunteers, etc., etc. Pray remember that in some shape I want to go.

As he signed the letter, Roosevelt had no way of knowing that the date on which it was sent would go down in his life story as one of the most significant for himself and historic for the nation. It began with the arrival at his desk of a brief note in the hand of the courtly gentleman down the hall.

Secretary Long advised that he intended to absent himself from the department and the recent stresses for a day's quiet rest. He continued, "Do not take any such step affecting the policy of the Administration without consulting with the President or me. I am not away from town and my intention was to have you look after the routine of the office while I get a quiet day off. I write to you because I am anxious to have no unnecessary occasion for a sensation in the papers."

This was hope in vain.

Within minutes of reading the note, Roosevelt sprang into action as only he could. He produced a blizzard of paper: orders for the shipping of fuel and ammunition to wherever he felt it might be needed; directives for work around the clock on ships undergoing repair; instructions for redeploying ships; a list of auxiliary cruisers to be purchased; messages to leading powers on Capitol Hill requesting immediate legislation to authorize the enlistment of unlimited numbers of men; commands to shift officers so the best would be on the right ships. He vowed, "I am going to put water under everything that will float."

Then he turned his attention to the Far Pacific. In his view the number of ships at Commodore Dewey's disposal at Hong Kong was insufficient. Calling in the man who knew all there was to know about the disposition of ships, Arent S. Crowninshield, head of the Bureau of Navigation, he inquired about the deployment of the Asiatic Squadron. As they talked, Henry Cabot Lodge happened by.

Presently, Roosevelt showed the men a cable he intended to send out immediately:

Dewey, Hong Kong:

Order the squadron except the *Monocacy* to Hong Kong. Keep full of coal. In the event of a declaration of war Spain, your duty will be to see that the Spanish Squadron does not leave the Asiatic coast, and then offensive operations in Philippine Islands. Keep *Olympia* until further orders.

Roosevelt.

The two men in the office and, eventually, Dewey read the message and its meaning. In Dewey's words, Roosevelt "had seized the opportunity . . . to hasten preparations for a conflict which was inevitable."

The following day as Leonard Wood waited for Roosevelt to join him for one of their "afternoon tramps," he spotted Roosevelt trotting around the corner from Connecticut Avenue to Wood's house at 2000 R Street, "with a broad smile on his face."

Barely able to contain himself, Roosevelt blurted, "Well, I have had my chance, Leonard, and I have taken advantage of it."

With astonishment, Wood listened as Roosevelt told him all he had done.

Looking back on that day, Wood wrote, "Few men would have dared to assume this responsibility, but Theodore Roosevelt knew that there were certain things that ought to be done and that delay would be fatal. He felt the responsibility was his and he took it."

When Roosevelt finished his account of all that he had done in Long's absence, he told Wood, "I may not be supported, but I have done what I know to be right; someday they will understand."

Back at the office the next day, the secretary of the navy shuddered with horror at what had happened. He called Roosevelt "a bull in a china shop." It was as if "the very devil seemed to possess him yesterday afternoon." Reflecting on all that had been done and the person who had done them, Long confided to his diary, "Roosevelt, in his precipitate way, has come very near causing more than an explosion than happened to the *Maine*."

Yet, John Davis Long was a sensitive man. He knew that his assistant's wife was very ill and his little boy was recovering from a long and dangerous illness.

Should an individual with these personal worries and who possessed a natural nervousness be entrusted with responsibility for the Navy Department at such a critical time?

Long consulted with President McKinley. The chief executive listened patiently to Long's lament (McKinley thought of it as "grumbling psalm tunes") and nodded sympathetically as Long spoke of "action most discourteous to me, because it suggests there is a lack of attention [by Long himself]."

While this was all true, what had Roosevelt really done but take measures that most agreed would have to be carried out in the event of a war?

Although Long determined to never again leave Roosevelt in charge of the Navy Department, he did nothing to alter any of the decisions Roosevelt had made, nor did he revoke any of Roosevelt's orders, including the one to the wolfhound, still leashed, in Hong Kong.

While Roosevelt's mind was alive with plans for the navy in the event of war, he added a P.S. to a letter to an official of the Navy Department. The postscript read: "By the way, will you please find out from the Life Insurance Company if my policy would be vitiated if I should go to Cuba in the event of war?"

Confessing to friends that he felt "a little blue," he vowed to work and to do his best "to get the Navy in proper shape, and while I won't accomplish nearly as much as I would like, still I will accomplish something."

Similar moments of gloomy introspection had marked his two years as police commissioner, but he had always bounced back, as he did now. His momentarily sagging spirits were boosted by his coterie of friends and allies. Among the most important of these was a stalwart band of Harvard graduates who referred to themselves as the Cantabrigians. They were Leonard Wood, Owen Wister, William Astor Chanler (great-great-grandson of John Jacob Astor), and, of course, Henry Cabot Lodge. Expansionists and jingoes all, each had played a role in bringing the United States to the brink of a war they believed just, humanitarian, and vital to the nation.

The Cantabrigians and Roosevelt's other friends, the non-Harvard social Darwinists, scornfully referred to their opponents as "the peace faction." Primarily members of Congress, they had found leadership in the Speaker of the House, Thomas B. Reed, whom Roosevelt had favored over McKinley for the Republican nomination for president in 1896. Writing to Captain Mahan in May of 1897 about those who resisted building up the navy, Roosevelt had exclaimed, "Tom Reed to my astonishment and indignation takes this view."

The depth of Roosevelt's dismay over the peace faction burst forth in a letter to Brooks Adams on March 21, 1898: "The blood of the

Cubans, the blood of women and children who have perished by the hundred thousand in hideous misery, lies at our door; and the blood of the murdered men of the *Maine* calls not for indemnity but for the full measure of atonement which can only come by driving the Spaniard from the New World."

Writing to Sir William Laird Clowes, who had solicited from Roosevelt a revised edition of *The Naval War of 1812* for publication in England, his subject again was the *Maine:*

> It was a terrible calamity. Captain Sigsbee and Lieutenant Commander Wainwright are two of the best men in our service, and I am confident that the Court [of investigation into the explosion] will hold them blameless. Of course I cannot pass any judgment in the matter until we hear from the Court. The opinion of the other officers at Havana is nearly unanimous to the effect that there was no accident, but that the ship was destroyed by a floating mine from without. Our "yellow" newspapers have been shrieking forth the same view, but in their case wholly without any facts to back it.

Claiming that he was in search of facts, William Randolph Hearst had made up his mind to conduct his own investigation. At the end of February he had launched it—literally. Pressing into service the largest press boat he owned (the 170-foot *Anita*), he dipped into his deep pockets to finance five members of Congress on a junket to Cuba. Heading the so-called Congressional Cuban Commission was Senator John M. Thurston. A Kentucky Republican, he took his ailing wife along, presumably hoping the sea air would improve her health. They reached Havana on March 11. Not long after, the editor of the *Journal* received an offering from Mrs. Thurston: "Oh! Mothers of the Northland, who tenderly clasp your little ones to your loving hearts! Think of the black despair that filled each Cuban mother's heart as she felt her life-blood slipping away, and knew that she had left her little ones to perish from the pain of starvation and disease."

Three days later, at the town of Matanzas, Mrs. Thurston suffered a heart attack and died.

The Congressional Cuban Commission sailed for home.

An outraged editor of another New York newspaper, E. L. Godkin of the *Evening Post,* denounced Hearst as "the blackguard boy" and condemned the exponents of yellow journalism in general. He said, "Every one who knows anything about 'yellow journals' knows that everything they do and say is intended to promote sales. No one—absolutely no one—supposes a yellow journal cares five cents about the Cubans, the *Maine* victims, or any one else."

Undaunted, Hearst's *Journal* appealed to readers to write to their congressmen, then claimed that fifteen thousand letters had poured in demanding war. The paper staked its "reputation as a war prophet on this assertion: There will be a war with Spain as certain as the sun shines unless Spain abases herself in the dust and voluntarily consents to the freedom of Cuba."

In a quieter tone the *Washington Post* observed in the national mood a "consciousness of strength" and a "new appetite" among the people. It said, "The taste of empire is in the mouth of the people even as the taste of blood in the jungle."

At the center of this national clamor for war stood William McKinley, who had hoped and worked to avoid war. A kindly man of peace, in the words of Hearst biographer W. A. Swanberg, McKinley "could deal expertly with legislators but lacked the dynamism, the spark of leadership that grips and sways the public mind. The country was getting away from him. The Presidency of the United States was being preempted by batteries of cylinder presses."

In the meantime, Captain Sampson and the board of officers designated to investigate the cause of the sinking of the *Maine* completed their work and filed their report. It was their opinion that a submarine mine had caused the partial explosion of two or more of the forward magazines. But it did not explain its reasoning and offered no speculation as to who might have laid the mine and detonated it.

On March 28, 1898, the president forwarded the report to Congress. In an accompanying message he said, "The appalling calamity fell upon the people of our country with crushing force, and for a brief time an intense excitement prevailed, which, in a community less just and self-controlled than ours, might have led to hasty acts of blind resentment." Pointing out that no blame had been fixed by the investigators, he told Congress, "I have directed that the finding of the Court of Inquiry and the views of this Government thereon be communicated to the Government of Her Majesty, the Queen Regent [of Spain], and I do not permit myself to doubt that the sense of justice of the Spanish nation will dictate a course of action suggested by honor."

Considering itself the voice of the American people, the New York *Journal* thundered in response:

REMEMBER THE MAINE!

TO HELL WITH SPAIN!

Chapter 16

Bent on Peace

On the day Roosevelt cabled Commodore Dewey to prepare the Asiatic Squadron for warfare, he found time to write to his sister Anna, "Edith had more fever yesterday, and though she went down again last night she seems so weak that I have concluded to get Dr. Osler, the great Baltimore expert, in for consultation."

A few days earlier, an ominous swelling had been detected in Edith's abdomen. In summoning Sir William Osler of Johns Hopkins University, Roosevelt had called on a world-famous specialist in abdominal tumors. Having done so, Roosevelt went to work behind his massive desk to produce the flurry of war preparation orders that so offended the sensibilities of Secretary Long, but without which the U.S. Navy could not have been prepared for the crisis that Roosevelt was convinced was both inevitable and close at hand.

That weekend Dr. Osler examined Edith and discerned what he believed to be a noncancerous inflammatory growth. He recommended immediate surgery. Roosevelt hesitated. The reason is unclear. Although he had to have been tormented by the memory of the death of his first wife, fellow Cantabrigian Winthrop Chanler (brother of William) thought the reluctance was the result of Roosevelt's reliance on "a lot of perfectly incompetent doctors, taxidermists and veterinarians, sportsmen and excellent athletes" who led him to believe Edith could recover on her own.

Rather, her condition worsened. When Roosevelt found that she did not have the strength even to listen to him read to her, he acted at last. He turned to a local gynecologist, who examined her on the fifth and recommended surgery. Roosevelt relented. As ether was being administered, he held her hand.

When the operation was over, he was told that there had been a large abscess at the hip. It had been removed. A complete recovery could be anticipated. An enormously relieved Roosevelt wrote to Anna, "She behaved heroically; quiet and even laughing, while I held her hand until the ghastly preparations had been made."

Presently, the perplexing malady that had been plaguing their son Ted was also diagnosed. A doctor laid the cause of the boy's state of exhaustion at the feet of a too-demanding father. The child simply could not meet the standards of robustness and physical fitness that Roosevelt had set. In an instance of repentence that was rare, a chastened Roosevelt vowed, "Hereafter I shall never press Ted either in body or mind. The fact is that the little fellow, who is particularly dear to me, has bidden fair to be all the things I would like him to have been and wasn't, and it was a great temptation to push him."

However, pushing himself was another matter, especially on the issue of getting himself into battle. The theme appeared in letter after letter. "If there is war," he wrote to one Charles Henry Davis on March 9, 1898, "I want to get away from here and get to the front if I possibly can."

The same day, Roosevelt wrote again to General Tillinghast in New York. "I don't want to be in an office during war, I want to be at the front." He went on to predict that if he were ever to have an opportunity to "raise a regiment of volunteers," he could do so "in short order." Furthermore, he had in mind enlisting the help of "a man who rendered the most gallant service with the regular Army against the Apaches," the admirable and envied Leonard Wood. When an admirer of Theodore Roosevelt addressed a letter to him as "Colonel," he noted in response, "I swelled with pride."

After reading an article in the Baltimore *American* that had lauded his efforts to ready the navy for war, he wrote to the author, Bradley Tyler Johnson, a former brigadier general of the Confederate army, lawyer, and leader of the Democratic party in Maryland and Virginia: "Of course I am personally what is called a Jingo, so there are only a few generous souls like yourself who take kindly to my views. I wish we had one or two men like you in Congress."

Writing on March 9 to Henry White, secretary of the American embassy in London, he hoped that the loss of the *Maine* would not be "treated by itself, but as part of the whole Cuban business." The only possible solution of a permanent nature was "Cuban independence," and "the sooner we make up our minds to this the better."

To Alfred Thayer Mahan went a brief note, dated March 10, reporting, "Mrs. Roosevelt has been very sick. I think she is now a little better." He went on to "earnestly wish that my chief [Secretary Long] would get you on here to consult in the present crisis." Four days later, a missive to Mahan was much lengthier and burning with war fever:

> We should have struck a year and a half ago, when our superiority of forces was great, and when we could have saved Cuba before it was ruined. Every month since the situation has changed slightly to our disadvantage, and it will continue to so change. It is the case of the sibylline books again. We should fight this minute in my opinion, before the [Spanish] torpedo boats get over here. But we won't. We'll let them get over here and run the risk of serious damage from them, and very possibly we won't fight until the beginning of the rainy season, when to send an expeditionary force to Cuba means to see the men die like sheep.

Given his appreciation for history, it is possible that with the receipt of a letter on March 15, 1898, from General Francis V. Greene of the New York National Guard, Roosevelt recalled the fate of Julius Caesar on the Ides of March. Certainly, Greene's letter must have felt like a dagger in his heart. It informed Roosevelt that he should not count on getting to the front with Greene's regiment. Would not the nation be better served if Roosevelt remained at the Navy Department? Crestfallen, Roosevelt replied:

> All right. I didn't have much expectation that you could succeed, and I thank you very much for what you have done. I don't agree with you as to post of duty. I don't want to be in an office instead of at the front; but I daresay I shall have to be, and I shall try to do good work wherever I am put. I have long been accustomed, not to taking the position I should like, but to doing the best I was able to in a position I did not altogether like, and under conditions which I didn't like at all. But I shall hope that in the event of serious war I may have the chance to serve under you.

The following day the mood of a letter to William Astor Chanler sounded desperate. He asked Chanler if he were planning to raise a regiment. If so, might he go along? "I shall chafe my heart out if I am kept here instead of being at the front," he wrote, "and *I don't know how to get to the front*" (emphasis added).

The letter went on, "I thought I might go under Frank Greene [but] nobody knows how the National Guard will be used. If nothing else happens I hope I can get with you in any capacity, in any regiment that goes to the front. I have a man here, Leonard Wood, who is also very anxious to go. He is an Army surgeon, but he wants to go in the fighting line. He is a tremendous athlete. Can't you come on here [to Washington]? I will take you to [Secretary of War Russell A.] Alger, and I will get Wood, and you and I and he will go over the matter together. At present I am utterly in the air as to how to advise you, because I haven't the slightest idea what I could do myself."

Meanwhile at home, Edith appeared to be gaining, although slowly. But, Roosevelt told his sister on March 16, Ted's headaches had come back. "It has been a hard winter," he wrote Anna Roosevelt Cowles. "I am working hard at the Department, as everyone is; and as the strain tells more or less on the Secretary, there is very little chance of a let up on me."

Regarding a Cuban policy, he complained, "What the Administration will ultimately do I don't know; McKinley is bent on peace, I fear."

The president of the United States was not without a sense of humor, however. In an encounter with his personal surgeon, he asked, "Have you and Theodore declared war yet?"

"No, Mr. President," replied Leonard Wood, "but we think you should."

As McKinley continued wavering, Roosevelt complained again and again to like-minded friends, the Cantabrigians, and the war hawks of the Metropolitan Club. The man who was reported to have said that McKinley's backbone was as soft as an eclair did not hold back on characterizing the president. On one occasion as he left a meeting at the Executive Mansion he roared, "Do you know what that white-faced cur up there has done? He has prepared two messages, one for war and one for peace, and he doesn't know which one to send in!"

But there had been a glimmer of hope from the Executive Mansion. On March 8 the president reluctantly asked Congress for fifty million dollars, saying, "I must have money to get ready for war. I am doing everything possible to prevent war, but it must come, and we are not prepared for war."

Congress passed the Fifty-Million Bill promptly, thereby allocating funds to the Navy Department for the acquisition of whatever was deemed necessary to augment the fleet. Among the many dealers in ships and boats who rushed forward to take advantage of the windfall was Charles A. Flint. He was interested in selling the Brazilian ship *Nictheroy*.

Roosevelt asked, "What is the price?"

"Half a million dollars."

"I will take her."

Taken aback, Flint said, "I shall write you a letter—"

Roosevelt shook his head. "Don't bother me with a letter. I don't have time to read it."

Presently, Finch received a contract that had been dictated by Roosevelt. Finch had never seen anything like it, describing it as "one of the most concise and at the same time one of the cleverest" agreements in his experience. Roosevelt made it a condition of the sale that the ship be delivered under her own steam at a specific point and within a specific period. "In one sentence," Finch recalled, "he thus covered all that might have been set forth in pages and pages of specifications. For the vessel *had* to be in first-class condition to make the time scheduled in the contract!"

But the assistant secretary of the navy had more on his mind than ships. He got a visit from a Mr. Walcott, director of the Geological Survey, on March 24. What the caller had to say caught Roosevelt's imagination. Walcott told of a scientist by the name of Samuel Langley who was experimenting with a "flying machine."

Whether Roosevelt had heard of Langley is not known. Had he, he would have learned that the sixty-three-year-old engineer had set out to test his theories of aerodynamics by building a series of model "aeroplanes." By 1896 he had built two, called Aerodromes 5 and 6. Capable of sustained flights and powered by small steam engines, they flew more than thirteen hundred yards and became history's first mechanically propelled heavier-than-air machines capable of sustained flight.

Walcott had brought photographs. Finding them "interesting," Roosevelt glimpsed the possibilities and wasted no time in sending a memo on the subject to Long:

It seems to me worth while for this government to try whether it will not work on a large enough scale to be of use in the event of war. For this purpose I recommend that you appoint two officers of scientific attainments and practical ability, who in conjunction with two officers appointed by the Secretary of War, shall meet and examine into the flying machine, to inform us whether or not they think it could be duplicated on a large scale, to make recommendations as to its practicability and prepare estimates as to the cost.

I think this is well worth doing.

He then listed two "outside experts" whom he considered it advisable to consult: R. H. Thurston, president of Sibley College at Cornell University, and Octave Chanute, president of the American Society of Civil Engineers at Chicago.

Although Langley's airplanes would not take part in the war that Theodore Roosevelt was working to bring about, Langley did receive government backing to build and test a man-carrying aircraft. He made a tandem-wing monoplane with a forty-eight-foot wingspan, powered by a fifty-five-horsepower engine developed by Charles Manley, who was also the pilot. The craft was catapulted from the roof of a houseboat on the Potomac River on October 7, 1898. Unfortunately, its landing gear ran afoul of something on the roof. The plane toppled into the water. When another try on December 8 also failed, Langley abandoned the project, leaving it to the Wright brothers to prove the viability of airplanes, and to their successors to realize a role for aviation in the navy.

As the month drew to a close, the consummate and indefatigable letter writer produced a flood of missives.

To William Astor Chanler on the twenty-sixth:

Things look as if they were coming to a head. Now, can you start getting up that regiment when the time comes? Do you want me as lieutenant colonel?

To General Tillinghast, also on the twenty-sixth:

I wish the Governor [of New York] could say whether or not he believes that the State militia would be sent out of the State, that is, down to Cuba as part of an expeditionary force, or whether we shall raise volunteers. If the latter, will you present my regards to him and ask if I may not be allowed to raise a regiment? I think I can certainly do it, although I shall have to get you to exercise a little patience with me, as I must of course provide a substitute for myself here [at the Navy Department]; but I could leave raising the regiment in the hands of my subordinates for the first three or four days.

On March 26 to Secretary Long, he played the role of naval tactician:

> I am informed by the Bureau of Navigation that the Spanish torpedo-gunboat *Temerario,* which has been for two years at Montevideo left there yesterday, destination unknown. I suggest that orders be sent to the Commanding officers of both the *Marietta* and the *Oregon,* to reach them at their next port, to be on the lookout for this vessel. By keeping clear of places where there are United States consuls or ministers [the *Temerario*] might work her way into the Straits of Magellan and make a fatal attack on the *Oregon* or *Marietta* in the comparatively narrow channel of the Straits of Magellan. It might be well to consider sending the *Oregon* round the Horn if there is danger of her being waylaid in the Straits.

To his brother-in-law, Captain W. S. Cowles, still on duty with the navy in Havana on March 29, on the subject of McKinley's reluctance to act:

> Shilly shallying and half measures at this time will merely render us contemptible in the eyes of the world; and what is infinitely more important, in our own eyes too. Personally I cannot understand how the bulk of our people can tolerate the hideous infamy that has attended the last two years of Spanish rule in Cuba; and still more how they can tolerate the treacherous destruction of the *Maine* and the murder of our men!

That frustration boiled over in a meeting of the McKinley cabinet. He told the president that no other course but war was "compatible with our national honor, or with the claims of humanity on behalf of the wretched women and children of Cuba." He continued, "I am more grieved and indignant than I can say at there being any delay on our part in a matter like this. A great crisis is upon us, and if we do not rise level to it, we shall have spotted the pages of our history with a dark blot of shame."

On the last day of March he wrote to another brother-in-law, Douglas Robinson, "The trend of events is for war. Congress is for war. All it needs is a big leader; but the two biggest leaders, the President and the Speaker [of the House, Thomas Reed], both of whom have enormous power, are almost crazy in their eagerness for peace, and would make almost any sacrifice to get peace."

Chapter 17

Bitter Wrath

On the fifth of April a bemused Roosevelt informed a friend that he had lobbied President McKinley for so long and in such plain language for the war that McKinley would no longer see him.

He complained on April 7 of feeling "bitter wrath and humiliation" at the lack of general planning by the government. "We have our plans in the Navy, and beyond that there is absolutely nothing," he grumbled. "The President doesn't know what message he will send in or what we will do if we have war."

What Roosevelt did not know was that he had carried the day. The president had made up his mind, at last, to send a message to Congress asking for a declaration of belligerency with Spain. It arrived on Capitol Hill on April 11, 1898—the day after Easter.

"In the name of humanity, in the name of civilization," McKinley said, "I ask the Congress to authorize and empower the President to take measures to secure a full and final termination of hostilities between the government of Spain and the people of Cuba, and to secure in the island the establishment of a stable government [using] the military and naval forces of the United States as may be necessary."

After much debate and recriminations on both sides of the war issue, Congress fashioned a resolution for "the recognition of the independence of the Cuban people, demanding that the government of Spain at once withdraw its land and naval forces . . . and directing the President of the United States to use the entire land and naval forces of the United States . . . to carry these resolutions into effect."

It passed at three o'clock in the morning on April 19, 1898.

The significance of the date could not have gone unnoticed by Theodore Roosevelt. It had been exactly one year since he had become assistant secretary of the navy.

McKinley signed the document at 11:24 A.M. on April 20. Shortly thereafter the Spanish minister to Washington called at the State Department and asked for the passports of all Spanish diplomats, a signal they were severing diplomatic relations. In the Spanish capital, the American representative, Stewart Woodford, handed the premier an ultimatum: Spain must free Cuba by noon on April 23. Sagasta rejected the demand, declared an end to diplomacy, and said the action of Congress and the president amounted to a declaration of war. Woodford departed for Paris, and then for home.

On April 20, in four-inch type, Hearst's *Journal* trumpeted:

NOW TO AVENGE THE MAINE

The following Saturday, McKinley issued a call for 125,000 volunteers to augment the 28,000-man regular army. In response, Roosevelt's friend, William Astor Chanler, took out an ad in some newspapers asking for able-bodied men between the ages of eighteen and forty-five to join a regiment he intended to organize. In the next few days more than fifteen hundred men signed up at Chanler's recruitment office on New York's Sixth Avenue. Similar enthusiasm manifested itself in cities, towns, and villages from coast to coast.

This zeal to join the fight also infected a trio of fresh-faced and wide-eyed, but underage, youths from the Groton school. Having heard that the navy would be accepting recruits in Boston, Franklin Delano Roosevelt, Lathrop Brown (his closest friend), and a third patriotic stalwart approached a pie maker who sold his sweet merchandise to Groton boys and bribed him into agreeing to a plan to smuggle them out of school in his wagon. But the scheme went awry; the youths came down with scarlet fever. When Franklin's formidable mother, Sara, heard the news, she rushed to the school to discover her ill son, looking "like a *reconcentrado*."

Volunteer fever seemed to infect everyone. William F. Cody, popularly known as Buffalo Bill, the star and operator of a Wild West extravaganza, let it be known that he was prepared to raise a company of cavalry scouts with four hundred horses. General Nelson Miles, who had led soldiers, including Leonard Wood, in the capture of Geronimo, promptly took him up on the offer. But complications, legal and otherwise, kept the cowboys and their colorful leader far away from the action. Other celebrities had their names put forward, not the least of whom were heavyweight prizefighters James J. Corbett and Bob Fitzsimmons. William Randolph Hearst proposed that these "magnificent men" and other big and brawny athletes were ideally suited to "overawe any Spanish regiment by their mere appearance." The *Journal* also suggested a company of cowboys to be led by Frank James, the brother of Jesse, and six hundred Sioux with tomahawks.

Out of the New York City suburb of Westchester marched five hundred businessmen. Claiming to be sharpshooters, they signed up en masse. Not to be outdone, the gentlemen of Manhattan's café society announced their eagerness to leave behind the lobster and the champagne of Delmonico's and the bratwurst and boiled potatoes of Luchow's for the army and navy mess tables. John Jacob Astor IV offered to buy the nation a battery of artillery and proffered the use of two of his railroads to transport war matériel down to Florida. For this gesture he hoped to attain a post on the staff of a general.

The phenomenon also gripped Roosevelt's home at Oyster Bay. After attending an operetta in Manhattan, Alice and Ted paraphrased one of the songs in the show as they cavorted on the lawn at Sagamore Hill. They sang:

Unleash the dogs of war!
The enemy will find us relenting.
When our cannons roar,
The little King of Spain
Will be repenting.

Newspaper editor William Allen White noted in the *Emporia Gazette* that "everywhere in this good, fair land flags were flying. . . . Everywhere it was flags: tattered, smoke-grimed flags in [railway] engine cabs; flags in button-holes; flags on proud-poles; flags fluttering everywhere. . . ."

Not everyone was so enthusiastic. Many feared an immediate Spanish attack on the cities of the East Coast. Roosevelt looked back on this reaction as a "fairly comic panic which swept in waves over our seacoast, first when it became evident that war was about to be declared, and then when it was declared." In his autobiography, published in 1919, the chapter dealing with this period was given the title "The War of America the Unready."

With a scorn that remained fresh two decades later, he wrote:

The public waked up to the sufficiently obvious fact that the Government was in its usual state—perennial unreadiness for war.

Thereupon the people of the seaboard district passed at one bound from unreasoning confidence that war never could come to unreasoning fear as to what might happen now that it had come. . . . Our people had for decades scoffed at the thought of making ready for possible war. Now, when it was too late, they not only backed every measure, wise and unwise, that offered a chance of supplying a need that ought to have been met before, but they also fell into a condition of panic apprehension as to what the foe might do.

Not so at the Navy Department. It was "full of coal." Decks were cleared for action. Roosevelt noted in his diary, "I have the Navy in good shape."

"Posterity will not grudge him that boast," declared Roosevelt biographer Edmund Morris in *The Rise of Theodore Roosevelt*. "The Navy was, indeed, in superb fighting trim. . . . What it lacked in sheer weight of metal it made up in efficiency and combat toughness. Never before had it been so strategically deployed; never was it so ready for instant action. . . . He had personally set the stage for one of the greatest sea dramas in American history."

Was the navy in good enough shape for the man who had done all this to leave?

Roosevelt believed so. He saw no further role for himself in the navy during the war. He said, "I would be useless on a ship." He yearned to command men in land battles. Accordingly, when the president called for raising three regiments of frontiersmen, Roosevelt lost no time in going to see the secretary of war. Almost before McKinley's signature was dry on the appeal for volunteers, Roosevelt was called into Russell Alger's office and offered his own regiment.

To Alger's astonishment, Roosevelt demurred. Admitting that he had little military experience, he proposed that the new unit be placed in the hands of Leonard Wood, in the rank of colonel, with himself second in command as lieutenant colonel. After taking some time to think it over, Alger accepted the proposition.

He commissioned both men to head the First United States Volunteer Cavalry.

Before Lieutenant Colonel Roosevelt could join Colonel Leonard Wood in actually raising and training the regiment, however, there remained a considerable amount of work for the assistant secretary of the navy. A war on two oceans had to be organized and set in motion.

Chapter 18

Two Sea Dogs and One Warhorse

In addition to his regular duties, Roosevelt had been named by Long to be chair of the new Naval War Board. Its purpose was the implementation of the war plan.

While it was true that the navy was in good fighting shape, all the squadrons were understrength. On the day that the *Maine* had gone down in the harbor in Havana, the entire U.S. navy consisted of ninety vessels. Twenty-one of these had been deemed unserviceable, and twenty-seven were out of commission. That left six in the East Indies, eight on the coast of Africa, seven on the Pacific coast, six in the South Atlantic, three on European station, and a dozen in home ports. Orders needed to be issued as soon as possible to redeploy them according to the war plan.

Of equal urgency was obtaining new ships, either by buying them or commandeering and converting merchant marine vessels into men-of-war. In quick succession ninety-seven merchantmen were bought to be transformed into auxiliary cruisers, gunboats, and colliers. To purchase ships abroad, Captain W. H. Brownson was sent first to Europe. Most countries were reluctant to risk involvement in a war they cared little about, but Brownson's efforts in England provided a pair of torpedo boats and the gunboat *Diogenes*. In South America he met with better success, obtaining the cruisers *Amazones* and *Abreu* from Brazil.

Soon this ad hoc navy would join the pride and joy of the assistant secretary, the first-class battleships *Iowa, Indiana, Oregon,* and *Massachusetts,* and the only survivor in the second-class category, the *Texas.* All of these ships meant a great superiority in firepower and armor protection, compared to the Spanish squadron under the command of Admiral Pascual Cervera y Topete.

Yet many naval analysts gave the edge to Spain. Among these was the publication *London Engineer*. In considering the American battleships, the journal found it difficult to see "where the usefulness of these heavily armed floating citadels comes in. . . . There is a small chance of them catching even a glimpse of the swift and handy armored cruisers of the *Vizcaya* type, and still less chance of getting an effective shot at them. . . . In point of fact we do not believe that the Yankees thoroughly understand the spirit of the mischief that they seem so determined to evoke."

Madrid's leading newspaper, *Heraldo,* had an article on April 6 that attributed to a former secretary of the Spanish navy a low opinion of the Americans. He said, "We shall conquer on the sea and I am now going to give you my reasons. The first is the remarkable discipline that prevails on our warships; the second is, as soon as fire is opened the crews of the American ships will commence to desert, since we all know that among them are people of all nationalities."

In assessing personnel strength, Roosevelt found that this polyglot of a navy consisted of 13,750 enlisted men. They were led by 913 line officers, 209 engineer officers, 72 marine officers, and 198 warrant officers. To look after their health were 161 surgeons. They got their wage packets from 111 pay officers.

To augment these rolls, the state naval militias were called up. This was done without waiting for special legislation. In a report on the response, Secretary Long praised the militias for their "patriotic spirit" and their promptness in meeting the call to duty. In particular he cited the contingent from the First Naval Battalion of New York. Six hours after receiving notice, the men "reported uniformed, armed, equipped and ready for duty." A Massachusetts naval brigade, notified at one o'clock on a Saturday afternoon, arrived at the New York navy yard "fully prepared for service on the *Prairie,* at nine o'clock the next morning."

A major part of the duties of the naval militia, according to the navy war plan, was the manning of thirty-six signal-flag stations up and down the Atlantic coast. They formed crews of old monitors, dating to the Civil War, to protect ports from Maine to the Gulf of Mexico. They also patrolled in tugs and yachts.

Of the latter there were twenty-eight, their luxury appointments stripped and replaced with guns. The biggest was the *Mayflower*. Displacing 2,690 tons, she could make sixteen knots. In all, 123 vessels that had not belonged to the navy found their way into service. They ranged from fast auxiliary cruisers to two steamers of the Fish Commission. Their names were typically American: the *Scorpion, Badger, Buffalo, Dixie, Panther, Yosemite, Prairie, Eagle, Hawk, Vixen, Yankee,* and one that presumably heartened Roosevelt, the *Wasp.*

One of the yachts loaned to the navy was called the *Gloucester* and belonged to financier J. Pierpont Morgan. Soon, the beautiful craft that Morgan saw as "frail as a lady's fan" was outfitted with ten guns and placed under command of the former executive officer of the *Maine,* Lieutenant Commander Richard Wainwright. She was rechristened the *Corsair.*

Spanish warships carried names that sounded strange to American ears: the *Vizcaya,* which had beat a hasty retreat from New York City; the battleship *Pelayo;* the armored cruisers *Infanta Maria Teresa, Almirante Oquendo, Carlos V,* and *Numancia;* and one named for the explorer who three hundred years earlier had stumbled on the Pearl of the Antilles, which now provided so much trouble to the Spanish people: *Cristóbol Colón.*

On the first of May, 1898, the American people learned by cable that the Spanish fleet, under Cervera, had put to sea.

It was this news, more than anything else, that triggered the panic up and down the East Coast that Roosevelt would condemn in his memoirs. As a result of these fears, the Naval War Board was compelled to divide its resources. Ships intended for an offensive deployment were assigned to defensive postures, not because anyone in the Navy Department expected Spanish raids on America's coast, but to calm unwarranted public anxiety.

With the Spanish fleet at sea, Roosevelt's war board looked forward to the inevitable clash between Cervera's ships and those of what was now called the Main Squadron, based at Key West. It had been under the command of sixty-two-year-old Rear Admiral Montgomery Sicard. But soon after he had formed the board of inquiry into the sinking of the *Maine,* his health had faltered to such an extent that he was declared unfit to carry on at sea. Named to replace him was Roosevelt's old friend from the *Iowa.*

On April 21, Captain William T. Sampson received the message, "You are assigned to the command of U.S. forces on the North Atlantic Station with the rank of rear admiral immediately." He had been advanced over seventeen officers of greater seniority.

Unsurprisingly (in Roosevelt's view), Sampson immediately recommended that a blockade of Havana include a bombardment of the forts that protected the harbor. His expectation was that the port would soon surrender. The plan was daring, but it was also risky. Ships would have to move close to the city to carry out the bombardment. That would put them in range of shore guns. Sampson was told to limit himself and his ships to blockading.

No such restraints had been imposed upon Commodore Dewey, half a world away. The order from Secretary Long that had flashed to the commander in chief of the Asiatic Squadron on April 24 had been terse: "War has commenced between the United States and Spain. Proceed at once to the Philippine Islands. Begin operations at once, particularly against the Spanish fleet. You must capture vessels or destroy. Use utmost endeavors."

The squadron departed Hong Kong on the twenty-sixth and put in at Mirs Bay, some thirty miles away, to take on ammunition, have target practice, and make final preparations for the 620-mile voyage south. The destination: Luzon, Philippine Islands. It was there that the Spanish fleet was most likely to be found.

At daybreak Saturday morning, April 30, 1898, Dewey looked into his binoculars on the bridge of the *Olympia* and gazed at the mountains of the largest island of the Philippines. Through the tropical mists he surveyed the Boca Grande (Great Mouth) of the entrance to Manila Bay. Reconnoitering by two of his ships had located the fleet of Spain's Rear Admiral Patricio Montojo in the sheltered harbor, anchored within sight of the capital city of the Philippines.

With his white cap low over frosty gray hair, Dewey lowered the binoculars and rubbed his eyes. Fingering the tips of his mustache, he turned to the captain of the *Olympia,* Charles Gridley, and said, softly, "Now we have them."

In the event the crew members lacked the necessary enthusiasm for the coming fray, Dewey had read to them a letter written by the archbishop of the Manila See and published by the Spanish governor-general of the Philippines, Don Basilio Augustin Davila:

> Spaniards: The North American people, constituted of all the social excrescences, have exhausted our patience and provoked war with their perfidious machinations, with their acts of treachery, with their outrages against the law of nations and international conventions. The struggle will be short and decisive. The God of Victories will give us one as brilliant and complete as the righteousness and justice of our cause demand. Spain will emerge triumphantly, humiliating and blasting the adventurers from those states that, without a

history, offer to humanity only infamous traditions and . . . united insolence and defamation, cowardice and cynicism. A squadron manned by foreigners . . . is preparing to come to this archipelago, with the ruffianly intention of robbing us of all that means life, liberty, and honor. . . . Vain designs, ridiculous boastings! . . . The aggressors shall not profane the tombs of your ancestors, they shall not gratify their lustful passions at the cost of your wives' and daughters' honor . . . Filipinos, prepare for the struggle and unite under the glorious Spanish flag . . . let us fight with the conviction that victory will crown our efforts.

Dewey's sailors hooted and catcalled, then broke into a rousing rendition of "Yankee Doodle," followed by "The Star-Spangled Banner."

At a brief war council early in the evening, Dewey declared his intention to enter Manila Bay soon after dark, proceeding at slow speed so as to reach the Spanish anchorage at daybreak. At 11:30 P.M., all crews stood at battle stations.

Trailing the *Olympia* in a long column, moving at eight knots at intervals of four hundred yards, were the *Baltimore, Raleigh, Petrel, Concord, Boston, McCulloch, Zafiro,* and *Nan Shan.*

Skies were overcast as the ships moved with all lights out through waters that the Spanish admiral had had stripped of all channel markers.

Despite the exhortations of the archbishop, lookouts posted at forts overlooking the approach to the bay proved to be not as vigilant as their spiritual leader had hoped. The first six of Dewey's line of ships slipped past them. The next in line was detected only because of a shower of sparks from the smokestack of the *McCulloch*. The flare prompted a shot from a coastal gun that missed by a wide margin. The *McCulloch* replied with a burst from her rapid-fire six-pounders.

Safely past the forts, the line of gunboats continued slowly and silently up the bay. In the first glimmer of dawn they came upon Admiral Montojo's armada, arrayed in defensive formation.

On the first of May, at six minutes after five o'clock, a mine exploded near the *Olympia,* followed by a second blast, both harmless. Cannon fire from the city's ring of forts also fell short.

The Spanish ships opened fire, rapidly, just as ineffectively.

This barrage lasted twenty-five minutes before Dewey turned toward the *Olympia*'s skipper and said, "You may fire when ready, Gridley."

When the news reached New York, Theodore Roosevelt's least-favorite newspaper, Hearst's *Journal,* blared:

VICTORY, Complete . . . Glorious!

THE MAINE IS AVENGED

In a few hours the Spaniards had lost their entire Pacific squadron and 381 lives. On the *Reina Cristina* alone, there had been 150 killed, including the captain.

Dewey's ships had suffered only fifteen hits, only one of which caused extensive damage. A shell striking the *Baltimore* had set off a supply of ammunition and injured two officers and six enlisted men—the only American casualties.

Manila stood under Dewey's guns, and the Philippines lay before him for the taking. The islands would remain American possessions for half a century, save for four years when occupied by the Japanese during the Second World War. Liberated in 1945 by American forces under General Douglas MacArthur (and conveyed to victory by the successors to Theodore Roosevelt's battleship navy), the Filipinos received independence in 1948. It was a resolution that accorded with Roosevelt's ideas. He recorded in his autobiography that it was his belief that "we should train them for self-government as rapidly as possible, then leave them free to decide their own fate."

President McKinley held a similar view. Following the news of Dewey's victory, he jotted a note to himself: "While we are conducting war and until its conclusion, we must keep what we can get. When the war is over, we must keep what we want."

Assessing American control of the Philippines in 1919 (after having had direct responsibility for administering the islands as president of the United States), Roosevelt boasted, with a social Darwinist flair, "I know of no country ruled and administered by men of the white race where that rule and that administration have been exercised so emphatically with an eye single to the welfare of the natives themselves."

But none of that future was known to the jubilant jingoes dining at the Metropolitan Club, where the chef's specialty for that historic day was *poulet sauté à la Dewey.* In other dining rooms, desserts took the form of ice cream sculpted in the shape of the *Olympia,* now second only to the *Maine* in the sentiments of the American people. So overwhelmed were some parents that they called their newborns Dewey. Also named for the Hero of Manila were racehorses, pets, yachts, and one brand of cigars.

Even the country's most widely read humorist, Peter Finley Dunne, creator of "Martin Dooley," was heard. Regarding the Battle of Manila, Mister Dooley, who appeared in the *Chicago Journal* speaking with an Irish brogue on whatever subject that struck his fancy at the moment, observed, "Georgy has th' thraits iv th' family. 'Surrinder,' he says. 'Niver,' says the Dago. 'Well,' says Cousin George, 'I'll just have to push ye ar-round,' he says."

For a time there was serious consideration given to making May first into Dewey Day.

The Navy Department expressed its official regard by promoting Dewey to rear admiral.

Roosevelt had signaled Dewey: "Every American is in your debt." He then sent a letter to his wolfhound. "You have made a name for the nation and the Navy, and yourself." But Roosevelt could not overlook himself. "And I can't say how pleased I am to think that I had any share in getting you the opportunity that you have used so well."

Now it remained to be seen what Roosevelt's friend, Captain William Sampson, could do against the Spanish in the Atlantic. On board his flagship, the *New York,* he was plying the waters in the vicinity of Cuba, from Bahía Honda west of Havana to Cárdenas on the east. Blockading but not attacking, he awaited the arrival of Admiral Cervera's Spanish fleet and, he hoped, the climactic sea battle that would settle the Cuban situation for good. But on the day of Dewey's triumph in Manila Bay, Sampson's mighty armada had been making for Key West to take on coal.

Traveling with Sampson was one of Roosevelt's favorite reporters. Indeed, the fact that Richard Harding Davis was aboard the *New York* had been Roosevelt's doing. He had granted Davis a set of special credentials. Accustomed to being on press boats, Davis found the *New York* like "a luxurious yacht, with none of the ennui."

Certainly, there had been nothing boring on April 27 as the huge ship unlimbered its mighty guns to return the fire of Spanish cannons in shore fortifications at Matanzas, fifty miles east of Havana. He wrote for readers of the *Herald,* "The guns seemed to be ripping out the steel sides of the ship. . . . The thick deck of the super-structure jumped with the concussions, and vibrated like a suspension-bridge when an express train thunders across it. . . . Your eardrums tingled and strained and seemed to crack. The noise was physical, like a blow from a baseball bat."

Regarding Rear Admiral Sampson, Davis discerned "a professor of mathematics . . . an intellectual fighter, a man who impresses you as one who would fight and win entirely with his head."

To another correspondent who boarded the *New York,* Stephen Crane, Sampson was the Dewey of the Atlantic. "Men thought of glory, and he considered the management of ships. No bunting, no arches, no fireworks, nothing but the perfect management of a big fleet. . . . Just plain, pure unsauced accomplishment."

Crane's famous 1895 novel of the Civil War, *The Red Badge of Courage,* had been carved from the imagination of a writer born eleven years after the start of the war between the states. Never having been in battle himself, Crane had sought to close that gap in his experience by becoming a war correspondent. William Randolph Hearst had decided the youth was just the kind of writer he wanted for the *Journal:* the genuinely esteemed author of highly acclaimed literature.

After failing to get in contact with Cuban rebels in 1897 (as had Davis and Remington), Crane had gone eastward to cover the Greco-Turkish war, meeting Richard Harding Davis in London. Like Davis, he had hurried back to America to get in on the coverage of the war with Spain, although he had switched his allegiance from Hearst's *Journal* to Pulitzer's *World* to do so.

Of the impending clash of navies, Crane wrote, "Now is in progress a huge game, with wide and lonely stretches of ocean as the board, and with great steel ships as counters."

In the matching of wits at sea, the Spanish commander appeared to have won the day. Cervera outfoxed Sampson by slipping into the port at Santiago de Cuba by coming to the island by way of Martinique and Curaçao while the Americans refueled at Key West. Feeling pleased with himself, Cervera cabled Governor-General Blanco at Havana: "Have cast anchor to-day in this harbor, whence whole squadron sends you greeting, desirous of cooperating in the defense of the country."

Unfortunately for Cervera, this cable and other messages had to pass under the fingertips of telegraph operator Domingo Villaverde, who happened to be an agent in an intelligence network that had been set up between the U.S. Army and the Western Union Telegraph

Company. Consequently, the Spanish admiral's boastfully cheerful cable was also read in the Navy Department.

Although there was some doubt about the authenticity of the intelligence from Santiago de Cuba, on the morning of May 12 a cable went to Sampson advising that the Spanish fleet "might very well" be there and strongly advising that Sampson dispatch ships under the command of Admiral Winfield Scott Schley to investigate. Sampson answered that he preferred to "follow the plan already adopted" and change it only if it could be confirmed that Cervera was at Santiago. Not having found the Spaniards elsewhere by May 21, he cabled Washington, "Schley has been ordered to Santiago."

On the night of the twenty-eighth, Schley's squadron lay about ten miles south of the destination. Moving closer at dawn, Schley looked across the water at a sunwashed Cuba like that viewed by Christopher Columbus. In Schley's words, the land was "green with verdure, the white surf breaking along the coral reefs, and the picturesque old Morro [fort] in its coat of dirty yellow plaster standing grim guard over the entrance" to the harbor.

Five miles from the old fort, one of Schley's ships' signal lights flashed: "Just caught view of Spanish warship in harbor entrance." A second later aboard the *Iowa,* Lieutenant Commander Raymond P. Rodgers peered through binoculars and cried to Captain Robley D. "Fighting Bob" Evans, Sampson's successor on the *Iowa,* "Captain, there's the *Cristóbol Colón!*"

Ordering his ships to form a semicircle to block the harbor, Schley uttered almost the same words as had Dewey at Manila. "We've got them now," he said, confidently. "They'll never go home."

As the news of the bottling up of Cervera's fleet sent a new wave of patriotic fervor across the country, hard on the heels of Dewey's triumph in the Philippines, the success of the navy off Cuba raised the tantalizing prospect of an end to the war before it even got started. But to the man in Washington who had done more than anyone to make these sea victories possible, the idea of a negotiated settlement meant only that Theodore Roosevelt might be denied his chance to reap glory in a great land battle.

Although he told Secretary Long, "I hate to leave you more than I can say," he was rushing to get away.

He told friends, "It will be awful if we miss the fun."

On May 10 a message went to Colonel Leonard Wood, who was out in San Antonio, Texas, in the first stages of organizing the regiment. Roosevelt insisted that "drill or no drill" it was vital "to get our troops [to Cuba] with the first expedition."

In a frenzy of preparation in early May, Roosevelt pulled strings, at Wood's request, to obtain for the new regiment modern Krag-Jorgenson carbines that used smokeless powder, thus ensuring the regiment's sharpshooters would not lose sight of their targets in a pall of smoke. For himself, he got his hands on a navy revolver that had been salvaged from the *Maine*.

McKinley had called for the raising of three regiments "composed exclusively of frontiersmen possessing special qualifications as horsemen and marksmen." Roosevelt considered himself a good shot, but he had doubts about his equestrian abilities. In his memoirs he confessed that while he was fond of horseback riding, he had taken to it slowly and with difficulty, as he had done with boxing.

"It was a long time before I became a respectable rider, and I never got much higher," he wrote. "I mean by this that I never became a first-flight man in the hunting field, and never even approached the bronco-busting class in the West."

Now that he would be second in command of a cavalry unit, Roosevelt telegraphed to San Antonio for Wood to get him "a couple of good, stout, quiet horses for my own use . . . not gun-shy . . . trained and bridle-wise, no bucking."

From his optician, he ordered a dozen extra pairs of glasses, steel rimmed.

Brooks Brothers, New York, received an order for a "blue cravenette regular Lieutenant-Colonel's uniform without yellow on the collar and with leggings," to be ready in a week. From a proper hatter he ordered suitably dashing campaign headgear.

He took out a life insurance policy.

Someone gave him a going-away gift of spurs.

Although the new regiment was designated the First Volunteer Cavalry, far more colorful names had been suggested, including Teddy's Texas Tarantulas, Teddy's Terrors, Teddy's Gilded Gang, Teddy's Riotous Rounders, and Roosevelt's Rustler Regiment. The one that stuck was just as alliterative. Painted on a signboard pointing the way to Camp Wood, the training site near San Antonio, it proclaimed:

THIS WAY TO CAMP OF ROOSEVELT'S ROUGH RIDERS

Across the Atlantic Ocean there was some confusion as to the role of Theodore Roosevelt in America's war machine. A newspaper reported, "The Commander-in-Chief of the American Army, is one Ted Roosevelt, formerly a New York policeman . . . born near Harlem . . . emigrated to America when young . . . [educated at] Harvard Academy, a commercial school. . . . He goes about the country accompanied by a bodyguard of young toughs called the rough rioters."

At a desk decorated in a naval motif, Assistant Secretary Theodore Roosevelt worked to create a modern fleet led by battleships and issued orders to ready the navy for a war to drive Spain out of the Western Hemisphere.

Naval strategist Captain Alfred Thayer Mahan provided ideas and inspiration for Roosevelt's efforts to build up the navy in preparation for war.

Roosevelt's political mentor and confidant, Henry Cabot Lodge, was the leader of the jingoes in the U.S. Senate. These jingoes demanded military intervention to overthrow the Spanish regime in Cuba.

"The liveliest spot in Washington at present is the Navy Department. The decks are cleared for action. . . . It remains only to sand down the decks and pipe to quarters for action," or so said the *New York Sun* on August 23, 1897. (New York Public Library)

Admitting his riding skills could never equal those of the "bronco-busting class" of Rough Riders, Roosevelt asked for "a couple of good, stout, quiet horses . . . not gun-shy . . . trained and bridle-wise, no bucking." One of them was drowned during the landing on Cuba, but the survivor, Texas, carried Roosevelt as he led the charge up Kettle Hill.

Two months before the war, Roosevelt cabled Commodore George Dewey to "keep full of coal" in preparation to lead the Pacific Squadron against the Spanish fleet in the Philippines. Dewey's execution of the order helped provide the first victory of the war. (New York Public Library)

To prepare for war, Roosevelt ordered a uniform from Brooks Brothers and a dozen extra pairs of his trademark pince-nez eyeglasses from his optician.

When the Rough Riders were organized, Roosevelt demanded that Leonard Wood be appointed colonel. Troopers gave Wood the nicknames Old Poker Face and Icebox. In contrast, the dynamic and popular Roosevelt was known as Teddy, and Wood fully expected to be "kicked upstairs to make room for Roosevelt." The prediction came true shortly after their arrival in Cuba, when Wood was promoted to general.

Officers of the Rough Riders, including Lieutenant Colonel Roosevelt, take a break from a meal to pose for a photograph at their training camp near San Antonio.

Sent to Cuba with writer Richard Harding Davis to provide drawings of the revolution for William Randolph Hearst's *Journal*, artist Frederic Remington became so disgusted with conditions that he vowed to return to Cuba only with the U.S. Army. He kept his pledge in the company of the Rough Riders.

When Roosevelt's wife Edith visited him in Florida before the Rough Riders sailed for Cuba, she stayed at the posh Tampa Bay Hotel. It had been taken over by the army as headquarters and officers' billets, but Roosevelt took no part in what Richard Harding Davis called "the rocking chair period of the war"; he camped with his troops.

Frederic Remington's painting of his friend Theodore Roosevelt astride Texas.

Colonel Theodore Roosevelt and some of his Rough Riders pose for a victory photo on San Juan Hill.

"THE ROUGH RIDER."

Artist Bernard Partridge's view of Theodore Roosevelt for the British magazine *Punch*.

Welcomed home as a hero and hailed by many as the most famous man in America, Roosevelt was sketched by one of the most well-known artists in the country, Charles Dana Gibson.

Part V

Cowboy Cavalry

Chapter 19

Roosevelt's Room

The term *Rough Riders* did not sit well with their namesake.

"The objection to that term," Theodore Roosevelt explained to a throng of journalists in Washington on April 29, 1898, "is that people who read it may get the impression that the regiment is to be a hippodrome affair. Those who get that idea will discover that it is a mistake. The regiment may be one of rough riders, but they will be as orderly, obedient, and generally well disciplined a body as any equal number of men in any branch of the service. But they will not make a show. They go out for business, and when they do business no one will entertain for a moment the notion that they are part of a show."

For Secretary Long, as he observed "Roosevelt's room" in the Navy Department, the "interesting scene" he found must have looked like a circus. The office and the corridor without "bubbled over with enthusiasm" and was "filled with bright young fellows from all over the country, college graduates and old associates from the western ranches, all eager to serve Roosevelt."

Roosevelt wrote to his sister, Corinne, that he had "about 25 'gentlemen rankers'" begging to accompany him, including "five from the Knickerbocker Club and a dozen clean-cut, stalwart young fellows from Harvard; such fine boys."

To Lincoln Steffens, Roosevelt's journalist crony during his two years in the police department, he expressed his expectation that these youthful and energetic collegians would be "exactly on a level with the cowboys."

One who had dropped out of Harvard and rushed to sign up was William Sloan Simpson, described by Roosevelt in a letter to the former American consul in Cuba, Fitzhugh Lee, as "a gallant young man." However, Simpson was only one of a large number of young men recommended for inclusion in the regiment by friends and government associates.

"It seemed to me that almost every friend I had in every State had some one acquaintance who was bound to go with the Rough Riders, and for whom I had to make a place," Roosevelt recalled in his memoir, *The Rough Riders*. "I eventually consented to accept some one or two recruits, of course only after a most rigid examination into their physical capacity, and after they had shown that they knew how to ride and shoot."

Looking around Roosevelt's crowded office on the day Roosevelt was sworn in as lieutenant colonel on May 6, a reporter for the *New York Times* observed thirty-one young men in "an assemblage of cowboys, plainsmen, college students, and ex-policemen of the New York force." Mustered in the day before, the men were seen as "decidedly unique in appearance." The paper reported, "The plainsmen and rough riders were in broad brimmed sombreros, and gave an unmistakable evidence of their ability to round up a herd of refractory steers. They were all tall, well built, athletic fellows, bronzed from exposure, and a picture of health and endurance. There were several young Englishmen in the party who had preferred this service as more exciting than ranching."

Three former police officers looked to the *New York Times* man as "quite as stalwart as the ranchmen," while "a sprinkling . . . coming from the colleges and universities, as well as from the social centres" were described as "tenderfeet."

Having shaken Roosevelt's hand, continued the article, "the men were unanimous in pronouncing him a 'brick.' "

Accompanying this colorful account was an item of special interest to readers in Roosevelt's hometown, reflecting his apparent change of heart concerning the nickname of the regiment:

CLUB MEN AS ROUGH RIDERS

———

Many Famous Horsemen and Athletes
Have Joined Theodore Roosevelt's Regiment

The Cowboy Regiment or, as it is understood he prefers to have it called, "The Rough Riders Regiment," organized by Assistant Secretary of the Navy Roosevelt for service in the war with Spain, has from the start excited the greatest interest in the New York clubs. Mr. Roosevelt has had applications from almost every clubman of his acquaintance who is a horseman, not only in New York, but in Boston and other large cities. From these applicants he has selected several well-known cross-country riders and polo players.

The most notable accessions to the ranks of this regiment from the New York clubs are Woodbury Kane, William Tiffany, Craig Wadsworth, and Reginald Ronalds, who started for Washington on Wednesday. These men, all members of the Knickerbocker Club, are intimate friends of Mr. Roosevelt, and all have volunteered as troopers.

Two years younger than Roosevelt, thirty-eight-year-old Woodbury Kane was a bachelor and a noted polo player and cross-country rider who had chased hounds and foxes in the United States and England. Roosevelt had regarded him as a "close friend" at Harvard, and in *The Rough Riders* he wrote of him, "During the eighteen years that had passed since my graduation I had seen very little of him, though being always interested in sport, I occasionally met him on the hunting field, had seen him on the deck of the [racing boat] Defender when she vanquished the Valkyrie, and knew the part he had played on the Navajoe, when, in her most important race, that otherwise unlucky yacht vanquished her opponent, the Prince of Wales's Brittania. When the war [began], Kane felt it his duty to fight for his country. He did not seek any position of distinction. All he desired was the chance to do whatever work he was put to do well, and get to the front; and he enlisted as a trooper."

Also a bachelor with "an independent income," thirty-five-year-old Craig Wadsworth was regarded as one of the best riders of the Genesee Valley Hunt Club and, according to the *New York Times*, was "a skillful cotillion leader." But for true blue-bloodedness, no one compared to thirty-year-old William Tiffany. Nephew of August Belmont and a grand-nephew of Commodore Oliver H. Perry, the hero of the Battle of Lake Erie, Tiffany had forsaken his cattle-ranching business in the West to enlist along with an array of young scions of New York City's high society.

These included Townsend Burden, the son of a Troy, New York, iron and steel magnate whose elegant mansion overlooking Madison Square Park had been the scene of one of the most daring crimes during Roosevelt's two years as head of the New York Police Department. On the evening of December 27, 1895, as his parents enjoyed a performance of "Romeo and Juliet" at the Metropolitan Opera House, Burden had remained at home, snugly ensconced with a book in a comfortable chair in the downstairs parlor while burglars looted his mother's jewel box, which had been left unlocked in her bedroom. Although Roosevelt's detectives had suspected "an inside job," they had been unable to lay the crime at the feet of a pair of male servants. This embarrassment at not being able to make arrests had been compounded two months later with the collaring of the duo in London, England, by a Scotland Yard detective.

Other socially prominent volunteers were Hamilton Fish Jr., who had the distinction of being the ex-captain of the Columbia University racing crew, and Reginald Ronalds, son of Pierre Lorillard Ronalds and a graduate of Yale, where he had been one of the best players on the varsity football team.

College athletes proved eager to don the uniform of Roosevelt's Rough Riders. The *New York Times*'s roster of volunteers included Dudley Dean, the famous football player, whom Roosevelt regarded as the best quarterback who ever played on a Harvard eleven; Guy Munchie, the coach; Charles Bull of the Harvard varsity crew; and Stanley Hollister, one of the best half-mile runners in the country. All of these men were recent graduates of Roosevelt's alma mater.

"Harvard being my own college," he wrote, "I had such a swarm of applications from it that I could not take one in ten."

From Princeton had come "a crack football player," Horace Devereaux of Colorado Springs, and Basil Ricketts, the son of an army general.

Roosevelt noted that "they all sought entry into the ranks of the Rough Riders as eagerly as if it meant something widely different from hard work, rough fare, and the possibility of death; and the reason why they turned out to be such good soldiers lay largely in the fact that they were men who had thoroughly counted the cost before entering, and who went into the regiment because they believed that this offered their best chance for seeing hard and dangerous service."

He felt, he confessed, "many qualms at first in allowing men of this stamp to come in . . . and was afraid they would find it very hard to serve—not for a few days, but for months—in the ranks, while I, their former intimate associate, was a field officer."

One close acquaintance, however, encountered no disparity in rank. Roosevelt's frequent correspondent, William Astor Chanler, had gotten a regiment of his own. But the difference between Roosevelt's

First Volunteer Cavalry and Chanler's Sixth U.S. Cavalry was that Chanler had raised the regiment and funded it himself. "He is rich," noted a profile in *The New York Times Illustrated Magazine,* "and has equipped this force of men in order that he may do a little Cuban campaigning and see some excitement."

That Chanler would do so came as no surprise to the author of the article. After visiting the regiment in its encampment in Tampa, Florida, the anonymous reporter withheld no superlatives in a profile with the headline:

WILLIAM ASTOR CHANLER'S ROUGH RIDERS

He wrote:

Out to the west of the town where the new cavalry camps have been established, and even further in the same direction, toward the encampment of the Cuban volunteers, he who goes out early in the morning before the heat of the sun puts an end to daily drills, will see some things that will strike him as unique and absolutely original. In a small grove of pines, whose boughs are fancifully festooned with Spanish moss, screened from the sight of casual passers-by, are a body of hardy, rough riders, all of whom are American or European born, but who have enlisted to fight for Cuba Libre. Their leader is a man with a history. He has led expeditions into Central Africa; has fought against savage tribes there for years; has explored remote and hitherto unknown regions in the most inaccessible portion of the Dark Continent; has hunted tigers in India for the fun of the thing, and has done all sorts of unusual things, simply for adventure.

While Chanler appeared well on his way to readying his own band of rough riders, Roosevelt found himself impatient to do the same. Chafing at the bit, he wrote to Anna Roosevelt Cowles on May 8, 1898: "Well, I'm here still; I hope to get off in forty eight hours, but Wood keeps me here where I can hurry things at headquarters. We *hope* we have fixed matters so that our regiment will embark at Galveston with the 5th cavalry on the first expedition to Cuba—but it's largely a matter of chance, and we'll just have to take whatever comes."

Two days later the impatience was evident in a long letter to Wood. He began by informing him of

two more recruits whom we will have to take. . . . The first is the son of the Hon. John Russell Young, the Librarian of Congress, a warm, personal friend of Secretary [of War] Alger's, for whom I should do anything anyhow, and for whom Secretary Alger wishes us to do what we can. The boy's name is Howard Young. He will turn up about the time this letter does. The other is young Crowninshield, a nephew of Captain Crowninshield, Chief of the Bureau of Navigation; the champion pistol shot of the Mass. artillery.

The letter continued:

I spent a good deal of yesterday and today fussing with the Ordnance and Quartermaster General's Department. They have sent out tracers and tell me that by day after tomorrow the rifles and most of the supplies will be at San Antonio. I hope you have got your horses pretty well purchased by this time. . . . I really don't see that there is much left for me to do; and this afternoon I shall wire you hoping that you will allow me to start tomorrow (Thursday). I hate to be hanging around here with you in all the turmoil of bringing order out of chaos. I appreciate of course that it was absolutely necessary for me to stay until we got these things started, for sending out tracers undoubtedly hurried them, but now it seems as if everything was being done, and if you start early next week I should be cutting connections pretty closely if I waited here later than Thursday.

The tangles with red tape and the wrestling matches with government bureaucrats still rankled Roosevelt fifteen years later as he published his autobiography. He wrote, "In trying to get the equipment I met with checks and rebuffs, and in return was the cause of worry and concern to various bureau chiefs who were unquestionably estimable men in their private and domestic relations, and who doubtless had been good officers thirty years before, but who were unfit for modern war as if they were so many smoothbores."

One "fine old fellow" suggested that the Rough Riders be armed with old-fashioned black powder rifles, explaining with a paternal indulgence that no one yet knew just what the smokeless powder requested by Roosevelt might do, adding for good measure that "there was a good deal to be said about having smoke conceal us from the enemy."

Another official studied War Department regulations concerning uniforms and found a rule that required issuing winter clothing in July, so as to give ample time for getting it to all the various posts before cold weather set in. Going by the book, he proposed issuance of winter gear despite the fact that the Rough Riders were training in

Texas in hot weather and would then be sent to fight in tropical Cuba. Recalling in his autobiography what may be credited as his first victory of the war, Roosevelt noted, "I rectified this and got an order for khaki clothing."

Meanwhile, Wood's troopers in San Antonio were being issued regular army-blue uniforms. By May 14, New Yorkers Kane, Tiffany, Ronalds and the others were shedding their civilian clothing and, according to the *New York Times*'s Camp Wood correspondent, "being fitted out in shorter order than ever they were in their lives before."

The reporter looked on as Reginald Ronalds "laid aside his broad-brimmed sombrero for the service hat without a murmur, and selected one of the cotton undershirts as if he wanted it."

With the problem of seasonally appropriate uniforms settled, Roosevelt next learned that before any horses could be purchased, advertisements had to be run in various journals over a period of thirty days. This rule was set aside only after his direct appeal to Secretary of War Alger. When the waiver was presented to the bureaucrat in charge of horse-purchasing rules, he threw himself back in his chair and exclaimed with a sigh, "Oh, dear! I had this office running in such good shape—and then along came the war and upset everything!"

Of gravest concern to Roosevelt was that the ensnaring red tape might so delay the equipping of the regiment that it—and he—would miss out on the war. He wrote to Wood, "I do hope we can get our troops down with the first expedition, drill or no drill. They are an unusually fine lot of men, and at the very beginning we can use them for scouting and outpost duty, and they could be speedily drilled into shape on the field. I suppose you are drilling them now."

In a P.S. he continued, "Jack Astor has offered his mountain battery, and the Secretary [of War] seems to think we had better accept it."

This referred to a fully equipped artillery battery given to the government by Roosevelt's friend, John Jacob Astor, at a cost of more than $100,000. To recruit men, Astor had authorized his personal business representative, Henry B. Ely, to open a recruiting office at Astor Court. On the appointed day, 150 men showed up at 18 West Thirty-fourth Street to be screened by the commander of the battery, Lieutenant Payton C. March. The *New York Times* described them as "young fellows, mostly of fine physique, among them many college students." Addressing them, March expressed the same warning as had Roosevelt in eschewing any idea that the unit would be a fun affair. "Those who want to join this battery," he told them, "want to distinctly understand that it is organized for hard service, and not for parade or play." He then revealed that he had received word that morning (May 28) that the battery was to be sent, not to Cuba, but to the Philippines.

As to the man who had paid for the battery, John Jacob Astor IV would not serve with the unit. Instead, he joined the staff of General Levi P. Morton, going on to attain the rank of lieutenant colonel.

In concluding the impatient May 10 letter to Leonard Wood, Roosevelt again could not restrain his eagerness to fling himself into a battle. "I don't want to be unpatriotic," he said, "but I feel like saying 'Thank Heaven,' for I hear that the four Spanish cruisers are back in Cadiz. If true this means that instead of Sampson ending the war we will be put in to end it in Cuba."

Two days later he wrote exultingly to his sister Corinne:

At last I have my orders, and start tonight, only, I fear, for a period of weary waiting in San Antonio. It will be bitter if we don't get to Cuba, but we shall have to take things as they come. Edith and I have had a lovely last fortnight together; we have gone out to dinner, have driven through the beautiful country, have enjoyed the cunning children.

Goodbye, my darling little sister.
Your own brother.

Chapter 20

A Little Enthusiastic

On the day Roosevelt had expressed his misgivings about the Rough Riders possibly being mistaken for a military version of Buffalo Bill Cody's Wild West extravaganza, a slight, elderly man with world-weary eyes behind a frail pair of wire-rimmed spectacles had stood quietly at the back of Roosevelt's crowded office, but not without being noticed by one of the mob of Washington reporters. One of their breed, although from New York City, he was Jacob Riis, and he knew the object of all this attention better than any journalist in the room. To anyone with a knowledge of Riis, it would have come as no surprise that he would be near the friend he called TR as he set off to war.

Years later, as Roosevelt campaigned for the presidency in 1904, Riis looked back to that spring of 1898 and, in a worshipful book aimed at helping Roosevelt to victory (titled *Theodore Roosevelt, the Citizen*), he wrote, "Merely to sit in an office and hold down a job, a title, or a salary was not his way. He did not go lightly. His wife was lying sick, with a little baby; his other children needed him. I never had the good fortune to know a man who loves his children more devotedly and more sensibly than he. There was enough to keep him at home; there were plenty to plead with him. I did myself, for I hated to see him go. His answer was as if his father might have spoken: 'I have done all I could to bring on the war, because it is a just war, and the sooner we meet it the better. Now that it has come, I have no business to ask others to do the fighting and stay at home myself.'"

On the afternoon Roosevelt crossed the Potomac River for a connection with a southbound train, the mid-May skies were overcast and Riis thought Roosevelt looked unnaturally somber.

"To me," Riis recalled, "the leaden sky seemed drearier, the day more desolate than before."

Then Roosevelt gave a sudden wave of a hand, broke into his famous and often-caricatured toothy grin, and said, "It won't be long."

The unspoken, nagging anxiety was still whether he would reach the war in time, for events appeared to be unfolding so rapidly that others might settle the issue of Cuba Libre without him. Indeed, an invasion force already had set sail from the port of Tampa. On May 10, while Roosevelt still wrestled with bureaucrats for the proper outfitting of the Rough Riders, Companies E and G of the First Infantry, with seven thousand rifles and two hundred thousand rounds of ammunition, had boarded the steamer *Gussie* with the intention of a landing on the northern coast, west of Havana, to engage the Cuban army in Pinar del Río.

"This is a hostile expedition," reported the *New York Times* from Tampa. "It is prepared to fight and expects to fight. United with Cubans, it will at once give a nucleus of strength to those forces . . . but even before it reaches General Gómez it will be well able to take care of itself against a thousand Spaniards, and it is not likely to meet half that number."

As the *Gussie* sailed, the port of Tampa was alive with preparations for the forces that were to follow the First Infantry onto Cuban soil and, ultimately, form an army of occupation. Rows of transports stood at dockside to take on arms and ammunition, while the troopers they were to carry engaged in relentless drilling in camps surrounding the seaport.

"Mobilizing regulars, with their equipment all ready," said the *New York Times,* "is no small task, and mobilizing volunteers, much of whose equipment has to be provided outright, is a herculean undertaking which cannot be hurried beyond a certain rate of speed. Unless all signs here [Washington, D.C.] have been misread, the invasion of Cuba in full force will be delayed no longer than it takes to get the necessary number of troops together, equip and organize them, and provide transportation facilities. Just when that will be is the work of a prophet. Experts in the War Department decline to fix a date."

Undoubtedly with delight, Roosevelt learned that these same experts had acknowledged that the standard blue flannel uniform that had been the sartorial hallmark of the U.S. Army since the Civil War was much too heavy and warm for the climate of the West Indies. An urgent order had been placed for ten thousand khaki outfits like those Roosevelt had obtained for the Rough Riders.

Another bit of news affecting the army had proved even more heartening to the former assistant secretary of the navy, who now held the rank of lieutenant colonel of cavalry. The commander of the Fifth Corps mustering at Tampa would be General Nelson Miles, hero of the Civil and Indian Wars. He was to be sent to Florida to replace Major General William Rufus Shafter.

At the age of sixty-three, Shafter was a veteran of the same wars as General Miles and had been awarded the Congressional Medal of Honor in the Civil War. Having started his long army career as a private, he had risen to the rank of general without attending the U.S. Military Academy at West Point. Unfortunately, he weighed three hundred pounds and suffered from chronic gout, hardly the physical attributes appropriate to lead men into battle in the tropics.

In command of other units would be Fitzhugh Lee (Seventh Corps) and a hero of the Confederate army, Joseph "Fighting Joe" Wheeler. Called to the Executive Mansion by President McKinley at the age of sixty-two, he had told the nation's commander in chief that he had thought his fighting days were over. He was glad they weren't. In the war to free Cuba, he would have no qualms about wearing Union Blue (actually khaki) and taking command of the cavalry, both regular and volunteer.

As the preparations for a land war proceeded, the ships of the U.S. Navy had plied the waters around Cuba in search of Spaniards. Since the fifth of May, Admiral William Sampson had been in a game of hide-and-seek at sea. Looking to engage ships under the command of Admiral Cervera, he guessed that the enemy might put in at San Juan, Puerto Rico, for coal. Arriving there in the early hours of May 12, he was disappointed to find San Juan's harbor empty of Spanish warships. Having steamed more than a thousand miles to come up empty-handed, he settled for a bombardment of Morro Castle, with negligible destructive effects, and sailed back toward Cuba.

In Washington, Captain Alfred Thayer Mahan dismissed the action as "an eccentric movement." Secretary Long put the episode down as a failure. Meanwhile, as discussed, Cervera had scurried into the harbor of Santiago de Cuba to lie there unmolested until discovered by Commodore Winfield Scott Schley. Arriving off Santiago on May 27, Sampson proposed to a war council aboard his flagship that the Spanish ships be bottled up by the device of sinking a ship at the mouth of the harbor.

To achieve this goal, Sampson chose a young volunteer who was not a line officer. At age twenty-seven, Lieutenant Richard Pearson Hobson was a Naval Academy graduate (first in his class) and a naval constructor. Warned by Sampson that he was volunteering for what might be a suicide mission, Hobson and seven equally daring sailors boarded the collier *Merrimac* at flood tide and made for the mouth of the harbor.

Watching from the deck of the *New York,* Associated Press reporter William "Chappie" Goode waited breathlessly as the little ship entered the channel under the muzzles of Santiago de Cuba's Castle Morro fortifications. Presently, he reported, "The flash of a gun streamed out from Morro. Then came another, and in a few seconds the mouth of Santiago Harbor was livid with flames that shot viciously from both banks. . . . The dull sound of the cannonade and its fiery light were unmistakable evidences of the fierce attack that was being waged upon Hobson's gallant crew."

Gallant they were, but the mission failed. Spanish gunners sank the *Merrimac* at a spot that did not block the channel. Yet the heroism of Hobson and his crew so impressed Spain's Admiral Cervera that he sent Sampson a message under a flag of truce, revealing that Hobson and his men had survived and had been taken prisoner. He then complimented them on their heroism.

Were Theodore Roosevelt still assistant secretary of the navy, he certainly would have been thrilled to add his voice to the chorus of accolades for Hobson and the men of the *Merrimac,* but, by the date of Hobson's daring dash to close the harbor of Santiago de Cuba, Roosevelt had been at Camp Wood for nearly two weeks.

Arriving there on May 15, he had sported a crisp new fawn-colored uniform with canary-yellow trim.

"The only objection," said one of the Rough Riders who had greeted him with cheers, "was that he wore glasses."

Four days after setting foot on the dry, hard Texas dirt of Camp Wood, Roosevelt confessed in a letter to Henry Cabot Lodge, "I feel pretty homesick, of course. If it were not for that, I should really be enjoying myself thoroughly."

To his stalwart political mentor and ever-ready ally, Roosevelt wrote, "Here we are working like beavers and we are getting the regiment into shape. It has all the faults incident to an organization whose members have elected their own officers—some good and more very bad—and who have been recruited largely from among classes who putting it mildly, do not look at life in the spirit of decorum and conventionality that obtains in the East. Nevertheless, many of our officers have in them the making of first rate men, and the troopers, I believe, are on the average finer than are to be found in any other regiment in the whole country. It would do your heart good to see some of the riding. The Eastern men are getting along very well."

Writing again to Lodge six days later, he was, as ever, the unflagging jingo and expansionist. He could not resist pleading with the senator to use his influence in the capital to ensure that peace would not be made "until we get Porto Rico, while Cuba is made independent and the Philippines at any rate taken from the Spaniards."

As to the likelihood of himself leading men into battle, Roosevelt had analyzed the situation at sea, noting that "the Spanish squadron has so far eluded our people," and found in this inability of the navy to end the war an opportunity for "this regiment [to] move whenever the advance on Cuba is to be made."

The newest and most famous Rough Rider bragged, "I really doubt if there ever has been a regiment like this. I cannot help but being a little enthusiastic about it."

Chapter 21

Rank and File

Although the public considered Theodore Roosevelt the leader of the so-called cowboy cavalry, he harbored no illusions; he knew that he was subordinate to Leonard Wood. In letters dated May 25 to President McKinley and Henry Cabot Lodge from San Antonio, he wrote, "Wood is the ideal man for Colonel."

As to the Rough Riders, he boasted to McKinley, "I really think that the rank and file of this regiment are better than you would find in any other regiment anywhere. In fact, in all the world there is not a regiment I would so soon belong to. The men are picking up the drill wonderfully. They are very intelligent, and, rather to my surprise, they are very orderly—and they mean business."

In his letter to Lodge, he was even more enthusiastic about the troops:

> Three fourths of our men have at one time or another been cowboys or else are small stockmen; certainly two thirds have fathers who fought on one side or the other in the civil war. Of course, a regiment cannot be made in a week, but these men are in it because they want to be in it. They are intelligent as well as game, and they study the tactics, talking all the movements over among themselves; in consequence we have made remarkable progress. You would enjoy seeing the mounted drill, for the way these men have got their wild half-broken horses into order is something marvelous. . . . I have been both astonished and pleased at my own ability in the line of tactics.

From the vantage point of his autobiography, published in 1913, Roosevelt credited his abilities as a trainer of soldiers to his previous experience with the New York National Guard. He wrote, "It enabled me at once to train the men in simple drill without which they would have been a mob."

In truth, as noted by Roosevelt biographer Henry F. Pringle, during the first weeks it had been a mob. "Never, probably, had so novel a military organization been gathered together," wrote Pringle. "Mingling among the cowboys and momentarily reformed bad men from the West were polo players and steeplechase riders from Harvard, Yale, and Princeton clubs of New York City. They arrived wearing derby hats, and in clipped tones, foreign to San Antonio, where the regiment mobilized, they gave directions at the railroad station that wagonloads of smart leather trunks and hatboxes were to be transported to the camp."

Camp Wood had been established on a flat grassy piece of state fair grounds two miles from the most legendary and venerated spot in the history of Texas. Settled by Spaniards in the last decade of the seventeenth century, San Antonio de Bexar stood astride the San Antonio River. It had been a sleepy, dusty village with a small adobe mission standing in a grove of *alamo* (cottonwood) trees until history descended upon it on February 22, 1836.

History came in the form of the army of the Mexican general Santa Anna. Awaiting him and his soldiers within the church was a small group of men who had taken up weapons in the cause of securing the recently declared independence of Texas. Following a twelve-day siege, the church was overrun, thereby endowing Texan and American history with a fresh pantheon of heroes and a battle cry, "Remember the Alamo," that provided inspiration for the slogan "Remember the Maine," which rallied latter-day Americans to enlist in the war so fervently advocated by Theodore Roosevelt. Hundreds of these men had swarmed upon San Antonio to follow him.

By Roosevelt's arrival on May 15, the Alamo had become a shrine known as the cradle of Texas liberty. In the center of a city of nearly forty thousand residents, Alamo Plaza had been surrounded by structures in keeping with the Gilded Age of the 1890s and with San Antonio's status as the chief city of Texas. To the north was the handsome new Federal Building. Visitors who came as tourists or to engage in the city's lively commerce in cattle, wool, horses, and mules arrived on trains of the International and Great Northern Railway, among others, with lines extending to Austin, Houston, El Paso, and all points to the east, west, and north. Having arrived, they enjoyed the opulence of fine hotels, including the Menger, Southern, and Mahncke.

Always of strategic importance militarily, the city was the headquarters of the Department of Texas and, situated on Government

Hill overlooking the city, the site of Fort Sam Houston. As a result of this rich martial history, the people of San Antonio had become accustomed to men in army uniform. But they had seen nothing like the volunteers who had descended upon them in late spring of 1898.

Although Roosevelt was no stranger to the West, even he admitted in *The Rough Riders* that the regiment had a "peculiar character." He wrote, "They had come from the Four Territories which yet remained within the boundaries of the United States . . . in which the conditions of life are nearest those that obtained on the frontier when there was still a frontier."

He thought of them as a splendid set of men—tall, sinewy, with resolute, weather-beaten faces, and eyes that looked a man straight in the face without flinching.

"They included in their ranks men of every occupation," he continued, "but the three types were those of the cowboy, the hunter and the mining prospector—the man who wandered hither and thither, killing game for a living, and spending his life in the quest for metal wealth."

He believed that in all the world there could be no better material for soldiers than these grim hunters. "These wild rough riders of the plains" were all accustomed to handling wild horses and to following the chase with a rifle, both for sport and as a means of livelihood.

Varied though their occupations had been, almost all had, at one time or another, herded cattle and hunted big game, as had the man they had followed off to war, disconcerting nose-glasses notwithstanding.

"They had their natural leaders," Roosevelt wrote, "the men who had shown they could master other men, and could do more than hold their own in the eager driving life of the new settlements."

Elected by the rank and file, some captains and lieutenants had campaigned in the regular army against the Apache, Ute, and Cheyenne. Others had been sheriffs, marshals, deputy marshals, and deputy sheriffs (as had Roosevelt, who had been a deputy sheriff in Dakota a dozen years earlier).

One of the former law officers was William "Bucky" O'Neill. Captain of Troop A, he had been mayor of Prescott, Arizona, and gained fame as a sheriff and as a fighter in the Indian Wars. The son of a veteran of Meagher's Brigade in the Civil War, he struck Roosevelt as wild, reckless, of dauntless courage, and boundlessly ambitious.

From Las Cruces, New Mexico, had come Captain William H. H. Llewellen. "A good citizen, a political leader, and one of the most noted peace-officers of the country," Roosevelt wrote of him, "he had been shot four times in pitched fights with red marauders and white outlaws." He commanded Troop G.

H Troop's lieutenant, Charles Ballard of Roswell, New Mexico, had been involved in the breakup of the Black Jack Gang "of ill-omened notoriety." Named Black Jack because of his swarthy complexion, Will Christian had led his brother Bob and a band of followers in the plundering of stagecoaches, trains, and banks in Oklahoma, Arizona, and New Mexico. But Black Jack's life had reached a bullet-riddled end on April 28, 1897, in a shootout with law officers near Clifton, Arizona, in a cave that was subsequently named after him.

Ballard's captain, George Curry of Tularosa, New Mexico, also had been a sheriff.

Three officers had served in the regular army. Major Alexander Brodie had lived for twenty years in the Arizona Territory and had become, in Roosevelt's opinion, a thorough Westerner without sinking the West Pointer—a soldier by taste as well as training, whose men worshiped him and would follow him anywhere. Before signing up for duty with the Rough Riders, he had been in charge of a mining business. But when the *Maine* was blown up, he abandoned everything, telegraphing "right and left to bid his friends get ready for the fight he saw impending."

The regular army's Micah Jenkins, the captain of Troop K, hailed from South Carolina. Roosevelt found him to be at the same time gently courteous and "a perfect gamecock."

The third regular was Allyn Capron. The fifth generation of Caprons to serve in the U.S. Army, he was tall and lithe with yellow hair and piercing blue eyes, and he immediately won Roosevelt's heart because he was a boxer and a walker, as well as a first-class rider and shot. "He had under him one of the two companies from the Indian Territory," Roosevelt recalled in *The Rough Riders,* "and he soon impressed himself upon the wild spirit of his followers, that he got them ahead in discipline faster than any other troop in the regiment. . . . He required instant obedience, and tolerated not the slightest evasion of duty; but his mastery of his art was so thorough and his performance of his own duty so rigid that he won not merely the admiration, but that soldierly affection so readily given by the man in the ranks of the superior who cares for his men and leads them fearlessly in battle."

Discipline and adherence to military ritual proved hard to come by. One cowboy took an oath to salute no one, while another cowpuncher greeted each noncommissioned officer who crossed his path with a snappy salute and a "How are you, Captain?"

Although disconcerting, this lax, even rebellious, attitude was not surprising. The men in the ranks were mostly young and had been living happily in the freedoms afforded in the rough-and-tumble frontier ranches and rudimentary, often fly-by-night towns of the great cattle drives. Many had taken part in the killing of the buffalo herds and then had fought against the Plains Indians who had struck out in fury against those who had deprived them of the buffalo, the substance of their existence.

Some had come from the East in search of adventure. Others had been born and bred on the frontier and had never seen a large town. Many of these latter youths, whom Roosevelt hoped to see boarding ships to cross the sea to Cuba, had never seen a body of water larger than the prairie watering holes and countless rivers to be forded while herding cattle along the Chisholm, Goodnight, Northern, and other trails to railheads in Kansas, Missouri, and California.

Exactly who some of these men were proved to be a problem. For various reasons (frequently to avoid the long arm of the law), many had changed their names. A good many went by colorful aliases, such as Cherokee Bill and Happy Jack of Arizona. Smoky Moore had earned his moniker as a tamer of vicious wild horses, known to cowboys as "smoky" broncos. Rattlesnake Pete had lived among the Hopi and had taken part in snake dances.

The men who had not adopted an alias in their lives before they joined the Rough Riders quickly gave camp nicknames to one another. A brave but fastidious member of a well-known eastern club who was serving in the ranks was renamed Tough Ike. His tent mate, a leathery cowpuncher, was dubbed Dude. One unlucky cowhand, who had never been east of the Great Plains in his life, unwarily boasted that he had an aunt in New York, earning himself the sobriquet Metropolitan Bill. A huge red-headed Irishman got the handle Sheeny Solomon. A young Jewish volunteer became Pork Chop. One of a number of professional gamblers was called Hell Roarer, while another former cardsharp was ironically named Prayerful James.

"There was one characteristic and distinctive contingent which could have appeared only in such a regiment as ours," wrote Roosevelt in his memoir of the regiment. "From Indian Territory there came a number of Indians— Cherokees, Chickasaws, Choctaws and Creeks."

One who stood out was a full-blooded Pawnee named Pollock. A silent and solitary figure, he had been educated in an "Indian school" and had exhibited a natural talent for drawing. By the time Roosevelt met him he had developed into the regimental clerk. He also had a sense of humor. Locating a trooper who had taken on the role of barber, he asked for his hair to be cut. "Don't want to wear my hair long like a wild Indian," he explained, "when I'm in civilized warfare."

Another Native American was a Texan by the name of Colbert. While working for the Southern Pacific Railroad, he had written a letter to Roosevelt seeking enlistment. Roosevelt recognized the name as that of one of the chiefs of the Chickasaw. Supposing the writer of the letter to be a descendent of the chief, he summoned Colbert for a personal interview, liked what he found, and signed him up.

One Cherokee named Adair had spent the best part of his life as a trader and agent. A second from that tribe, named Holderman, was described by Roosevelt as "a half-breed [who] came from a soldier stock on both sides and through both races."

"I don't know that I ever came across a man with a really sweeter nature," he wrote of Holderman in *The Rough Riders*. "He explained to me once why he had come to war; that it was because his people always had fought when there was a war, and he could not feel happy to stay at home when the flag was going into battle."

He also found men who had won fame as Rocky Mountain stage drivers, who had spent endless days guiding the lumbering wagon trains across expanses of grassy plains. A North Carolina mountaineer had hunted moonshiners. Another had been chief of scouts in the wild northwest reaches of Canada during the Kiel Rebellion.

Down from Colorado had ventured large, hawkeyed Benjamin Franklin Daniels. A former marshal of Dodge City, the most unruly of the Kansas cow towns, he explained to Roosevelt that he had only half of one ear because it had been bitten off in a fight. A friend who rode into Camp Wood with him was Sherman Bell, who had been a deputy marshal in Cripple Creek. Sizing him up as an "excellent man," Roosevelt enlisted him despite the fact that Bell had a hernia.

"Then there was Little McGinty, the bronco-buster from Oklahoma, who never had walked a hundred yards if by any possibility he could ride," Roosevelt recorded for posterity. "When McGinty was reproved for his absolute inability to keep step on the drill ground, he responded that he was pretty sure he could keep step on horseback."

Scattered among the unfamiliar faces were those of old friends. One of the first to be spotted was Woodbury Kane, happily cooking and washing dishes for a troop of New Mexicans. Soon after his arrival, Roosevelt ran into Fred Herrig, whom he had encountered some years earlier while hunting for mountain sheep and deer in Idaho to lay in a stock of meat for his ranch. Herrig said he had come to join his old "boss" and comrade in what Roosevelt called "the bigger hunting which we were to carry on through the tropic mid-summer."

The intensity of his admiration and respect for these men would find its way into *The Rough Riders:*

> There were men who had roped wild steers in the mesquite brush of the Nueces, and who, year in and year out, had driven the trail herds northward over desolate wastes and across the fords of shrunken rivers to the fattening grounds of the Powder and Yellowstone. They were hardened to the scorching heat and the bitter cold of the dry plains and pine-clad mountains. They were accustomed to sleep in the open, while the picketed horses grazed beside them near some shallow, reedy pool. They had wandered hither and thither across the vast desolation of the wilderness, alone or with comrades. They had cowered in the shelter of cut banks from the icy blast of the norther, and far out on the midsummer prairies they had known the luxury of lying in the shade of the wagon during the noonday rest. They had lived in brush lean-tos for weeks at a time, or with only the wagon sheet as an occasional house. They had fared hard when exploring the unknown; they had fared well on the round-up; and they had known the plenty of the log ranch-houses, where the tables were spread with smoked venison and calf-ribs and milk and bread, and vegetables from the garden-patch.
>
> Such were the men we had as recruits: soldiers ready made, as far as concerned their capacity as individual fighters. What was necessary was to teach them to act together, and to obey orders. Our special task was to make them ready for action in the shortest possible time. We were bound to see fighting, and therefore to be with the first expedition that left the United States; for we could not know how long the war would last.

Roosevelt was not alone in his eagerness to whip the regiment into shape. Colonel Leonard Wood quipped, "If we don't get them to Cuba quickly to fight Spaniards there is a great danger that they'll be fighting one another."

Chapter 22

Damndest Ass within Ten Miles

No one who ventured to San Antonio with hopes of becoming a Rough Rider brought with him into Camp Wood more experience with the rigors of life in the West than the man for whom the training ground had been named. Certainly, none enjoyed the admiration and confidence of Roosevelt more than Leonard Wood. Nor could any of the volunteers claim a closer kinship with Roosevelt in terms of personal character, nor a stronger bond of friendship, forged in the close proximity of their recent duties in Washington.

During the preceding year, Roosevelt had relished the congenial companionship of a man he regarded as a person of utmost conscientiousness, but one who had found time to keep himself, even at the age of thirty-seven, a first-class football player and hiker.

"No soldier could outwalk him," Roosevelt would write of Wood in *The Outlook* in 1899. "[None] could live with more indifference on hard and scanty fare, could endure hardship better, or do better without sleep; no officer ever showed more ceaseless energy in providing for his soldiers, in reconnoitering, in overseeing personally all the countless details of life in camp."

According to Roosevelt's and Wood's mutual friend Owen Wister, Wood appreciated the tedium and boredom of life in the military and to what lengths idle soldiers would go to relieve it. Writing of Wood in his autobiography, Wister declared, "In my life I have known nobody, except Roosevelt, who served his country in the grand manner more nobly and effectively than Leonard Wood." Yet, if a story Wister had heard from a friend were true, this paradigm of soldierly propriety and virtue had not always been so.

"As we went walking and talking along the pavements of Washington," Wister wrote, "I grew very curious to know the exact truth about an anecdote I had been told in San Francisco in 1887, something that the more I looked at him the less it seemed to fit the serious man that he so patently was."

Overcome with curiosity, Wister asked Wood, "Did you ever know Hugh Travis?"

Wood turned in surprise.

"Why, yes," he said.

"When you were stationed in Huachuca, Arizona, and he was on a ranch of his father's in that region?"

"Why, yes."

"He went to school with me, and to Harvard for a while, and after that I saw him a great deal in San Francisco," Wister explained. "He was the first person who ever mentioned your name to me. He told me that you and he took hashish once in Huachuca."

Wood answered with a nod. "We did."

Astonished, Wister gasped, "You really did?"

"That's exactly what we did."

"Well, well, well," said the novelist. "Some day I'll put that in a story, if you don't mind."

Many years later he did so, lacing the story with other incidents of life on the frontier army posts, intending, in his words, "to paint the infinite ennui of that life."

Despite this history, Wood demonstrated slight sympathy with any signs of boredom in the eccentric Rough Riders and thought Roosevelt showed too much. He found in his lieutenant colonel a decidedly unofficerlike desire to be liked by the men under him, which evidenced itself in a willingness to talk with them man to man instead of officer to recruit.

One day Roosevelt transgressed even farther. As he led a mounted troop back to the campground in the parching afternoon heat, they came to a resort called Riverside Park. Calling a halt, he shouted, "The men can go in and drink all the beer they want, which I will pay for."

That night he found himself summoned to Wood's tent and, for the next few minutes, upbraided in a manner that he had not experienced since Secretary Long had wigged him after the speech to the naval militia at Sandusky, Ohio.

An officer who drank with his men, Wood declared, was not fit for a commission.

Flushed and speechless, Roosevelt saluted, turned around and left, only to reappear a few moments later.

"Sir," he blurted, "I consider myself the damndest ass within ten miles of this camp. Good night, sir!"

Concerning Wood's experiences in pursuit of Geronimo, Roosevelt's admiration (and envy) were boundless. He wrote, "No one who has not lived in the West can appreciate the incredible, the extraordinary fatigue and hardship attendant upon these campaigns [against the Apaches]. There was not much fighting, but what there was, was of an exceedingly dangerous type; and the severity of the marches through the waterless mountains of Arizona, New Mexico, and the northern regions of Old Mexico (whither the Apache bands had retreated) was such that only men of iron could stand them. But the young contract doctor, tall, broad-chested, with his light-yellow hair and blue eyes, soon showed the stuff of which he was made."

In such campaigns, Roosevelt noted, it soon became essential to push forward the one actually fitted for command, whatever his accidental position may be. Such had been the case with Wood. Despite his being a physician, he had ended the campaign against the Apaches by serving as commanding officer of some of the detachments, showing "such conspicuous gallantry that he won the most coveted of military distinctions, the medal of honor."

Jacob Riis thought the combination of Wood and Roosevelt was ideal. "I liked to see them together because they are men of the same strong type," he wrote in *Theodore Roosevelt, the Citizen*. "While the Roosevelts and the Woods come when they are needed, as they always have come, our country is safe."

Observing the men they commanded, Riis found them to be the latest incarnation of western manhood rallying to serve the country. He wrote:

> In the War of the Revolution they came out of the West and killed or captured the whole of the British forces at King's Mountain. They furnished the backbone of Andrew Jackson's forces in the War of 1812. As the Texas Rangers they became famous in the troubles with Mexico. They conquered the French towns on the Illinois, and won the West from the Indians in a hundred bloody fights. In the Civil War they lost, to a great extent, their identity, but not their place in

the van and the thick of the fight. Theodore Roosevelt as a historian knew their record and value; as a hunter and plainsman he knew where to find the material to fill up the long-broken ranks. It came at his summons from the plains and cattle-ranges of the great West, from the mines of the Rocky Mountains, from the counting-rooms and colleges of the East, and from the hunting-trail of the wilderness, wherever the spirit of adventure had sent the young men out with the rifle to hunt big game or engage in the outdoor sports that train mind and body to endure uncomplainingly the hardships of campaigning. The Rough Riders were the most composite lot that ever gathered under a regimental standard, but they were at the same time singularly typical of the spirit that conquered a continent in three generations, eminently American.

By the time of Roosevelt's arrival, the regiment's roll call of names had lengthened to nearly a thousand. What he discerned in the men was a regiment that in his opinion "could whip Caesar's Tenth Legion." Credit for whatever military organization and discipline existed belonged entirely to Wood's leadership and his mastery of the military bureaucracy that had frustrated Roosevelt. Yet the medal-of-honor winner understood the meaning of the sign pointing the way to Camp Wood; the training site bore his name, but the Rough Riders belonged to Roosevelt.

In a regiment with a passionate penchant for assigning nicknames, the stiff-mannered Wood was dubbed Old Poker Face and Icebox. A Dakota Indian had given the boisterous and bespectacled Roosevelt the handle Laughing Horse. But to most of the troopers he was simply Teddy. Recognizing the dynamism of his second in command, his popularity among the men, and the attention being paid to Roosevelt by the press and public, Wood conceded, "If this campaign lasted for any considerable length of time I would be kicked upstairs to make room for Roosevelt."

How long the war would last remained, as the New York Times had suggested, a question for a prophet. Every hour that passed heightened Roosevelt's sense of urgency. He expressed to President McKinley his earnest "hope that we will be put into Cuba with the very first troops," and "the sooner the better."

Meanwhile, as Wood looked to the logistics of moving the regiment should the order to pull out of Texas be received, the primary responsibility for drilling the troops became Roosevelt's.

The day began with a bugler sounding reveille at 5:30. Next came roll call. At ten past six, the men fell out for stable call, some twenty minutes of feeding and rubbing down the horses. Then it was time for breakfast. Between 8:30 and 9:30, the horses were led to the river for watering in preparation for saddling and a morning of mounted drill. Roosevelt found the experience "bade fair to offer opportunities for excitement."

Riding out from the camp, they came onto open ground for practicing various column formations or throwing out the line to one side or the other, sometimes at a trot, sometimes at a gallop. As the men grew accustomed to these simple maneuvers, Roosevelt turned them to more complex and challenging skirmish drills. He found their riding skills "consummate."

"In fact," he wrote, "the men were immensely interested in making their horses perform each evolution with the utmost speed and accuracy, and in forcing each unquiet, vicious brute [of a horse] to get into line and stay in line. The guidon-bearers held their plunging steeds true to the line, no matter what they tried to do; and each wild rider brought his wild horse into his proper place with dash and ease which showed the natural cavalryman. In short, from the very beginning the horseback drills were good fun, and everyone enjoyed them."

To Roosevelt's delight, the foxhunters and polo players from the East, whom the leathery cowhands from the West teased as the Fifth Avenue Boys, turned out to be superb mounted soldiers. One of the first to prove it was Craig Wadsworth. When dubious westerners dared him to break an especially wild Texas mustang, he swung into the saddle, reigned up its head, heeled the horse's flanks, gave a tip of his hat, and cantered off with all the grace of the blue-ribbon winners at a Madison Square Garden equestrian competition. The cowpunchers attributed the facility for orderly movement shown by Wadsworth and the other eastern riders to their having spent so much of their time ballroom dancing.

Back from their mounted drills at midday, they were served dinner at 1:30, followed by hours of marching on foot. "We were not always right about our intervals," Roosevelt recorded, "our lines were somewhat irregular, and our more difficult movements were executed at times in rather a haphazard way, but the essential commands and the essential movements we learned without any difficulty, and the men performed with great dash."

While the men mustered for drill on foot, their horses were left to rest. Regarding the mounts, Roosevelt had misgivings about their suitability. "Judging from what I saw," he wrote, "I do not think we got heavy enough animals, and of those purchased certainly a half were nearly unbroken. It was no easy matter to handle them on the picket-lines, and to provide for feeding and watering; and the efforts to shoe and ride them were at first productive of much vigorous excitement."

To shoe those that were wild from the range, the men had to throw them down and tie them. Half the horses bucked or possessed "some other amiable weaknesses incident to the horse life on the great ranches," but, noted Roosevelt, "we had an abundance of men who were utterly unmoved by any antic a horse might commit."

His own horses had been bought for him by a Texas friend, John Moore, with whom he had once hunted peccaries on the Nueces River. The horses had cost fifty dollars each. With great relief, Roosevelt found they were not "showy," but "tough and hardy" and well suited to his purpose.

Afternoon stable call sounded at 4:00, followed by another roll call before a dress parade. Watching the marchers in their blue shirts, loosely knotted handkerchiefs around their necks, brown pants, leggings, boots, and slouch-brimmed hats that quickly became the regiment's hallmark, Roosevelt thought they appeared "exactly as a body of cowboy cavalry should look."

Supper was at 7:00 with final roll call an hour later, followed by night school for the officers and noncommissioned officers and, finally, at 9:00, the bugler's plaintive taps, signaling lights out.

But Roosevelt's tent went dark much later. There were notes to jot in his diary and, as on almost every day of his life, letters to write. On one of these sweltering, mosquito-infested nights as Roosevelt and Wood talked in the colonel's tent, one of the western territory recruits barged in, thrust his hand toward Wood, and declared, "Well, Colonel, I want to shake hands and say we're with you. We didn't know how we would like you fellars at first; but you're all right, and you know your business, and you mean business, and you can count on us every time."

That same night when Roosevelt and Wood stepped out for air, they looked with amusement at a sentinel as the youth muttered a curse, threw aside his rifle, dropped to the ground, and started wildly scratching at his badly bitten legs. Unabashed and not at all intimidated by being watched, he grinned at the regiment's top officers and asked as he continued to swat at mosquitoes, "Ain't they bad?"

Rigid guard duty had been established at the outset, as had the policing of the camp for sanitary purposes (not a surprising requirement in a unit whose commander was not only a veteran of the army but a physician—and not just any doctor, but recently the personal surgeon of the president of the United States).

"As always with new troops," Roosevelt wrote, "they were at first indifferent to the necessity for cleanliness in camp arrangements; but in this point Colonel Wood brooked no laxity, and in a very little while the hygienic conditions of the camp were as good as those of any regular regiment."

If a trooper discovered the waiting lines too long at washup facilities, he simply took his soap to the nearby river.

The rifles issued to the troops were regular army carbines, although a few men carried favorite Winchesters. They also were issued army revolvers. But the traditional symbol of the cavalry, the sabre, was abandoned. To issue the swords and try to train men to use a weapon that was utterly alien to them, Roosevelt and Wood agreed, would be worse than a waste of time.

All of this training was, in Roosevelt's words, "rough and ready drill," suited to the men. He found it "astonishing what a difference was made by two or three weeks' training."

The thorough performance of guard and police duties had helped the men to become soldiers. The officers studied hard as well and grew to realize, as Roosevelt had, that they were not to be overly familiar with those they commanded. The men, in return, acquired the habits of attention to soldierly detail.

"Above all," Roosevelt wrote in *The Rough Riders*, "every man felt, and had constantly instilled into him, a keen pride of the regiment, and a resolute purpose to do his whole duty uncomplainingly, and, above all, to win glory by the way he handled himself in battle."

But the questions haunting everyone's mind were *where* and *when*.

Chapter 23

On the Move

On the morning of May 30, 1898, William McKinley crossed the Potomac River to Virginia and a sprawling military cemetery on a hillside in Arlington to pay homage to those Union soldiers who had given what Abraham Lincoln had called "the last full measure of devotion." But on this thirtieth commemoration since General John A. Logan had proposed a Decoration Day to mark the graves of Civil War dead, the president of the United States, who had tried in vain to restrain the war hawks and expansionists of the jingo wing of the Republican party, would return to the Executive Mansion for a conference with the three men who had been charged with the responsibility of conducting the war he never wanted. Awaiting him in the Cabinet Room were Secretary of War Alger, Secretary of the Navy Long, and Major General Nelson A. Miles.

As the commander of the U.S. Army, Miles brought to the table a memorandum showing the disposition of the military forces concentrated at various encampments throughout the country, with details concerning the troop strength of both the regular army and the volunteer units at Tampa and other southern sites, including their readiness to embark on a Cuban invasion. Regular forces at Tampa numbered twenty thousand, comprising seventeen regiments of infantry. Volunteers numbered thirteen thousand, also encompassing seventeen infantry regiments. Artillery units consisted of twelve battalions with a total of twelve hundred men. The regular cavalry formed five regiments. Additional volunteer units stood ready to be deployed from camps at Mobile (Alabama), New Orleans (Louisiana), and Chickamauga National Park (Tennessee). Other forces in various stages of training elsewhere included the one that had captured the popular imagination: Teddy Roosevelt's Rough Riders.

The next day, the *New York Times* headlined:

TROOPS ORDERED TO INVADE CUBA

Tampa Forces to Be Loaded at Once on Transports

MAY MOVE ON SANTIAGO

An Invasion of Puerto Rico Not Improbable

PLANS KEPT SECRET

Thirty-three Thousand Men to Be Sent from Tampa—
Others to Go from Mobile

The lead of the story declared, "The military invasion of Cuba has begun."

With the caveat "unless the orders of the War Department had miscarried," the paper stated that the troops gathered at the gulf ports would have begun to break camp and march aboard transports waiting to carry them to the enemy's territory. "How many troops are to be moved and where they are bound are questions which the directing spirits of the campaign refuse positively to answer. They have no desire that the Spanish should have opportunity afforded them to gather forces to attack our soldiers as they land."

This lesson had been learned with the failure of the steamer *Gussie* to land troops and supplies on May 14. Nonetheless, the newspaper reported with confidence that the new plan called for twenty-five ships to board some thirty thousand men from the ports of Tampa and Mobile for a rendezvous at Key West with convoys of warships provided by Admiral Sampson to protect the troopships during passage across the Florida Straits.

Secrecy extended, as well, to the commander of the forces. "Concerning his movements, Gen. Miles will not state where his headquarters will be located, and it is probable that he will move from place to place as circumstances may demand," said the *New York Times*. "It is learned that precautions have been taken to prevent reports by correspondents with the army from coming out of Tampa, and, as the army commanders have control over the writers stationed there and might cancel their passes if they should overstep the bounds regarded as prudent by the men who control, it is believed that no publication of details will come from that quarter."

Among the reporters at Tampa was Roosevelt's friend, Richard Harding Davis, employed by the New York *Herald*. After observing the volunteers in their encampments, he praised them for possessing the "enthusiasm of volunteers," but faulted them for their ignorance. He admired the army regulars for their proficiency, but deprecated them for their indifference. But he found that regular and volunteer respected each other and got on well. In a letter to his mother, he said, "War takes all the littleness out of men."

Like most reporters in Tampa, he expected that the first target of the invasion would not be in Cuba. He envisioned the strike coming at Puerto Rico. The *New York Times* reporter (filing without benefit of a byline and therefore remaining anonymous) joined in speculating that Puerto Rico would be chosen, citing "the smaller [Spanish] force to be encountered, together with the comparable lack of preparation on that island." Another important factor was "the greater healthfulness of the Island of Puerto Rico over Cuba."

Indeed, the military planners worried about the effects of Cuba's rampant tropical diseases, including yellow fever, cholera, and malaria. The latter was of special concern since a particular variety of it had been defined by George Kennan of the Red Cross, who traveled to Cuba with Clara Barton. Its symptoms were chills, delirium, a ragingly high temperature, a swollen face, back pains, and severe headaches. Although it could be abated with doses of quinine, calomel, and sulphate of magnesia, relapses were common, leaving victims languorous and prostrate. No one had any idea that the infection was spread by mosquitoes.

Nevertheless, in a meeting on May 28 at the Red Cross Hospital on West 100th Street in New York City, a group of physicians who had been in Cuba and other South American countries during epidemics of tropical diseases readily offered recommendations as to how the Army could avoid these ravages. With a sublime naïveté, the thirty-four doctors proposed that soldiers "should live, whenever possible, in the high altitudes and no lower than 1000 feet above the level of the sea." Precisely how amphibious invaders might find their way immediately into highlands from sea-level landing sites was not ventured. Nor did the medical experts offer any ideas as to how to ensure, as they advised, that the troops be housed in "rooms" that had been "thoroughly ventilated and disinfected before occupancy."

"The clothing must be light," the panel insisted, unwittingly justifying Roosevelt's demands for khaki uniforms. "Flannels should not be worn."

Although well-intentioned, their next recommendation was on its face ludicrous. They declared, "Walking in the sun is dangerous and all movements should be made in the cool of the day."

For the soldiers preparing for action, the camps they had been inhabiting around Tampa had provided plenty of experience in dealing with the discomforts of the tropics. Instead of the rooms envisioned by the doctors in their meeting in New York, the soldiers had pitched tents amidst expanses of scrub pine, palmetto trees, and almost impenetrable jungles of undergrowth, all surrounded by swamps aswarm with nettlesome insects.

"The great city of tents at Tampa has been growing so rapidly that it is impossible to see it all in a single day," said the *New York Times* correspondent who had been sent to Florida with a camera to record the activities of William Astor Chanler's volunteer cavalry. "The sleepy little town, which for a century has sweltered in the sun and sand, has experienced such an awakening as its staid inhabitants never dreamed possible, and has done more business in the last two months than ever before in its history."

One of those who had cashed in on the arrival of the U.S. Army had been Henry Bradley Plant. Seventy-nine years old, he had discerned entrepreneurial possibilities in the port of Tampa Bay, nine miles south of the town, long before the war over Cuba. Among his innovations before the army and navy came to town were a mile-long wharf with connections by way of a railroad to the city; an amusement park; and a trolley line. He also owned a steamship line among whose intrepid vessels was the *Olivette,* the boat that had carried Richard Harding Davis and Frederic Remington to Cuba in January 1897.

The gemstone of Plant's enterprises was the Tampa Bay Hotel. Created in a vaguely Moorish motif, it had silver-tipped towers and minarets, stood five stories high, and boasted five hundred rooms. Ample spaces within or on verandas allowed guests to sip cooling drinks while gazing at the azure waters of the Gulf of Mexico, all to the accompaniment of bands offering waltzes and other fashionable melodies. Should anyone decide to chance the prospect of heatstroke for a whirl round the dance floor, they could do so to the strains of

"After the Ball Is Over" or "Sidewalks of New York," better known as "East Side, West Side."

Occupying two floors of the hotel were the headquarters and rooms of the officers in charge of the troops, whose accommodations were blankets on the hard ground in tents or hammocks strung between palmettos. Gawking in amazement at the grandeur of the hotel with its casino and peacocks strutting on the lawns and wandering onto the greens of the golf course, a cavalry general declared, "Only God knows why Plant built a hotel here, but thank God he did."

Equally grateful, if not as reverent, were more than one hundred members of the press, including Richard Harding Davis. Seeing himself "writing history," he roamed the lobby, the lounges, and the veranda and ventured out to the camps looking for stories for the *Herald* and, possibly, a book on the war. Deep in the lap of luxury, he regarded the interlude of waiting as "the rocking chair period of the war."

Davis wrote, "It was an army of occupation, but it occupied the piazza of a big hotel."

On the last day of May, he picked up a piece of news that was even more of a reason to be thankful. He learned that heading his way from the dusty drill fields of Camp Wood was none other than his old friend Theodore Roosevelt. The Rough Riders had left San Antonio on May 29.

"Finally," Roosevelt wrote in *The Rough Riders,* "just as the last rifles, revolvers and saddles came, we were ordered by wire at once to proceed by train to Tampa. Instantly, all was joyful excitement. We had enjoyed San Antonio, and were glad that our regiment had been organized in the city where the Alamo commemorates the death fight of Crockett, Bowie, and their famous band of frontier heroes. All of us had worked hard . . . but we were glad to leave the hot camp, where every day the strong wind sifted the dust through everything, and to start for the gathering-place of the army which was to invade Cuba."

During the busy but brief stay at San Antonio, Woodbury Kane had comported himself so well that he had been promoted to the rank of captain. Elevated to lieutenant were Horace Devereaux, a Princeton graduate; John Greenway, a footballer and catcher for Yale's baseball team; and David Goodrich, the Harvard crew captain. Roosevelt had found them to be natural soldiers whose "only thought was how to perfect themselves in their own duties, and how to take care of the men under them, so as to bring them to the highest point of soldierly perfection."

Suddenly, the preparing was behind them. The horses and men were in good shape. The regiment was well enough equipped to warrant starting on the campaign. Every man, in Roosevelt's view, "was filled with dread of being out of the fighting."

The time had come, at last, for Teedie to reap glory.

The plan called for proceeding by railway. With the train split into seven sections, the first three would be commanded by Wood and the remainder by Roosevelt. The loading of men, horses, and equipment was to be done on a Sunday, May 29. The railroad promised to convey them to Tampa in forty-eight hours. But it became immediately apparent to Roosevelt that this would turn out to be an unrealistic timetable.

Apparatus for getting the horses onto the cars proved to be nonexistent. Nothing had been done to provide for their watering and feeding. The few hours that had been anticipated in sending Wood's three sections on their way took the entire day. Because Wood had insisted on minimal personal luggage, the troops had only what they could carry on their backs, and the officers had little more. Roosevelt managed to pack his roll of clothes and bedding on his spare horse.

"It was dusk when I marched my long files of dusty troopers into the station-yard," he recalled. "I then made all dismount, excepting the troop which I first intended to load." But he soon realized that the process of getting the men and their horses aboard was going to take all night. To make matters worse, the passenger cars were delayed in arriving. Consequently, the restless and bored troops did exactly what idle soldiers had done throughout history. In Roosevelt's quaint phrasing, "some had drifted off to the vile drinking-booths around the stock-yards."

This required him to send details out to round them up while trumpeters blew assembly until the first sergeant could account for all the men. To preclude any more such wanderings, he ordered the men to lie down where they had been gathered, "by the tracks and in the brush, to sleep until morning."

The tardy passenger cars appeared at dawn.

Of the next four hot and dusty days, Roosevelt said, "I doubt if anybody who was on the trip will forget it. There was enough delay and failure to make connections on the part of the railroad people to keep me entirely busy, not to speak of seeing at the stopping-places that the inexperienced officers got enough hay for their horses, and that the water given to them was both ample in quantity and drinkable. It happened that we usually made our longest stops at night, and this meant that we were up all night long."

Offsetting these travails of travel, however, was what the troops encountered along the way. Recording it in *The Rough Riders,* Roosevelt dipped into his lexicon of poetic phrases and his knowledge of history:

> Everywhere the people came out to greet us and cheer us. They brought us flowers; they brought us watermelons and other fruits, and sometimes jugs and pails of milk—all of which we greatly appreciated. We were travelling through a region where practically all the older men had served in the Confederate Army, and where the younger men had all their lives drunk in the endless tales told by their elders, at home, and at the crossroads taverns, and in the courthouse squares, about the cavalry of Forrest and Morgan and the infantry of Jackson and Hood. The blood of the old men stirred to the distant breath of battle; the blood of the young leaped hot with eager desire to accompany us. The older women, who remembered the dreadful misery of war—the misery that presses its iron weight most heavily on the wives and the little ones—looked sadly at us; but the young girls drove down in bevies, arrayed in their finery, to wave flags in farewell to the troopers and to beg cartridges and buttons as mementos. Everywhere we saw the Stars and Stripes, and everywhere we were told, half-laughing, by grizzled ex-Confederates that they had never dreamed in the bygone days of bitterness to greet the old flag as they now were greeting it, and to send their sons, as now they were sending them, to fight and die under it.

Although in "a perfect welter of confusion," the regiment got to Tampa only to find no one to meet them at the end of the one-track railway, nor to tell them where to find their camp. Presently, they learned that the site was six miles distant from the rail terminus, requiring them to saddle horses and then make a weary ride to find it. Like their encampment at San Antonio, the new camp soon became, under Leonard Wood's strict and watchful gaze, an orderly tent city.

Sprawled around them lay the largest assembly of American men under arms since the Civil War.

Confident that his men had been properly settled in camp, Roosevelt headed into town to afford himself a luxury that was not available to the rank and file whom he left behind. Awaiting him in

Henry Plant's incongruous hotel was his wife, Edith. Informed by telegram from Roosevelt that the regiment would transfer to Tampa, however temporarily, she rushed down to be with him, arriving on June 1. She thought he looked "thin but rugged and well."

Upon his going off to the war he had labored to bring about, she had written to him, "Come back safe darling 'pigeon' and we shall be happy, but it is quite right you should be where you are."

Having been advised that her husband was leaving Texas for Tampa, she had pointed out the new location to young Theodore. Studying the map, Ted had said, "I suppose Father will get the war wind full in his face."

In relating the boy's excitement to Roosevelt, Edith said, "He says he should think every boy should want to go to war and wished you could have taken him just to clean your guns for, of course, he would not expect a shot at the enemy! He subsequently remarked he was sure he would be angry in a battle and ping away at the foe as fast as he could cram in cartridges. Ted hopes there will be one battle so that you can be in it, but come out safe. Not every boy has a father who has seen a battle."

The morning after arriving in Tampa, Edith wrote home to the children, "We were both hungry for supper and glad to get to bed at once."

A provision of Wood's permission to Roosevelt to spend time with Edith was that Roosevelt return to camp for reveille at four in the morning. But the next noon he was at the hotel for lunch and had brought Wood along. When the meal was over they took her to the camp for a tour and to watch the mounted drill and meet the regiment mascots, a little dog named Cuba and a temperamental mountain lion cub.

Roosevelt wrote home to the children he delighted in calling "Blessed Bunnies":

> It has been a real holiday to have darling mother here. Yesterday I brought her out to the camp, and she saw it all—the men drilling, the tents in long company streets, the horses being taken to water, my little horse Texas, the colonel and the majors, and finally the mountain lion and the jolly little dog Cuba, who had several fights while she looked on. The mountain lion is not much more than a kitten as yet, but it is very cross and treacherous. . . . Mother stays at a big hotel. . . . There are nearly thirty thousand troops here now,

besides the sailors from the war-ships in the bay. At night the corridors and piazzas are thronged with officers of the army and navy, and now they are all going to Cuba to war against the Spaniards. Most of them are in blue, but our rough-riders are in brown. Our camp is on a great flat, on sandy soil without a tree, though round about are pines and palmettos. It is very hot, indeed, but there are no mosquitoes.

He then wrote to Henry Cabot Lodge, "Edith has been down here for the last three days and it has been a perfect treat having her here."

On the last day of her visit, she returned to the camp, escorted by Richard Harding Davis, to watch the entire cavalry in a mass drill.

"We have had a regular spree here," Roosevelt wrote to his sister Corinne. "As the Chanlers and Jack Astor and various diplomats were down here, together with some other people whom we knew, [Edith] has had a few companions besides."

A letter to Anna on the sixth said, "I am very glad that she saw the regiment, because it will make her understand more just what I am doing."

Chapter 24

Higgledy-Piggledy

While an impatient Theodore Roosevelt penned letters on the sixth of June, two lines of U.S. Navy warships steamed toward the entrance channel of Santiago de Cuba. Within the harbor lay the ships of the elusive Spanish armada, bottled up at last, with Admiral Pascual Cervera awaiting the next move by the Americans. Aboard the *New York* was Roosevelt's friend, Admiral William Sampson. On the bridge of the leading ship of the second column, the *Brooklyn,* was the officer whom Sampson had superseded as commander in chief of the Flying Squadron, Admiral Winfield Scott Schley. Although Schley had pledged loyalty in all of his conduct, Sampson had harbored doubts as to the sincerity of the vow. The result was a prickly relationship. But now, with Cervera's fleet within range of their guns, nothing mattered to them but smashing the enemy and, perhaps, earning for the U.S. Navy the honorable distinction of compelling a quick end to the war.

Peeling out of columns, the American ships swung right and left and, at a distance of two thousand yards, opened fire on the coastal defenses of Morro Castle, Socapa Heights, and Punta Gorda. As shells pummeled them, others arched overhead to come down in the harbor. Several splashed and exploded harmlessly but close to Cervera's flagship, *Maria Teresa.* But the ship that had fled New York Harbor in fear of attack, the *Vizcaya,* took two hits, and the *Furor* suffered one. Many peppered the *Reina Mercedes,* one of which blasted away the right leg and hand of the executive officer, Commander Emilio Acosta y Eyermann. "Esta es nada" (This is nothing), he gasped as he died and his ship slowly sank, "Viva España!"

Spanish guns aimed at the American ships did not fare well. One scored a hit on a mast of the *Massachusetts.* Another struck the little gunboat *Suwanee* and wounded one sailor.

For 175 minutes, according to the count of Spanish artillery captain Severo Gómez, a hundred guns fired two thousand shells, yet Sampson found in this barrage no threat to his ships. Rather, he believed that if an amphibious attack were launched on the fortifications, they could be captured and silenced. In a cable to the War Department, he confidently predicted, "If 10,000 men were here, city and fleet would be ours within 48 hours. Every consideration demands immediate army movement. If delayed, city will be defended more strongly by guns taken from the fleet."

Meanwhile, east of Santiago de Cuba, a smaller American expedition, including the *Marblehead, Yankee,* and *St. Louis*, was taking steps to cut communications between Cuba and Spain by locating a telegraph cable linking Cuba with Haiti. They found and cut the cable on June 7, leaving Cuba isolated. In addition, the skipper of the *Marblehead,* Commander Bowman McCalla (one of Roosevelt's frequent correspondents), was in receipt of an order from the Navy Department that was to affect Cuban-American relations for more than a century.

A cable from the Naval War Board instructed McCalla to expect the arrival of a contingent of 650 men of the First Marine Battalion, then en route aboard the *Panther* from their training camp at Key West. They were to rendezvous on June 10 at a point about forty miles east of Santiago de Cuba, a point carried on McCalla's navigational chart as Guantánamo Bay. However, this was little more than a sideshow compared to the action that had been sparked in Washington by the urgent message from Sampson off Santiago de Cuba.

With the message in hand, Secretary of War Alger rushed to see the commander in chief. After a brief conference, President McKinley authorized the War Room to cable General Shafter at the Tampa Bay Hotel: "You will sail immediately as you are needed at destination at once."

Shafter replied that because "steam could not be gotten up earlier," the ships could not begin to take on troops before the morning of the seventh. Meanwhile, word was passed to the commanders in the tent cities amongst the pines and palmettos to break camp and move out for Port Tampa, nine miles away.

The order reached Roosevelt that evening. The Rough Riders were to be at dockside by daybreak. If the men were not aboard by that time, they would have to be left behind. To keep the appointment,

Roosevelt noted, the regiment would need to be "at a certain track with all our baggage at midnight, there to take a train."

The Rough Riders made it on time. The train did not. While the men settled down to sleep, Roosevelt and Leonard Wood set out to see what had gone wrong. They discovered that no one, including a major general, could provide an answer. Three o'clock came and with it an order to march to another track. Expecting to find a train waiting, Roosevelt was again disappointed. With each passing moment increasing the likelihood of ships sailing to war without him, he grew angrier by the minute. But the daybreak revealed an opportunity. At six o'clock, a train of coal cars rattled into view. Exhibiting the decisiveness he had shown in the absence of Secretary Long, he commandeered the empty, sooty gondolas and persuaded the locomotive engineer to back the train down the nine miles to Port Tampa.

Arriving at the dock with all their belongings and khakis soiled with coal dust, the Rough Riders gazed with dismay at the troopships anchored in the middle of a canal that connected to the bay. Nobody knew which of them was theirs. Told to locate the depot quartermaster, a colonel named Humphrey, Roosevelt dashed off to find him, dodging and weaving along a quay that was crammed with some ten thousand men who appeared lost and bewildered. His term for the chaos was "a good deal of higglety-pigglety."

When the elusive quartermaster was finally located, the harried officer pointed to the *Yucatan,* anchored in the middle of the canal. However, this was not the end of the problems; it turned out that the ship actually had been designated to the Second Regular Infantry and the Seventy-first New York Volunteers.

Neither Roosevelt nor any other source recorded his state of mind at learning this disconcerting news. History in the form of Roosevelt's book on the Rough Riders recorded only that he took off running at full speed to rouse his grimy cowboy cavalry and race them doublequick to the dock, and then "to hold her against the Second Regulars and the Seventy-first."

Those units "arrived a little too late," Roosevelt gleefully wrote of his first military face-off of the war, "being a shade less ready than we were in the matter of individual initiative."

As his men scrambled to board, Roosevelt peered curiously through his pince-nez at a pair of suspicious-looking figures on the dock. Between them stood a tripod topped by what appeared to be a very large and odd-looking camera. Striding over to them, he demanded, "What are you young men up to?"

"We are the Vitagraph Company, Colonel Roosevelt," came the reply from Albert Smith. "We are going to Cuba to take moving pictures of the war."

The already overcrowded ship notwithstanding, the public-relations-savvy Roosevelt said, "I might be able to handle two more," pointing Smith and his partner to the gangplank barred to the Johnny-come-latelies of the Second and Seventy-first.

By nightfall the Rough Riders were aboard a ship anchored again in midstream. They were "packed like sardines, not only below but upon the decks," Roosevelt wrote, so that at night it was only possible to walk about by stepping over them as they slept.

They were also hungry. Travel rations that had been issued for the voyage to Cuba proved insufficient, and much of it turned out to be spoiled and inedible. There were no facilities for the men to cook anything. There was no ice. The water was bad. They had no fresh meat or vegetables. Yet, all these things seemed of small importance to Roosevelt if compared to the fact that they were embarked. However, the next morning came maddening word that the plan to sail had been countermanded. Pending fresh orders, they were told to stay put.

Why there had been this last-minute hitch was not explained to the troops on the ships. All that was known was that General Shafter had received a cryptic cable from Secretary of War Alger: "Wait until you get orders before you sail. Answer quick." Only when Shafter returned to shore did he learn that the navy's ship *Eagle* had reported sighting a Spanish cruiser and destroyer in the Nicholas Channel off Cuba's northern coast. If the report were true, this "phantom fleet" would lie directly across the course to be followed by the invasion ships.

In the dark about this development and in a fuming mood, the man who had made *efficiency* his byword in government service with the Civil Service Commission, the New York City police force, and the Navy Department shot off a letter to his man in Washington, Senator Henry Cabot Lodge:

> No words could describe to you the confusion and lack of system and the general mismanagement of affairs here; a good deal is the inevitable accompaniment of a sudden war where people have resolutely refused to make the needed preparations, but a very good deal

could be avoided. For a month the troops have been gathering here in a country where lines of temporary railroad could be laid down for miles in 24 hours, yet to this day, while the troops are at Tampa there is but a single line connecting them with the point of debarkation 9 miles off and there are no switches to speak of and no facilities whatever for unloading freight or troops. . . . We have been here two days now; the troops jammed together under the tropical sun on these crowded troop ships. We are in a sewer; a canal which is festering as if it were Havana harbor. The steamer on which we are contains nearly one thousand men, there being room for about five hundred comfortably. We have given up the entire deck to the men, so that the officers have to sit in the cabin, and even so several companies are down in the lower hold, which is unpleasantly suggestive of the Black Hole of Calcutta. The officers' horses were disembarked last Sunday with the artillery horses; they have had to disembark them for the simple reason that they began to die. Of course there was no shadow of a reason for putting them aboard until the last moment.

Faced with the alarming possibility that the Rough Riders might become a cavalry without horses, Roosevelt pleaded to Lodge to do what he could with his influence in the capital to see that the animals would be forwarded as soon as possible.

"With two brigades of cavalry we can do a tremendous amount of work in Cuba," he argued. "We can drive the Spanish foragers from the fields and take the small towns and close the larger ones—and it is a shame to dismount all our men. Do, old man, try to see that the expedition is not longer deferred, because the bad effects of so deferring it are evident to everyone, and so see that our horses are sent after us at the earliest moment."

A June 12 letter to sister Corinne sounded a stoic tone regarding the mystifying delay in going: "I suppose it is simply the ordinary fortune of war for most irritating delays to happen, but it seems to me that the people in Washington are inexcusable for putting us aboard ship and then keeping us crowded to suffocation on these transports for six days in Tampa harbor in a semitropical sun."

To sister Anna on the same date, he held out the possibility of forgiveness for the stall, "if only we *do* start and get into the fun." He added, enviously, that so far all the "fun" had belonged to the navy.

Two days later on Friday, June 10, Commander McCalla's gunners laid down a withering barrage to cover seafaring soldiers, whom sailors called leathernecks, as the First Marine Battalion swept ashore at Guantánamo Bay. They reached the land with so little opposition that Stephen Crane, as he watched from an accompanying press boat, thought the scene was "rather comic." But he was premature in that assessment.

On Saturday a corps of three thousand of Spain's finest soldiers counterattacked. Having landed by then as well, Crane hunkered in a shallow trench as the fighting raged for thirteen hours. All through the night he longed for sunrise, and when dawn finally broke he was furious with "this wretched sunrise" that seemed to be taking so long that he thought he could have "walked around the world in the time required for the old thing to get above the horizon."

When the fighting ended, with one hundred Spaniards dead and the rest routed, the U.S. Marines held a portion of Cuba that would remain in American hands through the whole of the next century, providing the United States with the extracontinental naval base that had been advocated by Captain Mahan and coveted by his disciple, Theodore Roosevelt.

Two days after the marines had secured the base they named Camp McCalla, the House of Representatives overwhelmingly passed a resolution providing for the annexation of Hawaii. In doing so they gave the navy the forward position in the Pacific that Roosevelt had for so long agitated to obtain.

Meanwhile, the mighty warships following the flag of Admiral William Sampson had maintained position within gunnery range of the Spanish ships trapped in Santiago's harbor and awaited the arrival of the army. Sampson's impatience, however, was no match for Roosevelt's.

He had told Corinne in his June 12 letter, "The interminable delays and the vacillation and utter absence of efficient organization are really discouraging."

All this ended on the evening of June 13. Confident that the *Eagle* had not spotted Spanish warships but American ones, the War Department flashed orders to the troopships at Tampa to sail.

Of this exhilarating spectacle, the author who had penned *The Naval War of 1812* wrote:

> Ship after ship weighed anchor and went slowly ahead under half-steam for the distant mouth of the harbor, the bands playing, the flags flying, the rigging black with the clustered soldiers, cheering

and shouting to those left behind on the quay and to their fellows on the other ships. The channel was very tortuous; and we anchored before we had gone far down it, after coming within an ace of a bad collision with another transport. The next morning we were all again under way, and in the afternoon the great fleet steamed southeast until Tampa Light sank in the distance.

Before sailing he had written to his brother-in-law, Douglas Robinson (Corinne's husband), "Those of us who come out of it safe will be bound together all our lives by a very strong tie. You may rest assured I have not the slightest idea of taking any risk I do not feel I absolutely must take."

Chapter 25

Beneath the Southern Cross

As Theodore Roosevelt and a thousand horseless Rough Riders sailed as part of the largest war fleet ever to leave American shores, they found themselves in the company of a new but rapidly evolving fraternity of journalists who prided themselves in the title *war correspondents*. The first to have claimed to have gone to war armed with nothing more than a pen and a notepad had been William Howard Russell. He witnessed and reported on the charge of the Light Brigade for the *Times* of London. That this had made him "the miserable parent of a luckless tribe" was validated on his epitaph in Saint Paul's Cathedral, which named him "the first and greatest" war correspondent. Whether he had been the first was open to debate, yet there was no doubting that press coverage of the Crimean War spawned numerous descendants of the species. In the American Civil War at least five hundred of them turned out to cover the conflict on the northern side alone. Following the sinking of the *Maine*, no less than two hundred of Russell's breed had joined the ink-stained ranks.

The two who had surveyed Cuba in January 1897 on behalf of William Randolph Hearst and then disagreed as to whether there was a war, Richard Harding Davis and Frederic Remington, found themselves together again as the invasion ships of June 1898 made for the island. They had boarded General Shafter's *Segurança*.

Davis recorded the fleet rolling along with the lights they had been ordered to extinguish "blazing defiantly to the stars." Bands banging out ragtime music made so much of a racket that he wondered how Spanish torpedo boats could resist such a "happy-go-lucky" target.

Once a strange ship did steam up too close, provoking a torpedo boat to investigate while Roosevelt watched it "slip like a greyhound from the leash, and speed across the water toward it." When the stranger proved friendly, "the swift, delicate, death-fraught" type of boat that had been so close to his heart since his earliest days as assistant secretary of the navy fell back into line.

Never having enjoyed being at sea, Remington found little to get excited about on the voyage. "I hate a ship," he said, "in a compound, triple-expansion, forced draft way. Make me a feather in a sick chicken's tail on shore and I will thank you."

Theodore Roosevelt had become accustomed to being the focus of journalists and he even put up with one who routinely called him Teethadore. He had cultivated friendships with Davis, Remington, Jake Riis, Lincoln Steffens, and Joseph Bucklin Bishop. But his chance encounter on the dock at Tampa with Alfred Smith of the Vitagraph Company introduced him to something new to the field of reporting: the newsreel.

While the first use of motion pictures to record an event had been Louis Lumière's *La Sortie des Usines Lumière,* it merely showed workers leaving a factory. But within months, cameras were turned on all varieties of human affairs, including news events. A newsreel camera had recorded the coronation of Czar Nicholas II in Moscow and the inauguration of President McKinley in 1897.

Among the cinematic pioneers had been J. Stewart Blackton. Born in England in 1875, he emigrated to the United States at the age of ten and grew up to work as a journalist-illustrator for Joseph Pulitzer's *World*. Interviewing Thomas A. Edison for that paper in 1896, he so impressed the inventor with his drawings that Edison asked to make a short film of them with his motion picture camera, the kinetograph. Fascinated by the new technology, Blackton bought a kinetograph for himself and went into the motion picture business with a friend, Alfred Smith. Establishing a studio atop the More Building at 140 Nassau Street in Manhattan, they produced a film, *The Burglar on the Roof*, with Blackton in the title role, and exhibited it under their new company's name, Vitagraph. They also employed little wooden ship models to stage the bombardment of Santiago as they imagined it had happened.

Now, on June 15, 1898, invited onto the *Yucatan* by Theodore Roosevelt, a Vitagraph camera was on its way to make motion picture history by filming the actual invasion of Cuba. But Smith was not the only man with high hopes for the future of the camera in war. Dr. D. S. Elmendorf, a photographer who was employed by the American Museum of Natural History to illustrate lectures, planned to use what he called a cinematograph to take pictures of "the bombard-ment-in-progress" of Havana, if and when it took place. While waiting to travel to the event, he spent his time taking pictures of a presentation of the colors at a ceremony, an artillery drill, and a cavalry parade in the camps at Tampa. To photograph the shelling of Havana, he had in his possession three thousand feet of film.

Yet another technological innovator with an eye toward the battlefield was William E. Eddy of Bayonne, New Jersey. It was his idea to employ his invention, a "sliding messenger kite," to carry a "camera apparatus" for exploring enemy territory "as soon as the regular army invades Cuba." He also envisioned using kites to float dynamite charges weighing seventy-two pounds and then drop them on enemy troops.

Eddy also thought kites could be used for battlefield communication, and he had conducted a demonstration. According to a report in the *New York Times* of May 31, 1898, two kites, each seven feet in diameter, and another kite four feet in diameter had been sent up in tandem with piano wire to guide them. The report continued:

> A little distance under the kites was fastened a large American flag, which was kept flying all the afternoon. To the piano wire was made fast a thin copper wire, the free end of which was allowed to trail.
>
> As the kites ascending raised the point of contact higher into the air and further from the starting point, the copper wire trailed over the trees, houses and barns toward the Kill van Kull, the end of it finally resting on the Jersey shore, where it was secured by Dr. W. H. Mitchell [an associate].
>
> To it was attached a telephone similar to those used in the field. A similar instrument was attached to the kite wire at Mr. Eddy's house, a mile or so away on the base line. Conversation was thus had between Dr. Mitchell and Mr. Eddy, the communication being perfect.

Thus, by well more than two-thirds of a century, the kite-flying experimenter anticipated unmanned and wire-guided airborne cruise missiles and spy-in-the-sky reconnaissance.

Already available for use over Cuban battlefields by both the navy and army was a device that the U.S. Army's Signal Corps called one of "the most important military experiments of the century." Two fully equipped war balloons had been obtained. Similar to those in use in the French navy, they had been delivered to Governor's Island in New York Harbor from Liverpool, England, for shipping to Key West and then forwarding to the fleet off Santiago. Each of the balloons could carry three or four men and an equal weight of war paraphernalia, such as searchlights and dynamite. In addition to these balloons, the army had at its disposal larger ones for carrying aloft spotters for artillery batteries.

More down-to-earth matters concerned Roosevelt. His cowboy cavalry was on its way to war without all its horses. He could only hope that his letter to Henry Cabot Lodge would result in a quick remedy. Meanwhile, he basked in the knowledge that he was on his way. He wrote to Corinne on June 15:

> On Board U.S. Transport *Yucatan,* In the Gulf of Mexico.
>
> Today we are steaming southward through a sapphire sea, windrippled under an almost cloudless sky. There are some forty-eight craft in all, in three columns, the black hulls of the transports setting off the gray hulls of the men-of-war. Last evening we stood on the bridge and watched the red sun sink and the lights blaze up on the ships, for miles ahead and astern, while the band played piece after piece, from the "Star Spangled Banner," at which we all rose and stood uncovered, to "The Girl I Left Behind Me." But it is a great historical expedition, and I thrill to feel that I am part of it.

To keep the men occupied, there was drill in the manual, with an emphasis on the pages dealing with firing. Officers and underofficers attended school. But all did not go well. A schooner had to be towed, forcing the *Yucatan* to stop, then fall back so as to accompany the disabled boat while the bulk of the fleet sailed ahead and out of sight.

In his mind lurked a fear that the city might already have fallen, in which case the expedition would have been wasted, or that the city would fight little or not at all.

"All day we have steamed close to the Cuban coast, high barren looking mountains rising abruptly from shore, and at this distance looking much like those of Montana," he continued in the letter to Corinne. "We are well within the tropics, and at night the Southern Cross shows low above the horizon."

Feeling uneasy at the enforced idleness of what seemed to be an interminable voyage toward his destiny, Roosevelt eavesdropped on the conversations of his men as they speculated on the immediate future and debated whether they were to attack Santiago or Puerto

Rico. At other times they lounged in groups and swapped stories of mining camps and cattle ranges, of hunting bear and deer, of Indian wars, of lawless deeds of violence in the cow towns, brawls in saloons, gunfighting in the streets, cavortings with women after months on the cattle drives from Texas and innumerable nights on the grassy plains with only a horse and a restless herd of long-horn cattle for companionship.

"Most of the men had simple souls," Roosevelt remembered in his book about them. "They could relate facts but they said very little about what they simply felt."

An exception was Bucky O'Neill, the iron-nerved, iron-willed sheriff from Arizona whose name had struck terror into every wrongdoer who crossed his path. Roosevelt found him "a visionary, an articulate emotionalist." At night when O'Neill and he leaned on a railing to gaze at the boundless sea, he was less likely to tell tales of his hard and stormy past than he was to speak of the mysteries behind courage, fear, lust, love, and hatred.

One night he confided to Roosevelt that he had taken so many chances with death that he felt that the odds were against him in Cuba, but with eyes fixed on the Southern Cross he asked, "Who would not risk his life for a star?"

Sharing O'Neill's melancholy and fatalistic mood, Roosevelt wrote, "We knew not whither we were bound, nor what we were to do, but we believed that the nearing future held for us many chances of death and hardship, of honor and renown. If we failed, we would share the fate of all who fail; but we were sure that we would win, that we should score the first great triumph in a mighty world-movement."

If the Spaniards had shown any enterprise, he said in a second letter to Corinne (the first had yet to be sent), "they would somewhere or other have cut into this straggling convoy, but they haven't any so we are safe."

From the outset of the voyage the troops had felt the trade wind blowing steadily in their faces. But on Sunday, June 19, as Roosevelt stood on deck following church services, he realized the wind was "on our quarter" and the fleet had been set on a southwesterly course that could only mean their destination was Santiago de Cuba. The next morning they cruised past Guantánamo with the Sierra Maestra in the background, looking like the Rockies. That afternoon he sighted Santiago's besieged harbor.

"All next day we rolled and wallowed in the seaway," he recorded, "waiting until the decision was reached as to where we should land."

The word came on the evening of Tuesday, June 21. The place was called Daiquirí.

Suddenly, Lieutenant Colonel Theodore Roosevelt the Rough Rider became Teedie again. With one hand on a hip and the other waving his slouching campaign hat, he broke into a lively dance while bellowing a song he had learned in his cowboy years:

Shout hurrah for Erin go Bragh
And all the Yankee Nation!

Part VI

Three O'Clock Courage

Chapter 26

A Squalid Little Village

As Christopher Columbus had done 406 years earlier, Richard Harding Davis gazed in wonder at the island. "Every feature of the landscape," he observed from the deck of the *Segurança*, "was painted in highlights; there was no shading, it was all brilliant, gorgeous, and glaring. The sea was an indigo blue, like the blue in a washtub; the green of the mountains was the green of corroded copper; the scarlet trees were the red of Tommy's jacket, and the sun was like a limelight in its fierceness."

Nearby, aboard the steamship *Sylvia* (borrowed from the Baltimore Fruit Company), was Davis's old employer, William Randolph Hearst. Also on the ship was a staff of reporters, typesetting equipment, and a lightweight printing press. They had been brought along because Hearst had determined to publish the first American newspaper in Cuba, the *Journal-Examiner*. For the occasion of his own "invasion" of Cuba, he had hired John C. Hemment, a photographer, and William Britz, who shared Alfred Smith's dream of capturing the war in motion pictures. Having set aside any hard feelings he might have had over Frederic Remington's 1897 "there is no war" cable, Hearst was also paying the artist's salary and expenses.

Although Hearst was the only newspaper publisher on hand for the long-awaited invasion in the cause of Cuba Libre and American jingoism, Admiral Sampson and General Shafter had to contend with eighty-nine journalists. A few such as Davis and Remington had been allowed aboard navy ships, but the bulk of the descendents of that "luckless tribe" sired by William Howard Russell were confined to their own fleet of boats, darting and dashing between the warships.

Among them, no correspondent quite got under the skin of the weighty army chief as did Richard Harding Davis. Elegantly clad for the action in khakis, pith helmet, and white turban sash, he had railed against an order from Shafter that no reporters were to be allowed to go ashore until the troops had succeeded in securing the area.

Davis insisted that he was not a reporter but a "descriptive writer."

Shafter growled, "I don't care who you are! I'll treat you all alike."

Although Davis had waxed poetic about the beauties of the spot Shafter had picked to land his liberators, Roosevelt peered shoreward from the *Yucatan* at the port of Daiquirí and found "a squalid little village."

In the eastern province of Oriente, it had a railway and iron works and a little beach. But its lone wharf offered nothing even approaching useable docking facilities. Daiquirí had a value militarily, however, because it was thought to be very lightly defended, perhaps by three hundred Spaniards, and was only fifteen miles from the real prize, Santiago de Cuba.

To assist the American invaders, a body of *insurrectos* under the command of General Calixto García lurked in the hills. For a counsel of war to forge this army-navy-rebel alliance, Sampson and Shafter had slipped ashore at Aserrados, a small town safely in rebel hands.

Watching the obese, gout-ridden old commander of the invasion force astride a pack mule, an *insurrecto* felt sorry for the laboring animal as it groaned under the weight "of the cargo with which it had been punished."

Going into the conference, Shafter had authorization from the War Department to use his army to assist Sampson by assaulting and capturing the land fortifications protecting the entrance to Santiago Bay, thereby enabling Sampson's guns to finally smash Cervera. But Shafter also had permission to drive the army five miles inland and to attack Santiago directly with the purpose of capturing it. Sampson believed that Shafter had given "cordial assent" to the former plan. He discovered to his dismay that he was wrong.

Shafter bluntly informed him that he intended to strike at Daiquirí, seize the fishing village of Siboney, proceed via the town of El Caney, and then take the heights at Santiago from the rear. The role of the navy, he explained, was to carry the troops to Daiquirí, lay down a barrage of shells in a pattern to confuse the enemy as to the precise point of landing, and then supply boats to ferry the men ashore. García's forces were to attack Daiquirí from inland.

Admiral Sampson had no option but to accede to the plan. Accordingly, he had ordered his ships into position off Daiquirí in the early, rainy hours of June 22.

At 3:30 A.M., bugles blared in all troop transports. Years later in his autobiography, Roosevelt wrote, "We are always told that three-o'clock-in-the-morning courage is the most desirable kind. Well, my men and the regulars of the cavalry had just that brand of courage."

Bolting into action, the men gathered blanket rolls, canteens, ammunition belts, knapsacks stuffed with rations for three days, and weapons. In addition to this equipment, they wrestled up to the deck a brace of rapid-fire Colt automatic guns, gifts of Woodbury Kane and William Tiffany. They also had a dynamite gun that had been put under the control of a particularly trustworthy and careful sergeant.

Carried officially on army records as the Second Brigade, First Regular Cavalry, they were under overall command of Major General "Fighting Joe" Wheeler. Their immediate commander was Brigadier General S. B. M. Young. Like so many officers, he was a Roosevelt friend. He had been a familiar face at meetings of the big-game hunters belonging to the Boone and Crockett Club. The previous winter in Washington he had lunched with Roosevelt and Wood at the Metropolitan Club and had promised both men that, should there be a war, he would want them in whatever regiment that he might be called on to raise. To Roosevelt's everlasting gratitude, he had proved true to his word.

Just before leaving Tampa, the Rough Riders had been brigaded to serve with the First, Third, and Sixth Brigades, made up of white troops, and the Ninth and Tenth, all black. Following the custom of his era, Roosevelt in all his reminiscences referred to African-Americans as *coloreds*. Although he embraced social Darwinism and its tenet that Caucasians were at a stage of evolution more advanced than that of the nonwhite races, he did not exhibit prejudice toward individuals. As president of the United States, he would extend the first invitation to an African-American man to dine at the White House. While blacks had served in the military since the Revolutionary War, American society in the 1890s did not permit the racial integration of individual military units. It would be half a century before President Harry S. Truman ordered the desegregation of the ranks. Furthermore, the state of Texas, where the Rough Riders mobilized, had made it illegal for African-Americans to enlist (a law that remained in effect well after the end of the war), so even if Roosevelt had been inclined to flaunt the prevalent racial atmosphere, he could not have done so at Camp Wood.

Now, with Texas and Tampa behind him and with Cuba in view, he had his campaign kit ready. A medicine chest contained soap, razor, brandy, toothbrush, a yellow slicker, and rations for three days. Heading up to the deck to supervise the Rough Riders' debarkation, he confronted again the painful truth of the soldiers' maxim "All you do in the army is hurry up and wait." Because of extremely rough surf, getting men into boats would be delayed.

In the meantime it would be the navy's show.

Led by the big batteries of the *New Orleans,* the warships of Sampson's fleet pounded the shoreline while brass bands provided accompaniment with patriotic tunes and frequent renditions of "There'll Be a Hot Time in the Old Town Tonight."

Observing the barrage from the deck of the *Yucatan*, Roosevelt had, at last, reached that moment for which he had longed a year before when he had declared that a war with Spain over Cuba, at the very least, would serve as a beneficial training exercise for the navy in how to carry out amphibious assaults.

Unfortunately, what transpired as the big guns fell silent shortly after ten in the morning proved that there was a great deal to learn.

"We did the landing as we had done everything else—that is, in a scramble," he recalled with undiminished disgust in *The Rough Riders*. "There were no facilities for landing, and the fleet did not have a quarter of the number of boats it should have had for the purpose."

With mounting anger and frustration, the nation's principal proponent of efficiency looked on helplessly as the transports got as near to land as possible to load the men into smaller boats, some of which were promptly swamped in the roiling waves. Most anchored a mile and a half from land, forcing troops to jump in the water and wade to shore. Under the weight of equipment, some drowned.

Those troops who did make it to the pier found getting out of their bobbing boats perilous. One slip of a foot, and a man fell between boat and dock and was crushed to death.

In a situation in which each commander was forced to shift for himself, Roosevelt ran into a piece of luck. It took the form of the man who had been his aide while he was assistant secretary of the navy. Now the skipper of a converted yacht called *Vixen*, Lieutenant Sharp pulled aside the *Yucatan* to offer help. Roosevelt and Leonard Wood immediately scrambled aboard. But not even the *Vixen* was able to go all the way. Roosevelt and Wood plunged into the water a few hundred yards out, causing Roosevelt to lose most of his gear. Wading ashore, he was left with only the slicker and, in its pockets, his toothbrush, some soggy food, and, fortunately, his extra pairs of eyeglasses.

Among the first ashore as the *Vixen* shuttled other Rough Riders to land, Bucky O'Neill gaped in horror as a boatful of African-American soldiers capsized. Plunging into the choppy sea in full uniform, he tried to save two, but before he could grab them they had been dragged under by heavy ammunition belts and drowned. New Yorker George Knoblauch, a trumpeter, used his talents as a champion swimmer to dive down again and again to retrieve most of the infantry unit's rifles.

Running through Leonard Wood's mind as he watched countless instances of men who had to sink or swim was the painful realization that the debacle was being seen by foreign military observers and a horde of newspaper reporters. He had written to his wife that it was fortunate that such a woefully unready country as the United States had chosen as its foe "a broken down power, for we should surely have had a deuced hard time with any other." Now he could only imagine what destruction might have been delivered on these struggling invaders had they been met by any opposition, even from the Spaniards. But the Spanish soldiers had turned and fled at the first naval salvo without even destroying the ramshackle wharf.

It was from that vantage point that Roosevelt looked out at the transport attempting to unload the few horses that had been loaded at Tampa. They included Roosevelt's Texas and Rain-in-the-Face. But as the latter hung in a belly sling from a boom while being lowered, a wave broke over the rig and carried the horse to its death.

Temporarily abandoning his newsreel camera, Alfred Smith observed Roosevelt "snorting like a bull" and splitting the air with "one obscenity after another" and yelling, "Stop that goddamned animal torture!"

Handled with what one observer saw as "the supreme deliberateness of an *accoucheur* delivering an heir apparent," Texas made it safely to land and to Roosevelt's welcoming embrace.

What happened next surely had to have taken some of the edge off his anger. Several of his men made their way to a hilltop and, after spirited discussion with one of William Randolph Hearst's employees, persuaded the reporter that the American flag that Hearst insisted be raised over Cuban soil simply was not grand enough for the purpose. Instead, the bigger banner brought by the Rough Riders was run up the flagpole of an abandoned Spanish blockhouse.

Not until March 1945 when U.S. Marines raised the Stars and Stripes on Iwo Jima would the unfurling of the flag be greeted with such a clamor of patriotic fervor. Malcolm McDowell of the *Chicago Record,* aboard Henry Plant's *Olivette,* reported that for fifteen minutes the ships offshore greeted the sight with steam whistles and foghorns.

"Then the noise ceased," McDowell wrote, "and out of it came the strains of the 'Star-Spangled Banner' from the regimental band on the *Mattewan.*"

Soldiers ashore and afloat turned quiet. But when the anthem came to an end, they let loose with "three full-lunged hurrahs."

By late afternoon the Rough Riders were all accounted for. Two had drowned. With whatever ammunition and rations the rest could carry, they were, in Roosevelt's opinion, "ready for anything that might turn up."

Chapter 27

Wood's Weary Walkers

Surrounded by soaring mountains, palm trees, mangroves, and bamboo thickets, the Rough Riders pitched their tents on a dusty, brush-covered flat beside the Daiquirí River. Strange-sounding birds screeched in the deep recesses of dense jungle that formed a green wall. Huge land-crabs scuttled noisily in and out of the underbrush. The heat and humidity stifled breathing.

Certainly, such conditions were a dramatic change in lifestyle for Captain Woodbury Kane, recently of 319 Fifth Avenue, New York, and even from the neat and orderly tent city of Camp Wood. Nor had Sergeant Reginald Ronalds (who listed his address on the roster of Kane's Troop K as the Knickerbocker Club, New York), Sergeant Craig Wadsworth (of Geneseo, New York), or Lieutenant William Tiffany (of Manhattan) encountered anything like Daiquirí, Cuba. Not even Roosevelt's mountaineering friend, Corporal Fred Herrig of Pleasant Valley, Montana, had experienced this sort of rugged environment.

For Kane's troopers and most of their comrades throughout the regiment, including Lieutenant Colonel Theodore Roosevelt, experience in roughing it had been garnered as adventurers and while gunning for quarry that could not shoot back. Even those who had soldiered, such as Colonel Wood and General Wheeler, had not faced the daunting challenge of making war in the suffocating heat and humidity of the almost impenetrable jungles of Cuba.

With immense relief they learned that the Spaniards of Daiquirí had chosen not to fight. Had they done so, as Roosevelt noted in recording the events of the landings, five hundred "resolute men" could have prevented the disembarkation at very little cost to themselves. "The country would have offered very great difficulties to an attacking force had there been resistance." But those who had been available to fight the Yankees had run for their lives.

In their place the Americans had found hundreds of Cuban insurgents. Roosevelt saw "a crew of as utter tatterdemalions as human eyes ever looked on, armed with every kind of rifle in all stages of dilapidation."

It was evident at a glance, he wrote, "that they would be of no use in serious fighting, but it was hoped that they might be of service in scouting."

This turned out to be a vain hope. The rebels did, however, confirm that the small Spanish force that had been expected to defend Daiquirí was retreating toward Santiago. Recognizing the necessity to pursue the fleeing Castilians, General Wheeler gave the job to Brigadier General Young's First Cavalry. He, in turn, announced that he would personally command two regiments of regular cavalry. Wood and Roosevelt would lead the volunteers.

The word to march came in the afternoon, but it would not be till morning that the Rough Riders set out in company with the black troopers of the Tenth Cavalry. Because most of the men had been cowboys they had never done much walking. ("They were really horse men," Roosevelt wrote.) Consequently, they found the going difficult.

"The heat was intense and their burdens very heavy," wrote the leader from whom their regiment took its name. "Whenever we halted they instantly took off their packs and threw themselves on their backs. Then at a word to start they would spring into place again."

As they tramped past a group of foot soldiers, the foot-sure men taunted them with a brazenly insulting new nickname: Wood's Weary Walkers.

Much of the time, Roosevelt found himself alongside Captain William H. H. Llewellen of Troop G, whose officers hailed from New Mexico, while the troopers were a mix of men from the West, East, and Midwest. Two (George H. McCarthy and Frank P. Miller) listed their hometown as Los Angeles. All appeared to Roosevelt to be following Llewellen "with entire devotion," if not sharing the attitude of Lieutenant Jack Greenway, to whom "the entire march was nothing but an enjoyable outing, the chance of a fight on the morrow simply adding spice to the excitement."

At nightfall, under a gathering of glowering storm clouds, they reached the coastal hamlet of Siboney, described by Roosevelt with the adjective he had applied to Daiquirí: "squalid." Fires were made for coffeepots and skillets to cook pork and hardtack. By the time all was ready, the rains came, drenching men and victuals for almost two hours.

With the downpour abating, Roosevelt paid a visit to Captain Allyn Capron's Troop L. He chatted with Lieutenants Richard C. Day and John R. Thomas, respectively from Vinita and Muscogee in the Indian territories. Joining them were Trooper Elliot Cowdin, once a member of Roosevelt's Oyster Bay polo team, and New Yorker Hamilton Fish, a "huge fellow of enormous strength and endurance and dauntless courage."

"As we stood around the flickering blaze that night," Roosevelt wrote in *The Rough Riders,* "I caught myself admiring the splendid bodily vigor of Capron and Fish—the captain and the sergeant. Their frames seemed of steel, to withstand all fatigue; they were flushed with health; in their eyes shone high resolve and fiery desire. Two finer types of the fighting man, two better representatives of the American soldier, there were not in the whole army."

As Capron went over his plans for the fight they expected in the morning and Fish asked questions, Roosevelt saw in them an eagerness "to show their mettle" and a confidence that they would win "honorable renown."

Back with his own men, Roosevelt was roused from light sleep at midnight by Wood, fresh from a strategy conference with General Young. They were to start by sunrise toward Santiago. Young and four troops of the Tenth and four from the First would proceed up the road leading through the valley. Eight troops of Rough Riders were to move along a hill trail to the left. This path ultimately linked with the valley road at a point where the road rose to cross a spur of the mountain chain, then downward toward Santiago. The enemy lines were likely to be formed at the juncture of the road and the trail. Cuban General Castillo had pledged that eight hundred of his *insurrectos* would join in the fight. Young's immediate command was to be a squadron of First Regular Cavalry, two hundred strong, and a squadron of 220 from the Tenth. He also had a pair of Hotchkiss mountain guns.

They set out at 5:45 with a patrol of two men in advance. At 7:30 at a high ridge at the junction of the road and trail, they found the enemy. Some had dug pits. Others had hunkered down in the thick cover of jungle. Still more had taken up positions on a large ranch. Named for a species of abundant hog-nut trees in the region, the place was called Las Guasimas.

Riding a mule, Young moved forward to survey the situation and terrain. Ordering the Hotchkiss gun advanced, he emplaced it in concealment about nine hundred yards from the Spanish lines, then deployed some regulars, with the Tenth in support. Satisfied, he sent a Cuban runner to locate the Rough Riders and warn Wood and Roosevelt of what lay ahead.

Having broken camp at Siboney at six o'clock, the walking cavalry first had to climb a steep hill. Already footsore from trudging the previous day, some quickly found the going too arduous and had to drop out of line. Choosing not to ride Texas while his men were without horses, Roosevelt sweated in his yellow slicker and also felt "rather inclined to grumble" because of the speedy pace. But on reflection he realized that a quick march was needed if General Young's two-pronged tactic had any chance of succeeding.

As Captain Capron's Troop L spearheaded the march, Sergeant Hamilton Fish led a squad of four soldiers. They were followed by a contingent of twenty. Much farther back came Capron and the rest of his troop, followed by Wood and a pair of lieutenants as aides on loan from Young's staff. Next was Roosevelt at the head of his three troops. Brodie's squadron brought up the rear, along with William Tiffany and a pair of mules he somehow had managed to locate to transport the two Colt automatic guns. Because more mules could not be found, the dynamite gun had to be left in camp. Slogging along beside Roosevelt were two favored reporters. Defiant of heat and mud, Richard Harding Davis sported a white tropical suit and matching white helmet. The other correspondent, in much more sensible attire, was Edward Marshall of the New York *Journal*. Both had earned Roosevelt's approval in their reporting of his efforts to clean up the New York City police. But another correspondent whom Roosevelt did not care for, Stephen Crane, had been relegated to the rear, walking along with the stragglers and Tiffany's gun-toting mules.

The trail was so narrow that the men had to march in single file. Tangled jungle rose like walls on all sides, making the sending out of flankers impossible. Once atop the hill, however, the march was, in Roosevelt's description, "very pleasant." Now and then they came to glades or rounded shoulders affording views for long distances.

"The tropical forest was very beautiful," wrote the man whose reputation as a naturalist had led to a subspecies of Olympic elk being named for him, "and it was a delight to see the strange trees, the splendid royal palms and a tree which looked like a flat-topped acacia, and which was covered with a mass of brilliant scarlet flowers. We heard many bird-notes, too, the cooing of doves and the call of a great brush cuckoo." (He later learned that Spanish soldiers had learned how to imitate these birds.) "It was very beautiful and very peaceful, and it seemed more as if we were off on some hunting expedition than as if we were about to go into a sharp and bloody little fight."

Indeed they were, for a mile to the west and two hundred feet lower than Roosevelt's hilltop vista, Young's soldiers had met the enemy at the crossing of road and trail. Recognizing that it would take those on the hill trail some time to reach the position, Young did not launch troops in an immediate attack, choosing to send word to Wood's Weary Walkers and to wait.

Having reached the hilltop, Roosevelt's troops had fallen out for a rest break. While a group of New Mexicans plopped on the ground to murmur, not about Spaniards, but about the conduct of a certain cowpuncher in quitting work on a ranch to open a saloon, Roosevelt reminisced with Edward Marshall about a lunch they once attended at the Astor Hotel with William Randolph Hearst. But as Roosevelt talked, his keen cattle rancher's eyes spotted a curl of loose barbed wire fencing at the side of the trail. Suddenly grabbing its end, he said, "This wire has been cut today."

With a reporter's skepticism, Marshall asked, "What makes you think so?"

"The end is bright," Roosevelt answered, wagging the wire, "and there has been enough dew, even since sunrise, to put a light rust on it."

At that moment the sultry air snapped with an unmistakable sound.

In writing of the first bullet fired at him in war, Roosevelt showed remarkable restraint, recording only that the Rough Riders "became engaged." However, that singular moment of history for both Roosevelt and the nation was provided to posterity in the words of Marshall:

> Perhaps a dozen of Roosevelt's men had passed into the thicket before he did. Then he stepped across the wire himself, and, from that instant, became the most magnificent soldier I have ever seen. It was as if that barbed-wire strand formed a dividing line in his life, and that when he stepped across it he left behind him in the bridle path all those unadmirable and conspicuous traits which have so often caused him to be justly criticized in civic life, and found on the other side of it, in that Cuban thicket, the coolness, the calm judgment, the towering heroism, which made him, perhaps, the most admired and best loved of all Americans in Cuba.

Regarding what happened immediately after the shot, Roosevelt wrote, "To the right the jungle was thick, and we had barely begun to deploy when the crash in front announced that the fight was on. It was evidently very hot, and L Troop had its hands full."

Indeed they had. Captain Capron's troopers found themselves raked by rifle fire. Rushing forward with men of Llewellen's K Troop, including Woodbury Kane's platoon, Roosevelt came out of the jungle on a shoulder that jutted over a ravine and separated him from a ridge to his right. Beyond it lay the valley road where General Young had run into Spaniards.

Knowing nothing of that engagement, Roosevelt concerned himself with determining the origin of the firing around him and his men. The fact that the Spaniards were hard to find justified Roosevelt's own faith in the value of smokeless gunpowder. The effect, he would write, "was remarkable . . . not the faintest trace of smoke was to be seen in any direction from whence the bullets came."

His account of the fight continued:

> We could hear the faint reports of the Hotchkiss guns and the re-ply of two Spanish guns, and the Mauser bullets were singing through the trees over our heads, making a noise like the humming of tele-phone wires; but exactly where they came from we could not tell. The Spaniards were firing high and for the most part by volleys and their shooting was not very good, which perhaps was not to be wondered at, as they were a long way off. Gradually, however, they began to get the range and occasionally one of our men would crumple up.

First to fall had been Hamilton Fish, dropping at the feet of Captain Allyn Capron. A moment later a Mauser bullet drilled into Capron's heart.

Angered by being exposed to fire and seeing his men dropping under it while unable to return fire, Roosevelt searched for a target until he heard the urgent shout of Richard Harding Davis.

"There they are, Colonel; look over there, " he said as he pointed to the right. "I can see their hats near that glade."

Spotting them and pointing them out to men he knew to be the best shots, Roosevelt estimated the range. When the shots had no effect, he raised the estimate of distance and, with delight, watched the Spaniards spring out of the cover and run. With more of his troops now at hand, he was able to see many of the enemy and direct pun-ishing fire at them.

As the Spaniards fled, the Rough Riders pursued, taking advantage of the cover, sinking down behind any mound, bush, or tree trunk. But trees furnished no protection from Mauser bullets, as Roosevelt discovered. While standing by a large palm with his head out to one side, a bullet hit the tree and threw dust and splinters into his left eye.

As to the seriously wounded and an order that no one be permitted to drop out of the pursuit of the enemy to lend help, he wrote, "It was hard to leave them there in the jungle, where they might not be found again until the vultures and the land-crabs came, but war is a grim game and there was no choice."

One of those shot was Harry Heffner of G Troop, mortally wounded through the hips. He fell without uttering a sound and was dragged behind a tree. Propping himself up, he asked for a canteen of water and his rifle. The last time Roosevelt saw him alive, he was firing, loading, and firing again.

Finding himself out of touch with troopers under the command of Bucky O'Neill, he sent Sergeant Marcus Russell of Troy, New York, and George Roland, a New Mexican cowboy, down into the valley to find out where they were. Russell did not return, and Roland came back bleeding from the side. Although Roland dismissed the wound as slight, Roosevelt recognized he had a broken rib and ordered him to the rear. After some grumbling, Roland went, only to show up at Roosevelt's side fifteen minutes later with the claim that he had not been able to find the hospital. Roosevelt let him go on fighting.

As they drove Spaniards from their position on the right, the firing seemed to let up in that area, though the rattle of guns remained lively elsewhere. Observing troops across the ravine where Spaniards had been seen previously, Roosevelt had his men withhold fire, fearing the men in their sights might be Cubans. After a closer look, he was happy he had not given an order to shoot. The men were Americans.

Still very much in the dark as to where the main body of the Spanish forces was located or exactly what lines the battle was following, and thus uncertain what to do, he decided he could not go wrong by pushing forward. He hoped to find Colonel Wood. He had not seen him since the beginning of the skirmish. At that moment as the firing began and troops started to curse, Wood had growled, "Don't swear—shoot!"

Now, Roosevelt confessed in *The Rough Riders,* "I was in a mood to cordially welcome guidance, for it was most bewildering to fight an enemy whom one so rarely saw."

At the head of G Troop as he led them back to the trail, he passed the dead and wounded of L Troop and found Hamilton Fish as he lay "with glazed eyes under the rank tropic growth to one side of the trail." Moving on, he found the men spread out in a thin skirmish line and advancing across fairly open ground, taking advantage of whatever cover they found.

Strolling about in their midst with his horse on slack reins was Wood. That he and his horse escaped being hit, Roosevelt could not believe. But moments after Roosevelt dashed to him, Wood's aide, Lieutenant Colonel Alexander Brodie, took a bullet that shattered an arm, spun him around, and left him unable to go on. Directed by Wood to replace him on the left wing, Roosevelt was suddenly in charge of Captain Maximilian Luna's Troop F, Frederick Muller's Troop E, and Captain R. B. Huston's Troop D. Ordered forward, they advanced in a well-spread-out formation through the high grass of an open forest. They were greeted by a hail of bullets.

Looking for the source of the fire, Roosevelt decided that it came from a group of large, red-tiled ranch buildings about five hundred yards in front. Fortunately, the enemy fire went high. Whether the shots aimed at the buildings with a rifle he picked out of the hands of a wounded trooper did any better is not known. Convinced that the incoming fire originated in the buildings, he sprang upright and ordered the men to charge.

Moments later, panting for breath, they reached the buildings to find heaps of empty cartridge shells and two dead Spaniards, shot through the head. Outside, the firing appeared to have died out. Then Roosevelt heard shocking, sickening news. A breathless trooper ran up shouting that Wood had been killed.

Unable to confirm the report, he had no choice but to assume it was true and take over the regiment. He ordered men here and there to fill canteens with water and to care for a few of the walking wounded and to help into the ranch buildings a dozen who were suffering from heat exhaustion. But as he started in the direction of the main body of troops, he grinned with relief and delight at the sight of Wood, alive and well and with the welcome news that the fighting was over and the Spanish were in retreat toward Santiago.

An hour and a half after the first shot, the battle left the Americans in possession of the entire Spanish position and the enemy troops in full flight. But 8 of the Rough Riders lay dead, and 34 had been wounded. The First Cavalry lost 7 men and had 8 wounded. The

Tenth suffered 1 dead and 10 wounded. Out of 964 men who had marched into the battle, 16 had died and 52 were wounded.

Although the commander of the Spanish forces claimed a loss of 7 soldiers, Roosevelt insisted that this figure was wrong. He claimed to have counted 11 dead Spaniards, thereby taking issue with the official U.S. position that 42 of the Spaniards had been killed. He said, "Indeed, I should doubt whether their loss was as heavy as ours, for they were undercover, while we advanced, often in the open, and their main lines fled long before we could get to close quarters. It was very difficult country, and a force of good soldiers resolutely handled could have held the pass with ease against two or three times their number. As it was, with a force half of regulars and half of volunteers, we drove out a superior number of Spanish troops, strongly posted, without suffering a very heavy loss."

It had been, he said, a trying fight beyond what the losses showed, "for it is hard upon raw soldiers to be pitted against an unseen foe, and to advance steadily when their comrades are falling around them."

In the sudden stillness of afternoon, the Rough Riders made camp and looked after their wounded. Those who could walk made their way to a little field hospital set up by the regimental surgeon, Dr. Robert Church. Joining in a search for the dead and badly wounded, Roosevelt gazed in disgust and horror at hideous land-crabs "gathered in a gruesome ring, waiting for life to be extinct." One of his men and most of the Spanish dead were found with eyes plucked out and gaping wounds, the work of vultures. Passing a couple of lank Oklahoma cowboys whom experience had trained to look on life and death philosophically, he heard one say in his flat drawl, "Well, some of the boys got it in the neck!"

The other replied with a sigh, "Many a good horse dies."

The next morning brought interments on the summit of the trail. The Episcopal service was by Chaplain Henry A. Brown of Prescott, Arizona. The hymn was "Rock of Ages." In the hot blue sky, vultures wheeled. For Roosevelt there was no "more honorable burial than in a common grave." Indian, cowboy, miner, packer, and college athlete—the man of unknown ancestry from lonely western plains and the man born in the comforts of an eastern city "made one in the way they had met death, just as during life they had been one in their daring and loyalty."

Chapter 28

Full of Beans

History is written by the winners. However, the first draft is done by journalists.

The two who had been in the thick of it at Las Guasimas saw the Americans as blunderers into a Spanish trap. Edward Marshall said the troops "met the Spanish before they expected to." Richard Harding Davis telegraphed to the *Herald* that the Rough Riders were "ambushed by receding Spaniards with the advantage all on the side of the enemy." In a letter written soon after the engagement, he said, "We were caught in a clear case of ambush."

Theodore Roosevelt insisted there had been no such thing. He said that "we struck the Spaniards exactly where we expected" and "every one of the officers had full knowledge of where he would find the enemy."

Whether there had been an ambush or not was of no concern to a Spanish officer speaking to a diplomat of the British consulate in besieged Santiago. "The Americans do not fight like other men," he complained. "When we fire, they run right toward us. We are not used to fighting men who act so."

As for the historians, one of Roosevelt's biographers, Henry Pringle, downplayed the issue of whether there had been an ambush and concentrated on the performance of the cowboy cavalry and the man who led them in their first battle. He wrote, "Very much confused, but standing their ground admirably, the Rough Riders fired back at an enemy they could not see, and in the end the Spaniards continued their flight toward Santiago."

In *Theodore Roosevelt, A Life,* Nathan Miller concluded, "He had shown coolness and bravery under fire and had earned the respect of his men." Edmund Morris, in *The Rise of Theodore Roosevelt*, wrote of this baptism, "Although he did not fully realize it, he had succeeded brilliantly in his first military skirmish."

Michael Blow wrote in *A Ship to Remember:* "Ambushed or not, the Rough Riders had shown extraordinary courage in dispersing and inflicting heavy casualties on a superior enemy force, later variously estimated at from twelve hundred to four thousand men, well entrenched, hidden from view in the jungle, and commanding the ridges above the trail."

Perhaps the finest tribute came from a Spanish soldier. "The Americans were beaten, but persisted in fighting," he said in amazement. A second bewildered Spaniard said, "They tried to catch us with their hands."

Roosevelt's understanding of the meaning of the outcome and his role in it was set out in his autobiography. He described an encounter with a captain of the Ninth Cavalry who was "very glum" because his troop of regulars had not arrived in time to join in the fighting, and continued:

> [He] congratulated me—with visible effort!—upon my share in our first victory. I thanked him cordially, not confiding in him that till that moment I myself knew exceeding little about the victory; and proceeded to where Generals Wheeler, [Henry] Lawton, and [Adna] Chaffee, who had just come up, in company with Wood, were seated on a bank. They expressed appreciation of the way that I had handled my troops, first on the right wing and then on the left. As I was quite prepared to find I had committed some awful sin, I did my best to accept this in a nonchalant manner and not to look as relieved as I felt. As throughout the morning I had persevered a specious aspect of wisdom and had commanded first one and then the other wing, the fight was really a capital thing for me, for practically all the men had served under my actual command, and thenceforth felt an enthusiastic belief that I would lead them aright.

On June 25 he wrote to Henry Cabot Lodge from Las Guasimas, "Well, whatever comes I shall feel contented with having left the Navy Department to go into the army for the war; for our regiment has been in the first fight and has done well."

In Washington, Theodore Roosevelt was once again the talk of the town. Someone floated the proposal that he be made a brigadier general, an idea viewed dimly by the top brass of the regular army, who felt embarrassed that a group of irregulars had stolen the limelight, not to mention the glory, in the first battle in Cuba. Farther north, Republican politicians in New York with an eye toward the forthcoming gubernatorial election wondered if the perfect candidate might make himself available for a draft. Across the country, newspapers heralded a national hero the like of which had not been seen since General Ulysses S. Grant or even Andrew Jackson, the hero of the Battle of New Orleans.

At Sagamore Hill on Oyster Bay, Edith Carow Roosevelt held a packet of letters from her husband and cared only that Theodore came through the fight alive and well. "Last night I slept better because I held your dear letters to my heart instead of under my pillow," she wrote to him on June 27. "I felt I was touching you when I pressed against me what your hand had touched."

On that same night, just five miles from Santiago de Cuba, Roosevelt wrote to her:

> We have a lovely camp here, by a beautiful stream which runs through jungle-lined banks. So far the country is lovely; plenty of grass and great open woods of palms . . . mango trees and many others; but most of the land is covered with a dense tropical jungle. This was what made it so hard for us in the fight. It was very hard to stand or advance slowly, while the men fell dead or wounded, shot down from we knew not whence; for smokeless powder renders it almost impossible to place a hidden foe.

He reported himself in excellent health, "in spite of having been obliged for the week since I landed, to violate all the rules of health which I was told I must observe. I've had to sleep steadily on the ground; for four days I never took off my clothes, which were always drenched with rain, dew or perspiration, and we had no chance to boil the water we drank. We had hardtack, bacon and coffee without sugar; now we haven't even salt; but last evening we got some beans."

This delicacy had counted as another major victory over the military bureaucracy. On the morning of June 26, Roosevelt had learned of a stockpile of at least eleven hundred pounds of beans on the beach. Presenting himself at the commissary, he demanded all of it for the regiment.

According to regulations, he was haughtily informed by the commissary officer, beans were for officers only.

Very well, then, Roosevelt asserted, he would require eleven hundred pounds of beans "for the officer's mess."

The incredulous commissary officer gasped, "Your officers cannot eat eleven hundred pounds of beans."

"You don't know what appetites my officers have!"

"I'll have to send the requisition to Washington."

"All right, only give me the beans."

"I'm afraid they'll take it out of your salary."

"That will be all right," Roosevelt answered with a smile full of teeth, "only give me the beans."

In the letter to Edith he exclaimed, "Oh! what a feast we had, and how we enjoyed it."

Chapter 29

A View from a Hill

Roosevelt's "lovely camp" stood a little west of the bloody ridge at Las Guasimas and near the small town of Sevilla, which was so close to Santiago that if there were not a war, a person might stroll there on the road the Cubans called El Camino Real. The encampment proved to be no Eden.

Aside from the commandeered beans, there was little in the way of food. Roosevelt viewed this failure of the Army Commissary Department as one more evidence of the nation's unpreparedness for war. "We were not given the proper amount of food," he wrote in *The Rough Riders*. "We got enough salt pork and hardtack for the men, but not the full ration of coffee and sugar, and nothing else."

Taking the strongest and best walkers and also some of the officers' horses and a stray mule or two, he organized foraging expeditions back to the coast in search of whatever victuals he could cajole from the commissary.

If these efforts came up empty, the men made a meal of what was available. They plucked mangoes and other fruit until the trees were stripped bare. When tobacco (or money to buy it on the Cuban black market) ran out, they dried grass, and in the most extreme of cases, manure, for smokes. Skilled traders could swap army equipment with the locals for enough rum to make any man forget the grumbles of an empty belly.

One of these forays for food proved to be almost a disaster for Sherman Bell, the former deputy marshall of Cripple Creek and Wells Fargo Express rider whom Roosevelt had accepted into the regiment despite Bell's hernia. In coming back to the camp with a load of food, through a blinding storm, he slipped and opened the old rupture.

"The agony was great and one of his comrades took his load," Roosevelt noted. "He, himself sometimes walking, and sometimes crawling, got back to camp."

Rather than obey the order of Dr. Church that he be returned to the United States, Bell crawled out of the hospital and into the jungle, lying there until an ambulance that had been sent to fetch him had turned around and departed. When Roosevelt found him, Bell explained that if he must die, he wanted to do so fighting. Roosevelt did not have the heart to send him back.

Nor was there anything like enough transportation, whether in the way of wagons or mule trains, "exactly as there had been no sufficient number of landing-boats with the transports," Roosevelt complained. When a load of tents arrived, they provided "only a partial protection against terrific downpours of rain that occurred almost every afternoon and turned the camp into a tarn, and the trails into torrents and quagmires."

Despite these travails, Roosevelt found, "From the generals to the privates, all were eager to march against Santiago."

How to get there was a decision belonging to the officer who had yet to leave the ship that had carried him to Cuba. Plagued by his gout and barely able to walk because of his obesity, General Rufus Shafter finally came ashore and into a groaning buckboard on the last day of June for a bog-filled journey over El Camino Real to survey the situation and terrain facing his eager troops.

Helped onto the back of the biggest and strongest mule to be found, he ascended to the best spot from which to see what lay between his army and its objective. The locals called the hilltop vantage point El Pozo. It provided a panoramic view of a basin of jungle with hills to the right and left. Beyond another ridge of hills at the far side of the shallow valley lay Santiago. After a look at the hills from atop El Pozo, Richard Harding Davis said, "These hills looked so quiet and sunny and well kept that they reminded one of a New England orchard."

Scanning the valley below El Pozo through his binoculars, Shafter observed, as he looked to his left, a village guarded by six wooden blockhouses, a stone fort, and a fortresslike stone church where Cortés was said to have prayed while on his way to win Mexico for Spain. Named El Caney, the town with its fort was clearly an impediment that would have to be removed if the American army were to reach and assault the formidable defenses occupying the ridge of neat hills before Santiago.

Compelling Shafter's attention on the summit at the center of this ridge was a blockhouse that dominated El Camino Real as it twisted and rose to cross the heights on its way into the city. These hills were known as the San Juan Heights. The highest point at the center was called San Juan Hill.

A man did not have to have graduated from the U.S. Military Academy to recognize the significance of the hills in the distance. Richard Harding Davis gazed from El Pozo at "a long yellow pit opened in the hillside . . . and in it . . . straw sombreros rising up and down."

When William Randolph Hearst climbed El Pozo to have a look, it was a singular moment not only in the military history of the United States but in the annals of American journalism. Here in person was the brash exponent of the style of journalism that Roosevelt detested, filing under his own byline a story on a war that both he and Roosevelt had worked to bring on.

The publisher and now war correspondent proved to be capable of a rather tortured wordiness:

It is satisfactory to be an American and to be here on the soil of Cuba, at the very threshold of what may prove to be the decisive battle of the war. The struggle for the possession of the City of Santiago and the capture of Cervera's fleet seems to be only hours away, and from the top of the rough, green ridge where I write this, we can see the monstrous forms of Sampson's fleet lying in a semi-circle in front of the entrance to Santiago harbor, while here at our feet masses of American soldiers are pouring from the beach into the scorching valley, where smells of stagnant and fermented vegetation ground under the feet of thousands of fighting men rise in the swooning hot mists through which vultures that have already fed on corpses of slain Spaniards wheel lazily above the thorny, poisonous jungle.

Santiago and the flower of the Spanish fleet are ours, although hundreds of men may have to die on the field before we take possession of them.

Neither Cervera's crews nor General Linares's battalion or squadrons can escape, for the American fleet bars the way by sea and our infantry and dismounted cavalry are gradually encircling the city, driving the Spanish pickets backward toward the tiers of trenches in which the defenders of Spanish aggression must make their last stand.

Regardless of the complex syntax (which must have caused the editors of the *Journal* back in New York to shudder), Hearst managed to capture the essence of the situation. It was obvious to all who looked that once the defenses on the San Juan Heights were taken, Santiago and Cervera's armada would be caught in the jaws of a nutcracker formed by an eager, freshly blooded army on land and an impatient navy blockading the harbor.

At this crucial and probably decisive moment, Admiral Sampson received an alarming message from the Navy Department. In it, Secretary Long advised him that three of his best warships, the *Iowa*, *Oregon,* and *Brooklyn,* and four others might soon be sent to the Eastern Squadron of Commodore John C. Watson. Should a Spanish fleet sail out of Cádiz with the intention of bolstering Spain's position in the Pacific, the ships taken from Sampson were to make trouble along the coast of Spain. The hope was that such a maneuver would force the Cádiz division to cancel any mission to the Pacific, thereby thwarting any threat against Dewey's vulnerable squadron at the Philippines.

Although Sampson appreciated this strategy, he believed it was shortsighted and dangerous to chance letting Cervera's fleet slip the noose. Reminding Long that Hobson's attempt to sink the *Merrimac* had failed to block the harbor's channel, he warned that "we must be prepared to meet the Spanish fleet if they attempt to escape."

Having viewed the land approaches to Santiago from El Pozo, Shafter descended at noon to return to his field headquarters between Sevilla and La Redonda for a strategy conference with his generals. The attack he outlined was three pronged:

1. Lawton's infantry division, with a battery of artillery, was to advance northward along El Camino Real toward El Caney, camp there for the night, and attack at dawn Friday. Lawton estimated a success after a fight of no more than two or three hours. He would then swing to the southwest to hit the heights on the left flank.

2. Troops of a Michigan regiment, newly landed, would move westerly along the coast from Siboney and make a feint at the town of Aguadores to pin down the forces of General Arsenio Linares and keep them from reinforcing San Juan Heights.

3. The First Division of General Jacob F. Kent, supported by cavalry on the right wing, would constitute a frontal attack on the hills.

Ordinarily, the cavalry would be under the command of the famed Confederate General, Fighting Joe Wheeler. (In the pitch of the recent rout of the Spaniards, he had become so excited that he had forgotten what war he was in and had yelled as the Spanish retreated, "We've got the damn Yankees on the run!") Unfortunately, the old man had been laid low with fever, as had his second in command, Samuel Young, thus devolving the overall command of the cavalry to General Samuel S. Sumner.

This required giving command of Young's brigade to Leonard Wood. That, in turn, elevated Roosevelt to command of the Rough Riders.

Informed of this, he exclaimed with unabashed delight, "I got my regiment."

Chapter 30

Biff Bang

"It is a very typical American regiment," wrote the correspondent for *Leslie's Illustrated Weekly*.

> All have the spirit of adventure strong within them, and they are there in the Cuban chapparal because they see perils, because they are patriotic, because, as some think, every gentleman owes a debt to his country, and this is the time to pay. And all these men, drawn from so many sources . . . have been roughly, quickly, and effectively moulded and formed into a fighting regiment by the skillful discipline of Leonard Wood, their colonel . . . and by the inspiration of Theodore Roosevelt, their lieutenant-colonel, who has laid down a high place in the administration at Washington and come hither to Cuba because thus only can he live up to his idea of conduct by offering his life to his country when war comes.

Many significant dates had been noted in the diaries Theodore Roosevelt had begun keeping as a sickly child confined to the house on East Twentieth Street where he had been born. The day on which the father he had idolized and called "great heart" died. Harvard graduation day. His wedding to Alice Hathaway Lee. The birth of their daughter. A day of double heartbreak when he lost both his wife and his mother. Memorable dates in Dakota. Election Day 1886, when he was not only defeated as Republican candidate for mayor of New York, but finished third. Taking Edith Carow as a bride that same year. Fine dinners in Washington, engaged in lively repartee with Rudyard Kipling. Midnight rambles along the sidewalks of New York as police commissioner, in search of slack cops. Contentious hours with enemies of reform. The speech at the Naval War College. A decisive afternoon when he brazenly ordered Dewey to keep full of coal so as to grab the Philippines. Days spent drilling dusty troopers at Camp Wood. Setting foot on Cuban soil. The first taste of battle on June 24.

But this day—June 30, 1898—was like no other. It dawned with him in command of the regiment.

The previous evening he had stood atop El Pozo with the man who had believed all along that he was destined to be "kicked upstairs to make room for Roosevelt." To the men of the regiment, Leonard Wood had been the reserved and cautious planner, while Roosevelt, in the words of Sergeant David Hughes, was all "biff-bang-do-it-right-now-can-not-put-it-off-another-minute."

Suddenly, Hughes and the rest could call themselves unquestionably *Roosevelt's* Rough Riders. Without horses, yes. Still the weary walkers. But Roosevelt watched them break camp "greatly overjoyed" because they were on order to hold themselves in readiness to march against Santiago.

"As always happened when we had to change camp," he noted, "everything the men could not carry, including, of course, the officers' baggage, was left behind."

With every man carrying three days' worth of rations and with borrowed mules to carry along the dynamite gun and the two Colt automatic firers, they struck camp at noon, drew up in column beside the road at the rear of the First Cavalry, then sat and waited while one regiment after another marched past them on a very narrow road.

As Roosevelt's biographer Edmund Morris wryly pointed out, a small detail had apparently escaped Shafter's attention: the mobilization of some sixteen thousand men along a road ten feet wide would cause certain problems.

Richard Harding Davis said, "It was as though fifteen regiments were encamped along the sidewalks of Fifth Avenue and were all ordered at the same moment to move into it and march down town. If Fifth Avenue were ten feet wide, you can imagine the confusion. . . . Twelve thousand men . . . treading on each other's heels in three inches of mud."

At last, toward midafternoon, Roosevelt led his men forward, only to be halted every few minutes by a stoppage in their front. From time to time they came to gaps in the surrounding walls of jungle to find that a regiment, apparently left out of its proper place, would break up their line of march. It was nearly eight o'clock before they fell out of ranks, threw down their belongings, and slept on the spot.

With the sunrise, they fell in as a battery of field guns rattled past to take up a position on a hill just beyond them. Roosevelt thought the horses straining as they dragged the guns uphill was "a fine sight to see."

Perhaps so, but Leonard Wood did not care for the disposition of the guns. He told Roosevelt he wished their brigade could be moved somewhere else, pointing out that they were directly in the range of shells should Spanish artillery return fire.

This fact notwithstanding, Roosevelt noted it was "a very lovely morning." The sky was of "cloudless blue, while the level, shimmering rays of the just-risen sun brought into fine relief the splendid palms which here and there towered above the lower growth."

He thought of the lofty and beautiful mountains hemming in the Santiago plain as an amphitheater for the battle. In the next minute, as he sat beside Wood, the American guns opened fire and belched great clouds of white smoke that hung on the crest of the ridge. A few moments later they heard a peculiar whistling and a clap of thunder as a Spanish shell exploded overhead, followed by a rain of shrapnel. As they sprang to their horses, a second round burst and a chunk of hot metal struck Roosevelt on the wrist, immediately raising a lump the size of a hickory nut. The same blast wounded four Rough Riders and several regulars. A third landed in the midst of some *insurrectos,* killing many while the rest scattered in panic. A shard of shrapnel also pierced Wood's horse in the lungs.

When the twenty-minute barrage lifted, Wood formed the brigade, with Roosevelt's regiment in front, and ordered them to follow the First Brigade. Forming a column of fours, they marched down the slope toward a fording spot in the San Juan River to be greeted by desultory firing from the Spanish blockhouses and surrounding trenches. Roosevelt's orders called for a march to the right to form with Lawton's regulars, following the regulars' taking of El Caney.

Because no reconnaissance had been made, the exact strength and position of the enemy was not known. In an attempt to close this gap in field intelligence, a stationary manned balloon had been sent up. This proved to be a bad mistake.

Roosevelt described the ensuing minutes this way:

> I was now ordered to cross the ford, march half a mile or so to the right, and then halt and await further orders; and I promptly hurried my men across, and the captive balloon, to the horror of everybody,

was coming down to the ford. Of course, it was a special target for the enemy's fire. I got my men across before it reached the ford. There it partly collapsed and remained, causing severe loss of life, as it indicated the exact position where the Tenth and the First Cavalry, and the infantry, were crossing.

The only thing hotter than the incoming Spanish fire was the temperature of the air. As it soared to over one hundred degrees, Roosevelt slowly led his sweltering troopers through the high grass of the open jungle. With the First Brigade on the left, they came to a sunken lane. Bounded by a wire fence, it led straight up to and then between two hills to their front. Upon the one to the left stood heavy blockhouses. The rise on the right was surmounted by large haciendas. Because the height was dominated by a huge iron sugar-refining pot, it had been named Kettle Hill.

Blocked from advancing by the stalled First Brigade, Roosevelt got his men as sheltered as possible and waited for orders. Many huddled close to the river bank. The rest threw themselves flat behind patches of bush and in tall grass. All gasped for air in the stifling heat and waited for a signal from Roosevelt.

In Texas's saddle, determined to set an example of courage, he presented a tempting but elusive target as the Mauser bullets zinged all around him. For future artists, he presented the pose of a hero. That morning he had put on a dark blue shirt. A stand-up collar bore the insignia of the Rough Riders. To hitch up his trousers, he wore yellow suspenders with silver fasteners. But as the heat rose during the day, he had taken off his blue and white polka-dot scarf, the unique emblem of the cowboy cavalry, and shaded the back of his neck by fastening it to the rear of the brim of his slouched hat. All he lacked to complete a Napoléon-like picture of horseback gallantry was one of the sabres that had been abandoned as useless at Camp Wood. (He had carried a sword into the battle at Las Guasimas, only to fling it aside because he kept tripping over it.) But dashing looks and a conspicuous presence on a warhorse were useless without a good plan of battle, and at the moment it appeared that something was terribly amiss with the one they had been following.

The strategy had gone wrong at the town of El Caney. On the previous evening, Richard Harding Davis had taken a look at men who expected to "march on it and eat it up before breakfast." They believed they would find fewer than six hundred Spaniards and that, at the first sight of the overwhelming number of Americans, the Spanish soldiers would turn and run. Unfortunately for General Lawton's division, attacking El Caney proved difficult. Unexpectedly strong resistance had delayed the taking of the citadel, and they had been unable to link up on schedule with the forces assaulting San Juan Hill.

The fighting there, Roosevelt recorded, "was now on in good earnest." The Spaniards raked the valley below them with Mauser bullets that rained in sheets through the trees and jungle grass.

"Some of the bullets seemed to pop in the air, so that we thought they were explosive," Roosevelt recalled, "and, indeed, many of those which were coated with brass did explode, in the sense that the brass was ripped off, making a thin plate of hard metal with a jagged edge, which inflicted a ghastly wound."

Very few of the wounded died, even under appalling conditions of treatment due to the lack of personnel and supplies in field hospitals. Almost all fatalities resulted from head wounds or direct hits to the heart or spine.

While pinned down in the gulch of the San Juan River (more creek than river, actually), Roosevelt observed that the Spanish fire did not appear to be aimed at particular targets, but swept the whole field of battle up to the edge of the water. The result was that man after man in the ranks fell dead or wounded.

One who was hit was Lieutenant Horace Devereaux. Struck as he lay on the edge of the stream, he suffered arm wounds. West Point cadet Ernest Haskell, who had taken his summer vacation to become an acting second lieutenant, was shot through the stomach. He said to Roosevelt, "All right, Colonel, I'm going to get well. Don't bother about me." Roosevelt expected him to die, but the plucky incipient officer proved him wrong.

Despite the withering gunfire sweeping down the hillside, Captain Bucky O'Neill appeared to stroll among Troop A, ignoring a trooper who shouted, "Captain, a bullet is sure to hit you."

The inveterate smoker took a cigarette from his lips, blew a cloud of smoke, and laughed. "Sergeant," he scoffed, "the Spanish bullet ain't made that will kill me."

Moments later a shot struck him in the mouth and came out the back of his head.

"Even before he fell," Roosevelt wrote in *The Rough Riders,* "his wild and gallant soul had gone out into the darkness."

After Roosevelt's orderly, "a brave young Harvard boy" by the name of Sanders, collapsed from the heat, he was replaced by a trooper whose name Roosevelt did not know. Shortly afterward, while sitting beside the bank, Roosevelt ordered him "to go back and ask whatever general he came across if I could advance, as my men were being cut up." The trooper stood up to salute and then pitched forward across Roosevelt's knees. A bullet had drilled through his neck and cut the carotid artery.

Sending "messenger after messenger" to try to find General Sumner or General Wood "and get permission to advance," Roosevelt was about to make up his mind that in the absence of orders he had better "march toward the guns" when a lieutenant rode up with "the welcome command" to move forward and support the regulars in an assault on the hills in front.

To the end of a life whose diary pages were filled with memorable events and would record historic achievements as president of the United States, Theodore Roosevelt would sum up all that followed in three words.

Chapter 31

The Crowded Hour

Arguably the most prolific writer in the political history of the United States, Theodore Roosevelt was, according to historian John Gabriel Hunt in his book *The Essential Theodore Roosevelt,* a man of bold ideas and enormous energy who pursued with equal enthusiasm his passions for politics, social reform, the outdoor life, and the printed word. He gave to the American language a veritable dictionary of quotations and catchphrases: *Bully!, muckrakers, trust-busting, the New Nationalism, honesty and efficiency, the Square Deal, speak softly but carry a big stick*; and, on the occasion of being shot in the chest by a would-be assassin, *it takes more than that to kill a bull moose.*

Having been through warfare, he also enunciated its heady essence. "All men who feel any power of joy in battle," he said, "know what it is like when the wolf rises in the heart."

Overwhelmed by this emotion as he received the order to attack on that blistering, bullet-riddled, bloody afternoon of the first of July, he leapt on his valiant horse and rode Texas up and down the line so he could "see the men better and they could see me better."

Exhorting the troopers to go forward and rasping brief directions to the captains and lieutenants, he came upon a man crouching behind a little bush. He ordered him to jump up. When the man did not respond, Roosevelt "bade him to rise, jeering him and saying, 'Are you afraid to stand up when I am on horseback?' "

Suddenly the man toppled forward on his face. A bullet had cut through him lengthwise.

With a tinge of cold-bloodedness and perhaps an inflated sense of his own importance, Roosevelt supposed that the bullet had been aimed at him. "At any rate, I, who was on horseback in the open," he would recall, "was unhurt, and the man lying flat on the ground in the cover beside me was killed."

He did not believe that a life lost in a just battle was a life wasted. "I freely sent the men for whom I cared most, to where death might meet them, and death often smote them—as it did the two best officers in my regiment, Allyn Capron and Bucky O'Neill," he asserted in his autobiography. "The life even of the most useful man, of the best citizen, is not to be hoarded if there be need to spend it. I felt, and feel, this about others; and of course also about myself."

Certainly, he had demonstrated his conviction on that scorching first of July, which sounded to his friend Frederic Remington like "a Fourth of July morning, when the boys are setting off their crackers."

With his men pinned down in the bed of the San Juan River (which thereafter bore the name Bloody Ford), Roosevelt dared the men with the Mausers unflinchingly. Astride Texas, he goaded the troops in the rear forward until they crowded the ones in front of them. To get all lines to advance, he egged the horse between one line and the next, parting them, in Edmund Morris's exquisite phrasing, "like waves under a Viking's prow."

Suddenly, he found himself—literally—at the head of the regiment.

Arrayed around the Rough Riders were the Ninth Regiment, immediately in front, and the First on the left. Behind were the Third, Sixth, and Tenth, so intermingled that the Tenth's Sergeant George Berry carried not only his regiment's colors but those of the Third, whose color-sergeant had been cut down. Following the commander of the Tenth, Captain Ayres, who yelled and lifted his hat, Berry waved both flags and shouted, "Dress on the colors, boys! Dress on the colors!"

That day the Tenth Cavalry would lose a greater proportion of its officers than any regiment in the battle—eleven out of twenty-two. But Roosevelt found little to fault in any of the officers he encountered as he prodded Texas through the lines. They cajoled and exhorted the troopers lying on the ground to rise and fight: "walking to and fro . . . the officers of the white and colored regiments alike took the greatest pride in seeing that the men more than did their duty; and the mortality among them was great."

Yet he found one officer, a captain in command of the rear platoons, who insisted that orders were orders and his were to keep his men where they were. Roosevelt expressed his judgment that the only way to take the hills was to rush them.

The elderly captain replied that he could not charge without orders and that his colonel was not around to change them.

"Then I am the ranking officer here," declared Lieutenant Colonel Roosevelt, "and I give the order to charge."

The captain hesitated.

Roosevelt demanded, "Then let my men through, sir!"

As he whipped off his hat with its blue and white polka-dot scarf and yelled at his men to charge the hill on their right, grinning Rough Riders surged behind him. But while they moved ahead, Roosevelt recalled with pride, "It proved too much for the regulars, and they jumped up and came along, their officers and troops mingling with mine, all being delighted at the chance."

Suddenly, there seemed to be movement everywhere. As Roosevelt saw it, "The whole line, tired of waiting and eager to close with the enemy, was straining to go forward."

As the forces "slipped the leash at almost the same moment" (although Roosevelt did not know it at the time), an astonished Richard Harding Davis looked at how few of them there were and noted, "One's instinct was to call them back. You felt that someone had blundered and that these few men were blindly following some madman's mad order."

Stephen Crane heard someone shout, "By God, there go our boys up the hill."

The British military attaché, Captain Arthur Lee, one more old friend whom Roosevelt had brought along, slapped Crane on the back. "It's plucky, you know! By Gawd it is plucky," he exclaimed. "But they can't do it."

Crane listened to what seemed to be the "noise of a million champagne corks." He would write of that moment of blazing guns and charging soldiers, "Yes, they were going up the hill. It was the best moment of anybody's life."

Theodore Roosevelt would evermore call it "my crowded hour."

It began with "all in the spirit of the thing and greatly excited by the charge, the men cheering and running forward between shots," while Roosevelt galloped Texas toward the hill and up and out of the sunken lane onto the slope.

Only his new orderly, Henry Bardshar, outpaced him. He rushed ahead "in order to get better shots at the Spaniards" and fired the only shots by Rough Riders other than himself that Roosevelt actually observed hitting Spaniards in open combat. (He had seen two Spaniards fall dead from trees during the Las Guasimas fight.)

Closely behind Roosevelt up Kettle Hill came Dudley Dean and a band of Arizonans, but almost immediately afterward the hill was swarmed with Rough Riders, the troopers of the Ninth, and a scattering of men from the First Cavalry. Rushing forward among the latter was Sergeant Charles Karsten. Hit by shrapnel, he continued on the line, firing until his arm went numb, then refused to go to the rear. Instead, he devoted himself to taking care of the other wounded, "utterly unmoved by the heavy fire." A wounded trooper, Hugh Brittain, carried his regimental standard forward, waving it to cheer on his comrades.

Some forty yards from the top of Kettle Hill, Roosevelt and Texas reached a wire fence. Both had been nicked by bullets, one of which had grazed Roosevelt's arm. Jumping from the saddle, he let Texas loose. Expecting never to see the horse again, he wriggled through the fence while bullets flew around him, sounding "like the ripping of a silk dress."

Brandishing the revolver that his brother-in-law, Commander Cowles, had salvaged from the *Maine,* he aimed ten yards ahead and dropped a Spaniard "neatly as a jackrabbit."

A breathless second later, he and Henry Bardshar reached the crest of the hill. Almost immediately, the Rough Riders and the Ninth's troops swarmed around them.

Still down the hill, having sprawled flat on his stomach to duck bullets, Frederic Remington noted a sudden quiet, lifted his head, and gazed upward. In that instant, as the yellow flags of the guidons unfurled, he heard a thrilling noise.

" 'Cheer' is the word for that sound," he wrote. "You have got to hear it once when it means so much, and ever after you will grin when Americans make that noise."

Roosevelt wrote in *The Rough Riders,* "There was the usual confusion, and afterward there was much discussion as to exactly who had been on the hill first. The first guidons planted there were those of the three New Mexican troops, G, E, and F, of my regiment, under the Captains, Llewellen, Luna, and Muller, but on the extreme right of the hill, at the opposite end where we struck it, Captains Taylor and McBain and their men of the Ninth were first up. Each of the five captains was firm in the belief that his troop was first up. As for the individual men, each of whom honestly thought he was the first on the summit, their name is legion."

American history assigned the glory to only one.

Chapter 32

They Can't Kill Him

No sooner were Americans on the crest of Kettle Hill than a burst of rifle fire from entrenched Spaniards sent them scurrying for cover behind the huge abandoned sugar-cooker. Simultaneously, cannons sent rounds with time fuses hurtling at them to explode overhead. Also in enemy range were troops still advancing up the hill toward the most prominent feature on the heights, a blockhouse surrounded by Spaniard-infested trenches. It stood at the crest of another knoll, separated from Kettle Hill by a shallow valley offering scant cover.

Recalling the panorama of battle he witnessed from Kettle Hill, Roosevelt wrote in his autobiography that his thoughts turned to Alfred Thayer Mahan's account of Britain's Lord Nelson. "Memory plays funny tricks in such a fight," he noted as he remembered that the hero of Trafalgar had a standing order that as each of his ships sailed forward, if it found another ship engaged in a fight with the enemy, it should rake the foe with cannon fire while it passed. How the cowboy cavalry followed the British admiral's dictum and thus came to the aid of Americans still struggling up the San Juan Heights was set down by Roosevelt in *The Rough Riders:*

> Obviously the proper thing to do was to help them, and I got the men together and started them volley-firing against the Spaniards in the blockhouse and the trenches around it. We could only see their heads; of course this was all we ever could see when we were firing at them in their trenches. . . . We kept up a brisk fire for some five or ten minutes; meanwhile we were much cut up ourselves. . . . The infantry got nearer and nearer the crest of the hill. At last we could see the Spaniards running from the rifle-pits as the Americans came on in their final rush.

Fearing that his men might accidentally wound the advancing Americans, he shouted for firing to cease. Pointing toward the trenches, he yelled, "Charge!"

Clearing a wire fence with a single bound, he was confident that his Rough Riders and a contingent of troopers racing after him would promptly silence the rifles in the trenches. But a hundred yards from the enemy, with bullets zinging through the air and ripping up the grass, he looked around and realized with shock that only five men had followed him. A moment later Spanish gunfire reduced the number by two when Winslow Clark and Clay Green were wounded. Recognizing the futility of only four men attacking trenches brimming with Spaniards, he told the three able-bodied men to keep in place while he dashed back to bring up the rest of the brigade.

"This was a decidedly cool request, for there was no possible point in letting them stay there while I went back," he confessed in *The Rough Riders,* "but at that moment it seemed perfectly natural to me, and apparently so for them, for they cheerfully nodded, and sat down in the grass, firing back at the line of trenches from which the Spaniards were shooting at them."

Running back and scaling the wire fence again, he went up to the crest of Kettle Hill, "filled with anger" against the troops; especially the Rough Riders.

The words used when he reached them were not memorialized in his memoirs. *The Rough Riders* records only that he "taunted them bitterly" and that on their faces was "the look of injury and surprise."

They protested, "We didn't hear you, we didn't see you go, Colonel; lead on now, we'll sure follow you."

The account in *The Rough Riders* continued with a charming measure of understatement: "I wanted the other regiments to come too, so I ran down to where General Sumner was and asked him if I might make the charge; and he told me to go and that he would see that the men followed. By this time everybody had his attention attracted."

Among the astonished onlookers was Captain Robert L. Howze. He had witnessed the first charge, when Roosevelt had "under a galling fire . . . jumped through the fence and by his enthusiasm and courage succeeded in leading to the crest of the hill a line sufficiently strong to capture it." Now he was watching another charge.

But daring and enthusiasm could not compensate for short legs. Roosevelt found himself outstripped by the long-legged Lieutenant

John Greenway, Trooper Hedrick Ben Goodrich, and sharpshooter William A. Proffit.

Keeping pace with Roosevelt as he had done during the first charge of the crowded hour, Henry Bardshar was "running up at the double" when two Spaniards popped up from a trench less than ten yards away.

As they turned to run, Roosevelt closed in and fired twice with the pistol from the *Maine*, killing one fleeing foe.

Supposing "my feat to be unique," he learned "weeks after" that "not very far from me" a first sergeant, Clarence Gould of the First Cavalry, also had employed a revolver to kill a Spanish soldier just as the Spaniard aimed at a Rough Rider. The Roosevelt reaction in learning that his deed had not been a singular one (as recorded in *The Rough Riders*) was that "it is astonishing what a limited area of vision and experience one has in the hurly-burly of a battle."

There *was* a great deal of confusion. Regiments had become intermingled. White and black regulars raced toward the trenches with Rough Riders so that Roosevelt's "mixed lot" advanced under heavy fire from Kettle Hill, through a line of palm trees in the valley, and up to the chain of hills to assault the dug-in Spanish troops. While many fled and a handful surrendered, the bodies of scores of men in the blue and white of the Spanish regular army filled the trenches.

"Most of the fallen had little holes in their heads from which their brains were oozing," Roosevelt noted, "for they were covered from the neck down by the trenches."

He found few wounded.

As Roosevelt re-formed his troops, Captain Howze rode up with orders for them to halt and "hold the hill at all hazards."

To do so, Roosevelt, being the highest ranking officer, had under him fragments of six cavalry regiments. Because they had taken a gently rounded and grassy hilltop that afforded a poor cover, he ordered them to "lie down on the hither slope." Yet even flat on their faces they were subject to the Mauser bullets, shells, and shrapnel sweeping over the hill and reaping a toll.

At this time Roosevelt noticed that a few African-American soldiers "began to get a little uneasy and drift to the rear," either to help wounded men or claiming that they wished to find their own regiments. "This I could not allow," he wrote, "as it was depleting my line."

Jumping up and walking a few yards to the rear, he drew his revolver. Halting them, he said he appreciated the gallantry with which they had performed, but he would not hesitate to shoot the first man who, on any pretense whatever, went to the rear.

"Now, I shall be very sorry to hurt you," he said, "and you don't know whether or not I will keep my word, but my men can tell you that I always do."

The former cowboys, hunters, and miners of the Rough Riders nodded their agreement, saying, "He always does; he always does." Roosevelt thought the scene was like something out of a comic opera.

Continuing the anecdote in *The Rough Riders,* Roosevelt penned a passage that reflects accurately, if badly, on him and the era he seemed to personify. He wrote, "This was the end of the trouble, for the 'smoked Yankees'—as the Spaniards called the colored soldiers—flashed their white teeth at one another, as they broke into broad grins, and I had no more trouble with them, they seeming to accept me as one of their own officers. The colored cavalrymen had already so accepted me; in return, the Rough Riders, although for the most part Southwesterners, who have a strong color prejudice, grew to accept them with hearty good-will as comrades, and were entirely willing, in their phrase, 'to drink out of the same canteen.' "

He went on to state that "a peculiar meed of praise should be given to the officers of the Ninth and Tenth for their work, and under their leadership the colored troops did as well as any soldiers could possibly do."

Of course, the officers he referred to were white. He felt that the black troops were "peculiarly dependent" on them. And he wrote, "Occasionally they produced non-commissioned officers who can take the initiative and accept responsibility precisely like the best class of whites; but this cannot be expected normally, nor is it fair to expect it. . . . Whereas, with the white regulars, as with my own Rough Riders, experience showed that the non-commissioned officers could usually carry on the fight by themselves if they were once started, no matter whether their officers were killed or not."

Colonel Roosevelt of the Rough Riders remained at heart a social Darwinist.

Concerning the fighting abilities of the enemy facing him on San Juan Hill, he had only contempt. When Spanish forces made an offensive movement following his second charge, he dismissed their action. "It could not be called a charge," he said, because it was "not pushed home, but was stopped almost as soon as it began, our men immediately running forward to the crest of the hill with shouts of delight at seeing their enemies at last came into the open. A few seconds' firing stopped their advance and drove them into the cover of the trenches."

He believed that no possible number of Spaniards coming at his men from in front could have driven the Rough Riders from the hill, and "there was not a man on the crest who did not eagerly and devoutly hope that their opponents would make the attempt, for it would surely have been followed, not merely by a repulse, but our immediately taking the city."

As night fell and the firing gradually died away, some men made their way back to the buildings on Kettle Hill to forage for food. Fourteen hours had passed since they had had a meal. What they found was even more exciting than the beans Roosevelt had commandeered from the beachfront commissary. In one of the buildings, they discovered the Spanish officers' mess with dinner still on the stoves. Large iron pots contained beef stew and boiled rice. There was a supply of salt fish, small cans of preserves, loaves of rice bread, and a demijohn of rum. Divided among the many, the windfall did not provide much per man. But, in Roosevelt's words, "it freshened us all."

Soon after dark General Wheeler was feeling well enough to visit the front and squelch a rumor making the rounds that there was to be a withdrawal from the hard-gained territory. He ordered the forces to entrench. Presently, the Rough Riders who rushed up Kettle Hill behind Roosevelt and then followed him in the assault on the ridge trenches were rejoined by those whom the fortunes of war had left behind. For the digging in, the troopers benefitted from another find. During the afternoon, Lieutenant Greenway had taken it upon himself to do some exploring and had run across a trove of Spanish entrenching tools, picks, and shovels.

During the lull in the fighting, Trooper Warren Crockett, a former revenue officer from Marietta, Georgia, had also gone reconnoitering and turned up a supply of coffee. Being slightly built and not very strong physically, he proposed to Roosevelt that he be excused from digging and permitted to brew the find. Roosevelt approved, and the coffee was "much appreciated" by all.

The end of battle and onset of night gave Roosevelt time to reckon the cost of his crowded hour. One who had died was Major Albert Forse, a noted soldier in the Indian Wars who had served with the First Cavalry.

The night also let him reflect on a Sergeant Greenly, who had hit the ground to avoid a Spanish volley and found himself lying beside Roosevelt. After a moment he had whispered, "Beg pardon, Colonel; I've been hit in the leg."

Roosevelt had asked, "Badly?"

"Yes, Colonel. Quite badly."

One of Greenly's comrades helped him "fix up his leg with a first-aid-to-the-injured bandage" and "he limped off toward the rear."

But not all the wounded sought to leave the field. Thirteen of the injured kept fighting until the end of the day. Among them were the Wallers (who were unrelated). John, a cowpoke from New Mexico who served as a wagoner in Troop A, was shot in the arm and left with paralyzed fingers. Edward, a champion Yale high diver from Chicago assigned to Troop E, suffered a grazed scalp. Both had deferred treatment and bandaging until nightfall ended the fighting.

Corporal G. Roland "Ben" Fortesque of New York was hit in the foot, a fact not realized by his old friend until Roosevelt noticed him "making wry faces" as he pulled off a bloody boot.

One who was forced to the rear but returned to the front was Captain Llewellen. A large, heavy man with a son in the ranks, he had started the day not feeling well but remained in command of Troop G throughout the day until he fell from exhaustion, wrenching his back. In excruciating pain on the morning after the ridge had been taken, he had to be ordered to a field hospital. Another was Lieutenant William C. Day (eventually promoted to the command of Troop L). Hit in the shoulder by a Mauser bullet on the summit of Kettle Hill and also forced to the rear, he refused to return to the United States and rejoined his troop before the wound had healed.

There would be more action the next morning. At the break of dawn, the Spanish cannons opened fire again. One of the artillery shells burst near a tree where Roosevelt had set up headquarters. When Roosevelt stood up and dusted himself off, unscathed, Ben Ferguson gazed in amazement and muttered, "I really believe now they can't kill him."

By Roosevelt's accounting, out of the 490 Rough Riders who had marched into the battle for the San Juan Heights, 89 had been killed or wounded, the heaviest loss suffered by any regiment in the cavalry division. He credited the Spaniards with having put up a stiff fight, "standing firm until we charged," and fighting much more stubbornly than at Las Guasimas.

That the Rough Riders had suffered more heavily than their opponents was a point of pride for Roosevelt; he attributed it to the fact that his men had done the charging.

But everyone who had witnessed both charges agreed that they had occurred only because of the man who had led them. Captain C. J. Stevens, whose Second Cavalry had been targeted by the firing from the trenches and thus motivated the second charge, asserted, "By his gallantry and strong personality he contributed most materially to the success of the charge of the Cavalry Division up San Juan Hill." Major M. J. Jenkins of the First Cavalry felt that "unhesitating gallantry in taking the initiative against intrenchments lined by men armed with rapid fire guns certainly won him the highest consideration and admiration of all who witnessed his conduct throughout the day."

Half a year after the two charges, General Sumner, whose men had been kept from reinforcing the assault against the San Juan Heights because of unexpected resistance at El Caney, recommended, "as a reward for conspicuous gallantry at the battle of San Juan," that Roosevelt be presented the Congressional Medal of Honor.

But, surely, the praise that had to mean the most to Theodore Roosevelt was this:

Colonel Roosevelt . . . led a very desperate and extremely gallant charge on San Juan Hill, thereby setting a splendid example to the troops and encouraging them to pass over the open country intervening between their position and the trenches of the enemy. In leading this charge, he started off first, as he supposed, with quite a following of men, but soon discovered that he was alone. He then returned and gathered up a few men and led them to the charge . . . an extremely gallant one, and the example set a most inspiring one to the troops in that part of the line [and] had a very encouraging effect and had great weight in bringing up the troops behind him.

A recommendation to Secretary of War Alger that Roosevelt be presented the Medal of Honor, it was signed by Leonard Wood.

Part VII

Crackerjacks

Chapter 33

Triumph Tasted

At one o'clock in the afternoon, July 1, 1898, as Edith Carow Roosevelt sat down for lunch with the children at Sagamore Hill, her husband was on his way to glory on Kettle Hill. Although the next day's newspapers were filled with accounts of the heroic deeds, it was a note from friend Bob Ferguson that couched it in personal terms:

Dear Mrs. Theodore
    . . . No hunting trip has ever equalled it in Theodore's eyes . . . all the way down to the next line of entrenchments he encouraged us to "look at these damned Spanish dead!" . . . Some of the men insist on his taking shelter sometimes, and he is becoming more amenable to discipline.

An urgent need for shelter for his men had impressed itself upon Roosevelt immediately after the shrapnel shell had blasted his open-air headquarters. Recognizing that "we had better settle down to solid siege work," troops who were not in trenches were dispersed toward the rear into the shelter of a valley. Then came the work of improving the entrenchments by constructing traverses that would allow the men to move between them and remain safe from the Spanish gunners, who were close by and equally well dug in.

While no one on the firing line believed the Spaniards had the capacity to break out, neither did anyone hold out the prospect of success in rushing the heavy earthworks and wire defenses of the Spanish line. It was a standoff—a foreshadowing of the prolonged trench warfare of World War I—with firing continuing all day long between opposing armies lying within sight of one another. Roosevelt estimated American strength at about eleven thousand, and Spanish at about nine thousand.

From time to time he ordered use of the dynamite gun and found that while it made "a terrific explosion," it "did not seem to go accurately." Nor was he impressed by the Colt automatics that had been detailed to the command of William Tiffany. In the absence of mules, the weapons proved too heavy for men to haul any distance. Even worse, the guns could not handle the standard Krag ammunition. Fortunately, they did take Mauser cartridges. These had been left behind in abundance by the retreating Spaniards.

As they settled in, the Rough Riders got a new official name. The regiment became the Eleventh United States Horse. Roosevelt felt it was deserved "by our conduct, not only in fighting and in marching, but in guarding the trenches and in policing camp."

He proudly wrote, "In less than sixty days the regiment had been raised, organized, armed, equipped, drilled, mounted, dismounted, kept for a fortnight on transports, and put through two victorious aggressive fights in very difficult country, the loss in killed and wounded amounting to a quarter of those engaged. This is a record which it is not easy to match in the history of the volunteer organizations. The loss was but small compared to that which befell hundreds of regiments in some of the great battles of the Civil War; but it may be doubted whether there was any regiment which made such a record during the first months of any of our wars."

Roosevelt made no allusion to the Battle of Gettysburg, but it seems reasonable to presume that the historian in him did not fail to realize that he had twice led daring charges on the thirty-fifth anniversary of that pivotal engagement of the Civil War. Nor is it likely he was unaware that detailed accounts of the charges would fill the newspapers of the nation on the Fourth of July.

On that date so dear to his patriotic heart, Roosevelt addressed to Leonard Wood his own almost hour-by-hour summation of how well Wood's Weary Walkers had comported themselves on July 1 and 2. Though the report began with the words "with myself in command," it was crowded with the names of men "who showed signal valor," from Captains Llewellen, Muller, and Luna to a roster of troopers covering the alphabet from Allerton to Waller. But he could not leave out a few gripes. He pointed out that while they continued to hold the ground, "the food has been short; and until today we could not get our blankets, coats or shelter tents, while the men lay all day under the fire from the Spanish batteries, intrenchments, and guerrillas in trees, and worked all night in the trenches, never even taking off their shoes."

Richard Harding Davis believed that the Americans on the San Juan Heights were hanging on "by their teeth and fingernails, and it seemed as though at any moment their hold would relax and they would fall."

Yet relief lay only four and a half miles offshore. It took the form of the big guns of Sampson's warships. In the opinion of Captain French Chadwick, commander of Sampson's flagship, a relentless barrage on Spanish fortifications in and around Santiago would so demoralize the Spanish forces that "the American troops could [enter] the city at once and with little or no difficulty."

Why did they not open fire?

The decision rested with Sampson and General Shafter, who was racked not only by his gout and a fever but by the sickening reality of the casualties. With more than two hundred dead and almost twelve hundred men wounded, Shafter's effective fighting force had been reduced by a tenth, and he had no stomach to accept more. The army had done its duty. He believed it was up to Sampson's navy to force the surrender of Santiago by finishing off the trapped Spanish fleet in the harbor. He messaged the admiral: "I urge that you make effort immediately to force the entrance, to avoid future losses among my men, which are already very heavy. You can now operate with less loss of life than I can."

Sampson had shot back, "Impossible to force entrance until we can clear channel of mines—a work of some time after forts are taken possession by your troops."

The general retorted, "I am at a loss to see why the Navy can not work under a destructive fire as well as the Army," and he called for a meeting with his division commanders for a discussion of the options available, absent the help of the navy. They convened at El Pozo, with Shafter reclining his great bulk on a door that had been removed from a nearby farmhouse.

The situation, he said to Wheeler, Kent, Lawton, and John C. Bates, was bleak. If Spanish forces at Manzanillo reinforced the Santiago garrison, a Spanish counterattack might drive the forces off San Juan Heights. Supply lines to Siboney were vulnerable. Malaria was beginning to take a toll among the troops. Even the weather was against them, in the form of torrential rains. There was intense pressure from President McKinley and Secretary of War Alger for a quick victory. What were the options?

Kent called for withdrawal from the heights. The rest voiced opposition. Shafter went along with the majority. For the moment, the troops were to maintain their positions. Meanwhile, Shafter would meet with Sampson in the hope that the admiral might have a change of heart.

Aboard his flagship, the cruiser *New York,* Sampson signaled to the fleet, "Disregard the movement of the commander-in-chief," indicating that while he was ashore for the meeting with Shafter, he would not be relinquishing command to Admiral Schley, his second in command. Because it was Saturday, the ships were preparing for Sunday inspection and religious services, and they had only enough steam to maintain their positions. Running low on coal, the *Massachusetts* had pulled out of line for a short voyage to Guantánamo Bay for replenishment. Its absence and the diversion of the *New York* to convey Sampson to the Siboney meeting reduced the number of blockaders to ten. Among them was the *Iowa,* whose bridge was now commanded by Sampson's successor, Fighting Bob Evans. She lay almost due south of the entrance to the harbor's channel. To *Iowa*'s port was the *Texas.* To the starboard, the *Oregon.* Aboard all, sailors faced a day that promised to be as boring as each of the thirty-five since the blockade had been established. But they were in for a surprise that had begun unfolding nine days earlier.

On June 24 Admiral Pascual Cervera had received a curt reminder from Spain's marine minister, Ramón Aunon, that Cervera's fleet operated under the overall command of the governor-general of Cuba, Ramón Blanco y Enenas. This was the start of increasingly bitter communications between Santiago and Havana regarding the use of Cervera's armada in support of the Spanish land forces. Blanco had urged Cervera to dare a breakout from the harbor to confront the American fleet. The admiral had demurred.

Citing deficiencies in ammunition, guns, coal, and men (many of his sailors had been sent ashore to back up the army in defending the city), Cervera insisted "it is absolutely impossible for [the] squadron to escape under these circumstances." To attempt a sortie, in which the ships would have to sail from the harbor in single file, he argued, would spell their doom.

"I, who am a man without ambitions, without mad passions," he said, "state most emphatically that I shall never be the one to decree the horrible and useless hecatomb which will be the only result of the sortie." It would be far better, he argued, if the ships remained in port to help in the fight to defend the city.

Blanco had replied that it was not a question of fighting "but [of] escaping from that prison in which the squadron is unfortunately shut in." This was especially wounding because Cervera had opposed the sending of the fleet to Cuba in the first place. But Blanco was not through. He warned Cervera, "The eyes of every nation are at present fixed on your squadron, on which the honor of our country depends, as I am sure your excellency realizes."

Cervera's reply sizzled. "I construe your excellency's telegram as an order to go out, and therefore ask . . . for reembarkation of forces which were landed at your excellency's suggestion. I beg that you will confirm the order to sortie."

Blanco responded that "if the fall of Santiago is believed near, the squadron will go out immediately, as best it can."

There the matter had stood until Americans swarmed up the San Juan Heights on July 1. In an order to José Toral, commander of the city's defenders, Blanco authorized the return of Cervera's sailors to their ships. Until the squadron departed, Toral was to maintain the defense of the city at any price.

"Main thing is that squadron go out at once," Blanco said, "for if Americans take possession of it Spain will be morally defeated and must ask for peace at mercy of enemy."

Thus for Spain, the future of Cuba hinged on national pride, as it always had for the Americans who had followed Theodore Roosevelt to war. And now, as Roosevelt had both planned for as assistant secretary of the navy and feared as leader of the Rough Riders, the outcome would rest in the hands of men in command of warships.

Forced to choose between a colonial city and his country's pride as embodied in Cervera's ships, Blanco did not hesitate to come down on the side of the navy. A city could be recovered, he said. The loss of the squadron—and Spain's honor—could not.

Consequently, at sunset on Saturday, July 2, while Roosevelt and his men desperately held on to the San Juan Heights, Lieutenant F. K. Hill, the deck officer of the *Iowa,* pointed out to Captain Evans columns of smoke rising beyond the protective hills of Santiago's harbor. Because the Spanish ships were known to maneuver in the bay, Evans thought nothing of the smoke. At 9:30 on Sunday morning, he learned differently. Again officer of the deck, Hill looked toward the mouth of the harbor's channel and recognized the black, gold-crested

prow of the Spanish gunboat *Alvarado*. A moment later he ordered
the man in charge of semaphore flags to run up Signal 250, and he
personally fired a six-pounder. These actions meant one thing to the
ships of the blockade: "They're coming out."

Five miles away, Admiral Sampson promptly scuttled the meeting
with General Shafter and ordered the *New York* about. "Let us get on
after the fleet," he said. "Not one must get away."

For Theodore Roosevelt and the Rough Riders, the second of July
had worn on, "the fight raging fitfully at intervals" and gradually
dying away. Most of the trouble had come from Spanish guerrillas,
whom Roosevelt credited with showing "great courage, exactly as did
[Spanish] soldiers who were defending the trenches." But he praised
only those guerrillas posted in front of his men, who he felt did "le-
gitimate work." They crept up before dawn and either hid in the thick
jungle or the foliage of trees. This cover and the use of smokeless
powder "betrayed not the slightest sign of their whereabouts and
caused us a great deal of annoyance and some little loss." For those
guerrillas posted in trees toward the rear, he had only contempt, finding them guilty of "wanton cruelty and barbarity" for firing at men
bearing wounded in litters and, despite their Red Cross brassards, at
doctors who came to the front.

To deal with the snipers during daylight, he picked a detail of
sharpshooters—"first-class woodsmen and mountain men"—who felt
"very vindictively toward these guerrillas." During the night he established pickets and outposts in the jungle well to the front, in hopes of
preventing all possibility of surprise. Meanwhile, the work on improving the siege trenches continued, as did his fulminations concerning
the quality of the army's generalship.

Roosevelt was delighted at the promotion of Wood to brigadier
general and hoped that he also might be elevated in rank, especially
because Wood had recommended him for the nation's highest military
decoration. "I think I earned my Colonelcy and medal of honor, and
hope I get them," he wrote to Lodge, "but it doesn't make much difference, for nothing can take away the fact that for the ten great days
of its life I commanded the regiment, and led it victoriously in hard
fought battle."

No military leader ever offered a more heartfelt expression of confidence in the civilian soldiers who followed him than that of Theodore
Roosevelt in his memoir of leading the Rough Riders. He wrote, "They

were natural fighters, men of great intelligence, great courage, great hardihood, and physical prowess; and I could draw on these qualities and upon their spirit of ready, soldierly obedience to make up for any deficiencies in the technique of the trade which they had temporarily adopted."

He admitted to Henry Cabot Lodge that he had not expected to come through. He had come through, and now he was "as strong as a bull moose." Proud and happy, he basked in the companionship of the men he had led. He felt connected as never before to the age-old bond of the hunter and the warrior, exemplified by the hardy souls of the American frontier—cowboys, buffalo hunters, and horse soldiers—about whom he had written in *The Winning of the West;* adventurers who had conquered plains and mountains with guts and guns and then banded together as Rough Riders. In khakis, slouching hat, and polka-dot scarf, he had fulfilled every fantasy of little Teedie Roosevelt and had left behind the sickly boy with the dogeared adventure books and the bedtime stories of wartime prowess and the toy gunboats. Now the man whose valor had been proved on the San Juan Heights and validated by Wood's recommendation for the Medal of Honor could get on with such time that remained of his life and meet whatever challenges fate held in store; that is, once the Spaniards were at last beaten and driven out of the Western Hemisphere for good.

At daybreak on July 3 they again opened fire from the trees and jungle. Grateful that only one of his men had been wounded but "very much annoyed," he made preparations to "fix them" the next day. He decided to send twenty of his best sharpshooters into the jungle between the lines before dawn. Each with a canteen of water and a little food, they were to "spend the day, getting as close to the Spanish lines as possible, moving about with great stealth, and picking off any hostile sharp-shooter, as well as any soldier who [left himself exposed] in the trenches."

But it was not to be. The issue of a Spanish colony on Cuban soil was being settled on water, as Spain's warships came out of the harbor of Santiago in a column—Admiral Cervera's *Infanta Maria Teresa* and the *Vizcaya, Almirante Oquendo, Cristóbol Colón, Pluton,* and *Furor.* Awaiting them were the American blockaders, now in the direct command of Admiral Schley while Sampson's cruiser rushed to reach the impending fray.

Asked by the *Infanta Maria Teresa*'s captain for permission to open fire on seven waiting American ships, Cervera answered with a shrug.

The captain muttered, "Poor Spain."

Not since the sea battles that Roosevelt had painstakingly researched and described in *The Naval War of 1812* had waters of the Western Hemisphere witnessed such a climactic clash as that which unfolded on July 3, 1898. First to be hit by Spanish shells was the cruiser *Brooklyn,* followed by the frantic efforts of the wounded warship's crew to avoid colliding with the battleship *Texas.* Disaster narrowly averted, the *Brooklyn* sped westward in pursuit of the Spanish ships emerging from the channel.

Moments later, the pride of Theodore Roosevelt's steel navy, the battleships *Texas, Oregon,* and *Iowa,* found the range for the *Infanta Maria Teresa* and launched salvo after salvo. Instantly afire and with her guns turned into useless wrecks, she turned toward shore and struck rocks. Three-quarters of an hour after Cervera's bid for the freedom of the high seas, his flagship was a burning, exploding ruin.

The *Almirante Oquendo* soon suffered the same fate.

Then it was the turn of the ship that once had panicked New Yorkers, the *Vizcaya.* Pounded at close range (ironically, by the *Brooklyn*), she managed to cause the only American fatality of the four-hour sea duel. As Chief Yeoman George Ellis attempted to set the range for Admiral Schley's gunners, a *Vizcaya* shell ripped off his head.

As the *Vizcaya* blazed, sailors on the *Texas* broke into cheers. Captain John Philip silenced them with, "Don't cheer boys. Those poor devils are dying."

The last of the armada to go was the newest and fastest ship, the *Cristóbol Colón.* Outsped and outgunned, she, too, headed for the ignominy of the rocks. This was also an irony; the Spanish empire in the New World came to its end on the shores of the Pearl of the Antilles with the destruction of a ship that honored the man who had established that empire: Christopher Columbus.

In the early hours of Monday morning, Admiral Sampson cabled the news of victory to the Navy Department: "The fleet under my command offers the nation as a Fourth of July present the whole of Cervera's fleet."

The previous morning, General Shafter had also sent a message to Washington. He informed Secretary of War Alger, "We have town [Santiago] well invested on the north and east, but with a very thin line." He warned that with Spanish defenses "so strong it will be impossible to carry it by storm with my present force and I am seriously considering withdrawing about five miles and taking up a new position."

After consulting with a desolate McKinley, Alger cabled in reply that Shafter was, of course, best qualified to judge the situation. He went on, "If, however, you can hold your present position, especially San Juan heights, the effect upon the country would be much better than falling back."

Richard Harding Davis had sent his own gloomy report. The situation in the rifle pits on the morning of the third, he said, was most critical. "One smelt disaster in the air."

Always ready to invoke political influence where it counted, Roosevelt assessed the plight of the army and wrote to Lodge in language that, if read by any of Roosevelt's immediate commanders, would mean a court-martial:

> Tell the President for Heaven's sake to send us every regiment and above all every battery possible. We have won so far at heavy cost; but the Spaniards fight very hard and charging these intrenchments against modern rifles is terrible. We are within measureable distance of a terrible military disaster; we *must* have help—thousands of men, batteries, and *food* and ammunition. The other volunteers are at a hideous disadvantage owing to their not having smokeless powder. Our General is poor; he is too unwieldy to get to the front.

Meanwhile, at Shafter's headquarters at Siboney, one of the general's aides, Colonel Edward McClernand, had a suggestion for the gouty and pouting general. "Let us make a demand on them to surrender."

Shafter ruminated a full minute, then said, "Well, try it."

At 8:30 Sunday morning, an hour before the ships of the U.S. Navy sighted Cervera's flagship in the harbor's channel, McClernand drafted the following on behalf of Shafter to General Toral:

> I shall be obliged, unless you surrender, to shell Santiago de Cuba. Please inform the citizens of foreign countries, and all women and children, that they should leave the city before 10 o'clock tomorrow morning.

Toral offered an enticing alternative at a meeting under a flag of truce on July 10. If the Americans were to fire over the city, too high to do any harm, Toral would be justified in evacuating under enemy fire, thereby saving lives on both sides and, incidentally, preserving the honor of Spain. Shafter, with his eyes on the likely carnage that would accompany an assault on the city and keenly aware of mounting numbers of his men felled by malaria, accepted the proposal.

When Roosevelt found out, his scorn for generalship filled a July 10 letter to Lodge that reverted to his naval lexicon to denounce the American commander: "We on the firing line are crazy just at present because Gen. Shafter is tacking and veering as to whether or not he will close with the Spaniards' request to allow them to walk out unmolested. It will be a great misfortune to accept less than unconditional surrender. We can surely get the whole Spanish army now, at the cost of probably not more than a couple days' fighting, chiefly bombardment."

When President McKinley learned of the Shafter-Toral deal, he also was horrified. He told Shafter, "Your message recommending that Spanish troops be permitted to evacuate . . . is a great surprise, and it is not approved."

On Sunday afternoon, July 10, a week after the massacre of the Spanish fleet, navy guns swiveled shoreward and opened fire on the city. The bombardment continued until evening, paused, and resumed Monday. It lasted until 1:00 P.M.

Then came silence and, as both sides considered what to do next, an uneasy, unspoken kind of truce took hold.

Roosevelt viewed the lull as "merely a further cessation of hostilities by tacit agreement" and kept his troops "equally vigilant, especially at night." Meeting his officers while inspecting their lines, he sat and talked with them and wondered what shape the outcome of the siege would take. He felt confident that Santiago would be captured, but he wasn't sure exactly how. Failure to establish any depot for provisions on the fighting line, where there was rarely more than a days' worth of food, made the risk very serious. Should a hurricane strike the transports, "scattering them to the four winds," or if three days of heavy rain broke up the lines of supply, starvation would be certain. Regarding an attack on the city, he foresaw the loss of a quarter of the men, and he hoped the order to attack would not be needed. Meanwhile, he and his men could only sit and wait.

"Each day we expected either to see the city surrender, or be told to begin fighting again," he wrote, "and toward the end it grew so irksome that we would have welcomed even an assault in preference to further inaction."

His old friend from the Dakota badlands, Fred Herrig, was especially frustrated. An Alsatian, he spoke with a heavy accent that turned "gun detail" into "GON-detel" and "guerrillas" into "gorillas." Inasmuch as the gorillas were now forbidden game, he asked Roosevelt, might he be allowed to go after guinea hens instead?

Roosevelt gave permission to him and another sharpshooter, with the result that several wild fowl were harvested. All were provided to men who had fallen ill with fever and were being cared for in a makeshift hospital set up by Dr. Church. Looking in on the stricken, Roosevelt found it pitiful to find them lying on their blankets, if they had any, or in the mud, with nothing to eat but hardtack and pork. Among them was Captain Llewellen, whom Roosevelt feared would die if he were not sent to a hospital in the rear. Despite Llewellen's protests, he was transferred. (He survived and was still in command of Troop G when the Rough Riders were mustered out of Cuba.)

An aspect of the uneasy truce that Roosevelt welcomed was the opportunity it afforded to spend time with various visiting military attachés and foreign observers. He especially enjoyed being able to spend time with Richard Harding Davis (by now regarded as a kind of public relations man for the Rough Riders).

Shortly after midday on July 10 when the fighting began again, it became evident to Roosevelt that the enemy troops did not have much heart in it. The next day the regiment was shifted to guard the El Caney road, long-since pacified. As the men settled down and Roosevelt organized his tent, the worst storm of their Cuban experience ripped through the camp. When a gust blew down his tent, Roosevelt, who had completely undressed for the first time since the landing at Daiquirí, groped blindly in the darkness for his clothes. At last finding them in a muddy puddle, he made his way to the kitchen tent. There, "good Holderman, the Cherokee," wrapped him in dry blankets and made a bed for him on a table that had been liberated from an abandoned house.

Encamped by the road to El Caney, the commander of the Rough Riders faced a new problem. The fighting had made thousands of women, children, elderly persons, and other noncombatants into refugees. Most were peasants, but he found "not a few of the best families" among them. Although low on rations themselves, the troops shared what they had until Roosevelt felt "duty bound to keep my own regiment at the highest pitch of fighting efficiency" and ordered them to "insist that the refugees should go to headquarters."

Three days after the move to El Caney, another meeting took place under a flag of truce between Shafter, General Nelson Miles (recently arrived), and General Toral. The Americans came to the talks with an unequivocal message from McKinley and Alger to the Spanish commander: "The way to surrender is to surrender."

In the agreement to end the hostilities, *surrender* became *capitulation*. A ceremony for the signing of papers ending the war was slated for Sunday, July 17, in Santiago's central plaza.

With the city securely in American hands, Roosevelt sent in a detail of six Rough Riders with a pack train and his own money to buy whatever "simple delicacies" they might lay their hands on to augment the meager rations in camp.

On July 19, peace afforded him the luxury of writing letters without the expectation of being fired upon. By far the longest went in reply to one from Lodge:

> I was, naturally, deeply touched, old man, by the whole tone of your note and especially by your thinking now that I was justified in coming. Somehow or other I always knew that if I did not go I never would forgive myself; and I really have been of use, I do not want to be vain, but I do not think that anybody else could have handled this regiment quite as I have handled it during the last three weeks and during those weeks it has done as well as any of the regular regiments, and indeed, frankly, I think it has done better than any of the regulars with the exception of one or two of the best regular regiments.

Along with the self-congratulations went a large measure of criticism of the war effort and how it could have been better handled. The fight was over in "a big triumph," so there was no use in washing dirty linen, he said, but ever the strenuous advocate of American readiness, he cautioned, "We ought to profit by our bitter experiences in the next expeditions."

To brother-in-law Douglas Robinson he sent thanks for a box of medicines and underclothes ("just what I needed") and a request that Douglas find out if an extra pair of breeches and a set of gaiters had been sent to Tampa and, if so, whether they could be forwarded to

Cuba. Personal comfort aside, he felt a need for introspection. "Whatever comes, I cannot say how glad I am to have been in this—I feel I now leave the children a memory that will partly offset the fact that I do not leave them much money."

The past three weeks with the regiment of Rough Riders, he said, were "the crowning weeks" of his life. "There is nothing I would have exchanged for having led it on horseback."

A note to "Darling Corinne" said simply, "Triumph tasted."

Chapter 34

Clear Skirts

When the news of the destruction of Admiral Cervera's Cuban armada reached Spain, the immediate reaction of stunned government ministers was to flash an urgent message to Admiral Manuel de la Cámara at Suez. It ordered him to return to the Spanish coast to guard against a possible attack by the U.S. Navy. This had brought welcome relief to the man Theodore Roosevelt had picked to handle the show in the Pacific. Though Admiral George Dewey had smashed the Spanish squadron in Manila Bay in May, he had not yet managed to capture the city.

The problem was not that Spanish defenders stood in his way. It was the arrival of warships flying the flag of Germany. Helmed by Vice-Admiral Otto von Diedrichs, Emperor William II's Asiatic fleet had been ordered to keep the Americans from taking islands that the Kaiser wished to add to his small but treasured list of colonies. Secret negotiations with Madrid to accomplish this grand scheme had been on the verge of consummation at the very moment that Dewey's warships wreaked havoc on Admiral Montojo's armada in Manila Bay.

With the arrival of Germany's men-of-war and an ostentatious demonstration of the Kaiser's intention to ally the gunboats with the Spaniards in Manila, a tense standoff developed in which American and German ships faced each other while German experts helped improve the Spanish defenses on land and set about establishing a German base at the tip of Bataan Peninsula. Had Cámara's squadron continued through the Suez Canal and onward to the Philippines, Dewey's position would have become untenable.

The recall of Cámara also set Admiral William Sampson's mind at ease. Ships that might have been stripped from his command to sail to the Spanish coast were now available to him in the next phase of American strategy to drive Spain from the Western Hemisphere, the capture of Puerto Rico. This enterprise had considerable appeal to Roosevelt. Again and again in letters to his friends and allies, he had spoken of the necessity of taking "Porto Rico."

Restless and unhappily encamped at El Caney, he anticipated receiving that prize for his battle-seasoned Rough Riders. Seeing them idle rankled him. In any army, it is a challenge to maintain discipline in a regiment with nothing to do. With men who had come primarily from the unbridled, footloose-and-fancy-free frontier and who prided themselves in the name Rough Riders, keeping order was even more of a task. Yet, men who were not used to being told to do something they did not want to do had learned to accept being ordered around, so long as the reason for the order was explained. And as long as they had work to do.

"It was a regiment which was sensitive about its dignity and was very keenly alive to justice and to courtesy," Roosevelt said in his autobiography, "but [the men] cordially approved absence of mollycoddling, insistence of performance of duty, and summary punishment of wrong-doing."

Sometimes the acceptance of an order proved hard, as in the case of John C. "Jack" Greenway. In the fighting at San Juan, he had taken a prisoner. Shortly afterward Roosevelt discovered him leading his captive with a string. He commanded Greenway to turn the man over to guards who were escorting other prisoners to the rear. With a look of astonishment and in a plaintive tone, Greenway blurted, "Why, Colonel, can't I keep him for myself?"

With evident amusement and perhaps more than a little sympathy for this trace of some ancient warrior ancestor in Greenway's soul, Roosevelt wrote, "I think he had an idea that as a trophy of his bow and spear the Spaniard would make a fine body servant."

Soon after making camp at El Caney, Greenway came down with malarial fever. His case was typical. For a few days the victim would be very sick. Apparently recovered, he was able to go back to work, only to be felled again. Although those on the sick list never exceeded 20 percent at one time, Roosevelt rarely had more than half the regiment fit for duty. Lithe college athletes had lost the spring in their step, and leathery cowhands and hunters lay listlessly in dog-tents that became steaming morasses in torrential rains and ovens when the sun blazed down.

One who was stricken and recovered was Henry Bardshar. The malady left Roosevelt's gallant companion eighty pounds lighter and "a mere walking skeleton."

Although the camping site was "a most beautiful spot beside a stream of clear water," Roosevelt found that "no ground in the neighborhood was healthy."

Because there were only a dozen ambulances for the entire army and because he was concerned about the bad conditions in the large rear hospitals, Roosevelt and Dr. Church agreed that the sick should be kept in the regiment's field infirmary. Meanwhile, he did all he could to obtain proper medicines and decent food. Details dispatched into Santiago and Siboney with Roosevelt's own money scrounged to find rice, flour, cornmeal, oatmeal, condensed milk, potatoes, and canned vegetables. Other supplies were pried loose from the commissary. Some came by way of direct appeals to Clara Barton's Red Cross.

To carry these goods, the regiment acquired carts, mules, and horses in every way available. One victim who had lost a horse to marauding Rough Riders warned another officer that if he ever found himself in the Rough Riders' vicinity, he would be wise not to dismount.

Amazingly, as Roosevelt worked without end to make his men as comfortable and healthy as possible, he found himself somehow immune to the illness. After observing him, Stephen Crane, who could never be counted in the ranks of Roosevelt admirers, wrote, "This fellow worked for his troopers like a cider press. He tried to feed them. He helped build latrines. He cursed the quartermasters and the— 'dogs'—on the transports to get quinine and grub for them."

Keenly aware that back in the States there was among savvy political bosses a growing excitement at the prospect of running Roosevelt for office, perhaps for governor of New York as soon as the November election, Crane continued, "Let him be a politician if he likes. He was a gentleman down there."

The possibility that Roosevelt's future might hold a return to politics had caught his wife's attention in the form of a mid-July letter to the editor of the New York *Sun*. It had been signed by three Democrats who recommended that the people of New York wrest political power from the party machines and demand the nomination of Roosevelt for governor. But whatever joy Edith felt on the matter was eclipsed by the death on Friday, July 15, of Roosevelt's uncle, James

Roosevelt. She had been fond of Uncle James, but in a letter to Theodore she confessed that she did not dare allow herself to weep. Were she to "once break down," she wrote to him, "all the longing for you and the terrible suspense and loneliness [will come] over me in a wave that I am helpless against."

Marveling at the endurance of women during the Civil War "who lived through four years of this," she felt relieved that there would be no more battles for Theodore. The only threat to him now was from the epidemic of fever that she read about in each day's newspapers and which her husband described in letters to members of the family, such as one to brother-in-law Douglas Robinson. He wrote, "We have no adequate transportation or hospitals nor a proper supply of food . . . the few delicacies—if beans and tomatoes can be called such—which they have I had to purchase myself."

Of the six hundred troops with whom he had landed, he said, "less than three hundred are left; the others are dead or in the hospital."

To make matters worse, yellow fever also broke out in the rear, primarily among Cubans. Although it never became epidemic, it caused, said Roosevelt, "a perfect panic in the minds of one or two generals and of the home authorities." He soon realized that whenever a man was sent to the rear, he was decreed to have yellow fever. If he was kept at the front, he most likely had malarial fever, and after a few days he was back at work.

The effect of this "absolutely groundless" panic was hesitation by authorities in Washington to bring the army home, out of dread that yellow fever might be imported to the United States.

"Our real foe was not yellow fever at all," Roosevelt wrote, "but malarial fever, which was not infectious, but which was certain, if the troops were left throughout the summer in Cuba, to destroy them, either by killing them outright, or weakening them so that they would have fallen victims to any disease that attacked them."

One tactic in dealing with disease was to have troops shift camp every two or three days. The plan failed. Sick men were incapable of the effort required. The moving from one camp site to another took at least three days. Roosevelt immediately saw that the exertion among the half-sick caused the next day's sick roll to double.

Regarding a proposal that the troops go to the mountains, he recognized that once the men were there, it would be impossible to feed them. "It was all that could be done, with the limited number of wagons and mule-trains on hand, to feed the men in the existing camps, for the travel and rain gradually rendered each road in succession wholly impassable. To have gone up the mountains would have meant early starvation."

A third plan devised by the War Department called for a move of some twenty-five miles to what was called a high interior plateau. It turned out to be sugarcane country, rife with malarial fever. To have sent troops there, Roosevelt railed, would be "simple butchery."

It seemed to him that the only alternative to leaving Cuba altogether (he hoped the destination would be Puerto Rico) was to stay where they were, with the hope that half the men would live to see the cool season. The challenge in this plan was to keep up the men's spirits in a situation affording nothing for them to do. Most were weak and languid. The wet and heat drained energy. An attempt at diversion by climbing the surrounding mountains resulted in half of Roosevelt's climbing party coming down with sickness the next day.

The city they had fought to capture, Santiago, offered very little in the way of either attractions or distractions. Quaint and old, it was "interesting to go in once or twice." One could wander through the narrow streets with curious little shops and low houses of stained stucco, elaborately wrought iron trellises in the windows, and curiously carved balconies. Other sites included the central palace, where there was a fine cathedral; the Café Venus; and the low, bare, rambling Governor's Palace, which had been taken over for the offices and convenience of the staff of the new American military governor, General Leonard Wood.

An adventurer with stamina might go out to the fort that had been the great stumbling block to Admiral Sampson, Morro Castle. Roosevelt went with Fitzhugh Lee as his guide, accompanied by Jack Greenway. Although the fortress proved of some interest, Roosevelt was, of course, fascinated by the blackened hulk of Richard Pearson Hobson's valiant but ill-fated *Merrimac*. Presently, he decided to swim out and explore it.

This was not an undertaking for anyone Lee's age, so he remained on the parapet as Roosevelt and Greenway shed their uniforms and plunged in. No sooner had they begun swimming than Lee began frantically waving his arms and yelling.

As Greenway told the story:

"Can you make out what he's trying to say," the old man asked, punctuating his words with long, overhand strokes.

"Sharks," says I, wishing I were back on shore.

"Sharks," says the colonel, blowing out a mouthful of water, "they" stroke "won't" stroke "bite." Stroke. "I've been" stroke "studying them" stroke "and I never" stroke "heard of one" stroke "bothering a swimmer." Stroke. "It's all" stroke "poppy cock."

Just then a big fellow, probably not more than ten or twelve feet long, but looking as big as a battleship to me, showed up alongside us. Then came another, till we had quite a group. The colonel didn't pay the least attention. . . .

Meantime the old general was doing a war dance up on the parapet, shouting and standing first on one foot and then on the other, and working his arms like he was doing something on a bet.

Finally we reached the wreck and I felt better. The colonel, of course, got busy looking things over. I had to pretend I was interested, but I was thinking of the sharks and getting back to shore. I didn't hurry the colonel on his inspection either.

After a while he had seen enough, and we went over the side again. Soon the sharks were all about us again, sort of pacing us in, as they had paced us out, while the old general did the second part of his war dance. He felt a whole lot better when we landed, and so did I.

Then it was back to the camp, with its disease-ravaged men struggling to survive under the brutal sun of a Cuban July. But there was one moment that must have brought the former assistant secretary of the navy a great deal of personal satisfaction.

On July 25, as the simmering crisis between Admiral Dewey and Germany's Pacific squadron seemed about to boil over, one of Admiral von Diedrichs's officers brought a written demand for Dewey to withdraw two cruisers from the vicinity of German ships. Theodore Roosevelt's unleashed wolfhound snapped his reply to the German courier. "Does Admiral von Diedrichs think he commands here, or do I? Tell your admiral if he wants war I am ready."

The German commander looked to the representative of Britain in Manila, Captain Sir Edward Chichester, hoping to find him an ally in the crisis. Once that appeared unlikely, Diedrichs sought British neutrality. When the question was put directly to Chichester, his reply was enigmatic. "What would I do if there were a conflict between your squadron and Dewey's? Ask Admiral Dewey." But Chichester's response did not remain a riddle for long. Shortly after Diedrichs had posed the question, the band on Chichester's gunboat, *Immortalite*, struck up "The Star-Spangled Banner."

Diedrichs decided that Germany at war with the United States was one thing, but Germany at war with the greatest naval power in the world was quite another.

Six days after Dewey dared the Germans to start a war with the United States, Roosevelt received, in his new role as commander of the Second Brigade, a summons from General Rufus Shafter to a conference of all the division and brigade commanders, to be held at Wood's palace. He traveled into Santiago with Generals Sumner and Wheeler. Upon arrival, he also found line officers of all the chief medical units. Each was a regular, trained to obey without protest, yet they caught him by surprise.

"They were ready to obey still," he recorded in *The Rough Riders*, "but they felt, quite rightly, that it was their duty to protest rather than to see the flower of the United States forces destroyed as the culminating act of a campaign in which the blunders that had been committed had been retrieved only by the valor and splendid soldierly qualities of the officers and enlisted men of the infantry and dismounted cavalry. There was not a dissenting voice; for there could not be. There was but one side of the question."

To plan for continually shifting camp or for moving up into the mountains or for moving to the interior was unacceptable. To convey this consensus, a record of the meeting was to be made in the form of a letter or report. It was to declare that keeping the army at Santiago meant its absolute and objectless ruin. The army had to be recalled from Cuban soil at once.

The difficulty that became apparent immediately was that the regulars did not care to risk their careers by writing such a report. Consequently, Roosevelt volunteered to be the author. He would also draft a letter, endorsing the report, to General Shafter. Only the letter would be circulated, in a round-robin fashion, for the signatures of all of Shafter's field commanders.

With a determination "that my skirts shall be kept clear of this particular form of murder," as Roosevelt would explain in a letter to Lodge, he crammed the report (dated August 3, 1898) with blunt language:

> There is no possible reason for not shipping practically the entire command North at once.
>
> Yellow-fever cases are very few . . . but there have been 1,500 cases of malarial fever. . . .

. . . The whole command is so weakened and shattered as to be ripe for dying like rotten sheep. . . .

If we are kept here it will in all human possibility mean an appalling disaster. . . .

If there were any object in keeping us here, we would face yellow fever with as much indifference as we faced bullets. But there is no object.

As agreed, only Roosevelt's name was affixed.

The letter to Shafter (with the same date) insisted that "this army must be moved at once, or perish." It was duly signed by Kent, Bates, Chaffee, Sumner, Will Ludlow of the First Brigade of the Second Division, Wood, and, lastly, Roosevelt.

Not since the cable to Dewey to "keep full of coal" had he written or done anything so daring and potentially disastrous to his future.

The message to Dewey had garnered him acclaim and gratitude in the War Department. The round-robin letter would set loose a firestorm of official fury and vindictiveness that resulted in a public rebuke and a deeply wounding personal disappointment.

Chapter 35

A Great Time

"I don't want to take it," declared General Rufus Shafter, brushing aside Roosevelt's hand with the written result of the meeting of the generals and medical officers. "Do whatever you wish with it."

Looking on was a correspondent for the Associated Press, who had been invited by Roosevelt to witness the presentation of the round-robin letter, signed by the generals, and the report of the meeting, signed only by Roosevelt.

He again pressed Shafter to accept.

The general shoved the documents toward the AP man. Roosevelt let him take them. The reporter's story, with the complete texts, date-lined "Santiago de Cuba, August 3d" and noting, "delayed in transmission," appeared in newspapers some days later.

One of those finding the story in his daily newspaper was the president of the United States, the constitutional commander in chief of the victorious forces in Cuba. Reading for the first time that these forces were evidently suffering and possibly mutinous did not leave William McKinley in a happy state of mind. Perhaps the only individual in Washington who felt angrier and more embarrassed was his secretary of war.

In his office in the grand Victorian edifice adjacent to the Executive Mansion, Secretary Alger mulled over court-martialing Roosevelt, but on reflection found a more satisfying means to deal with him. A long-standing recipient of letters and memorandums from Roosevelt (beginning even before Roosevelt had come to Washington to help run the Navy), he remembered a particularly bragging message that had come from Roosevelt in Cuba. It had extolled the merits of the Rough Riders and the regulars of the army (written with what Roosevelt later called "much complacency") and stated that each of the regiments was worth "three of the National Guard regiments." Fishing the letter from his files, Alger decided to play tit for tat by sending a reprimanding telegram to Roosevelt and then leaking the letter to the newspapers.

Roosevelt's old nemesis, William Randolph Hearst, in a case of the pot calling the Kettle Hill hero black, howled by way of the *Journal* that Roosevelt exhibited "irresistible self-assertion and egotism" that besmirched "really admirable services in the field." Many other papers took umbrage, as well, and some wondered aloud if the Roosevelt wealth of mouth might have torpedoed the growing public sentiment to seat him in the governor's chair in Albany.

That such an outcome might result also crossed the mind of Theodore Roosevelt. In an appendix to his account of the episode in his autobiography, he wryly suggested, "The publication of the extract from my letter was not calculated to secure the votes of the National Guard if I ever became a candidate for office."

The appendix went on, rather disingenuously, "However, I did not mind the matter much, for I had at the time no idea of being a candidate for anything—while in the campaign [the military one in Cuba] I ate and drank and thought and dreamed regiment and nothing but regiment, until I got the brigade, and then I devoted all my thoughts to handling the brigade. Anyhow, there was nothing I could do about the matter."

He could find consolation, however, in the fact that not all the nation's newspapers followed Hearst's tack. Many rallied to Roosevelt and turned on Alger, accusing the secretary of war of treachery in disclosing the contents of a private letter. So what if Roosevelt bragged about the Rough Riders? Hadn't they been worthy of praise? The *Baltimore American* noted that he had led the regiment "in one of the noblest fights of the century."

Several days later, a perhaps cowed Alger sent Roosevelt the following:

WAR DEPARTMENT,
WASHINGTON,
August 10, 1898.

Dear Col. Roosevelt:

You have been a most gallant officer and in the battle before Santiago showed superbly soldierly qualities. I would rather add to, rather than detract from, the honors you have so fairly won, and I wish you all good things. In a moment of aggravation under great stress of feeling, first because I thought you spoke in a disparaging manner of the volunteers (probably without intent, but because of your great enthusiasm for your own men), and second that I believed your published letter would embarrass the Department I sent you a telegram which with an extract from a private letter of yours I gave to the press. I would gladly recall both if I could, but unable to do that I write you this letter which I hope you will receive in the same friendly spirit in which I send it.

Come and see me at a very early day. No one will welcome you more heartily than I.

Yours very truly,
R. A. Alger.

Roosevelt thought it was "a manly letter" and "paid no more heed to the incident."

Unfortunately for Roosevelt, Alger's assertion that he did not wish to detract from Roosevelt's honors was hardly the truth. He declined to add an endorsement to Leonard Wood's recommendation (supported by Generals Sumner and Young, along with other officers and enlisted men who had been on the San Juan Heights) that Roosevelt get the Congressional Medal of Honor.

Edith later said the denial of the medal was "one of the bitterest disappointments of his life." It would be fifty-six years before a Roosevelt received the nation's highest military decoration, with its blue neck sash and citation for conspicuous gallantry. It was earned in Normandy, France, on D-Day, June 6, 1945, by Theodore Roosevelt Jr. It was awarded posthumously.

That Alger remained resentful of Ted's father may also have been the consequence of the sudden announcement of orders for the immediate withdrawal of the army from Cuba. The decision had been made before Roosevelt's letters became public, but the unexpected disclosure left the public impression that Roosevelt had precipitated the evacuation against Alger's will.

The Rough Riders got orders on August 6 to board the transport *Miami* the next morning. Although General Wheeler was the ranking officer on board, Fighting Joe put Roosevelt in charge of managing and policing the crowded ship (a squadron of the Third Cavalry was also aboard). With the ship barely to sea, trouble surfaced. The captain complained that his stokers and engineers were insubordinate because Roosevelt's Rough Riders had smuggled liquor on board and gotten them drunk.

With clenched teeth, Roosevelt warned that unless the contraband spirits were turned over to him, a search would be conducted and any liquor found would be thrown over the side. But any voluntarily surrendered alcohol would be returned upon debarkation. About seventy flasks were handed over. Twenty others were located and chucked into the sea. Order and discipline were restored among the ship's crew by appointing the Rough Riders to supervise them.

Because Roosevelt was "anxious to keep the men amused, and as the quarters were so crowded that it was out of the question for them to have any physical exercise," the vice of gambling in games of chance was overlooked, so long as no disorder followed.

One man who had been suffering from dysentery died. Wrapped in a hammock and draped with the flag, he was given a burial service by Chaplain Henry Brown. The Third Cavalry's band played a dirge. The flag was removed and the body went, in the phrasing of the historian of a previous American war at sea, "rushing down through the dark water to lie, till the Judgment Day, in the ooze that holds the timbers of so many gallant ships, and the bones of so many fearless adventurers."

Good weather favored the *Miami* as she plowed north, bound for Montauk, New York, at the eastern end of Long Island. To pass the time, the voyagers sat on deck and swapped yarns. Although he had many to spin of his experiences in the Dakota badlands or as a midnight rambler at the head of the police department in New York, Roosevelt preferred to listen to recollections of voyages around Cape Horn, yacht races for the America's Cup, football games famous in the annals of college sport, feats of desperate prowess in Indian Wars, or the breaking up of gangs of outlaws. He drank in, like little Teedie in his mother's lap at storytime, "adventures in hunting big game, in breaking wild horses, in tending great herds of cattle, and in wandering winter and summer among the mountains and across the lonely plains." Even old Fighting Joe Wheeler chipped in with sagas about "the great war, compared with which," Roosevelt wrote, "ours was such a small war—far reaching in their importance though its effects were destined to be."

Indeed so. As the *Miami* sailed peacefully toward the United States, Admiral George Dewey and the ships of the Asiatic Squadron, unimpeded by Admiral von Diedrichs, were engaged in ensuring the powerful presence of the United States in the Pacific. On August 13 he opened the final assault on Manila. Ready to swarm ashore and take the Philippines were eighty-five hundred soldiers under the command of Generals Wesley Merritt, Francis Greene (the friend in whose regiment Roosevelt once hoped to go soldiering), and Arthur MacArthur, whose son, Douglas, would loom large in the lives of Filipinos in an even more momentous future war.

Ironically, Dewey's capture of the Philippines came one day after American diplomats sat at a table with a Spanish delegation in Paris and signed a peace treaty. At the same time, President McKinley and a Spanish envoy signed a protocol in Washington in which Spain agreed to withdraw from Cuba. Spain would also cede to the United States the Philippines, Guam, and Puerto Rico—all in return for $20 million in cash.

What the onlooking rulers of other world empires did not expect was a renewed pledge by the Americans to turn the government of Cuba over to the Cuban people. That condition would take some time to achieve, however, and a portion of the island, priceless Guantánamo Bay, would stay in American possession, along with Guam and Puerto Rico, to provide the kind of defensive assets far from the coastlines of the United States that had been a goal of Alfred Thayer Mahan and his relentless disciple, Theodore Roosevelt, now only hours out from Montauk.

"I am on my way home," he wrote to a friend as the *Miami* steamed ahead on August 14, 1898. "We have had a great time and this is a regiment of crackerjacks—American from start to finish, in the best and fullest sense of the term."

Chapter 36

A Splendid Little War

The *Miami* slipped next to a pier in Montauk's Fort Pond Bay a little after eleven in the morning, August 15, 1898. Waving his campaign hat as he stood next to Fighting Joe Wheeler, Roosevelt scanned the crowd on the dock with binoculars with the same intensity with which he had looked for Spaniards. Out of the noise he heard the yell of someone asking if he was well. Since going to war he had lost twenty pounds, but the answer to the question, shouted back, was that he was "feeling disgracefully well."

After a pause, he added a full-lunged "I've had a bully time and a bully fight. I feel as big and as strong as a bull moose!"

As he bounded down the gangplank with the pistol from the *Maine* belted to his waist, a band blared "Rally Round the Flag" from another war and the timeless anthem of American warriors, "Home, Sweet Home."

Then came the Rough Riders and their mascot. The little dog Cuba appeared none the worse for wear, but to Jacob A. Riis the men seemed to be a worn and tired lot.

"So the army came home, his Rough Riders with it, ragged, sore, famished, enfeebled, with yawning gaps in its ranks, but saved," wrote Roosevelt's old friend from the press shack across from the Mulberry Street police headquarters, "they to tell of his courage and unwearying patience; how in the fight he was always where the bullets flew thickest, until he seemed to them to have a charmed life."

Might that enchantment grace him in politics? Did he even wish to run for office?

Everybody yearned to know.

He confided to John Hay, whom McKinley had just appointed secretary of state, "My Regiment will be mustered out in a few days, and then I shall be footloose. Just at the moment there is a vociferous demand to have me nominated for Governor, but I very gravely question whether it materializes and I haven't the slightest knack of making it materialize."

A man who might possess that knack was Lemuel Ely Quigg, a mentor in matters political who had guided Roosevelt for many years and through numerous shoals inhabited by sharks far more wily and hungry than the ones that scared the wits out of Jack Greenway and Fitzhugh Lee in Santiago. "Can you get out here tomorrow or Friday," Roosevelt telegraphed him. "Would particularly like to talk over matters with you."

Quigg's advice was that while he dealt with the boss of the New York Republicans, Thomas Platt, Roosevelt should keep his mouth shut and wait to see what the courtly Easy Boss had to say about the idea of one day addressing Roosevelt as Governor.

The old man had spent August in "a heap of thinking" about the idea and mulling over a dilemma. The man his political punch had propelled into the governor's mansion in the previous election, Frank Black, normally would be entitled as incumbent to the party's nomination for a second two-year term. Unfortunately, Black had alienated a considerable segment of voters because of his questionable and costly handling of a project to repair the Erie Canal, increasingly called the canal steal. With Black at the top of the GOP's ticket in November, the voters might define the election with the ugliest word in Platt's dictionary—*defeat*.

Consequently, despite his belief that Roosevelt was "a bull in a china shop," Platt decided to travel out to Montauk with hat in hand, hoping the hero of San Juan Hill would take it and toss it into the political ring.

Having bided his time, an uncommonly mum Roosevelt wrote to Lem Quigg, "I have absolutely refused to say anything as you have doubtless seen." Considering the likelihood that if he became a candidate for governor there probably would be a fight with the Black loyalists at the nominating convention, he assured Quigg, "If the organization wants me to go before the convention [to fight for the nomination], I will do it."

The man who had led two charges on the San Juan Heights also counseled Quigg against "uneasiness about my being frightened."

Francis Ellington Leupp, who would publish *The Man Roosevelt* in 1904, was told in a letter from Roosevelt dated September 3, 1898:

"I haven't bothered myself a particle about the nomination, and have no idea whether it will be made or not. In the first place, I would rather have led this regiment than be Governor of New York three times over. In the next place, while on the whole I should like the office of Governor and would not shirk it, the position will be one of such extreme difficulty and I shall have to offend so many good friends of mine, that I should breathe a sigh of relief were it not offered to me."

That Roosevelt would accept the nomination only on his own terms came as no surprise to Platt. The two had been battling one another for many years. Neither one liked or trusted the other. Platt also feared that Albany would prove to be a Roosevelt stepping stone to something grander.

"If he becomes Governor of New York," Platt said, "sooner or later, with his personality, he will have to be President of the United States."

The present bearer of that title, William McKinley, arrived at Montauk, accompanied by Secretary of War Alger, to visit the returned army. They were met at the railroad station by General Shafter. A carriage waited to take them to the sprawling base set up for the mustering out, Camp Wikoff. But as the coach was about to leave, McKinley spotted a familiar figure and exclaimed, "Why, there's Colonel Roosevelt." Then he waved and called out to him, "Colonel, I am glad to see you."

Stepping from the carriage, he cast aside protocol and the courtesies due him as president and commander in chief to hold out a hand to the man he knew to be the most famous and popular figure in America. Clearly caught by surprise by this gesture, Roosevelt struggled to take off his glove. He yanked at it with no effect and finally stuck the tips of its fingers between his formidable teeth. Tightly held and mightily tugged, it slipped off. Pumping the hand, McKinley said, "I'm glad indeed to see you looking so well."

Roosevelt took advantage of the moment to get McKinley to promise that in addition to a general review of all the men of the army that day, he would make a special visit to "my boys."

The next day Roosevelt wrote that McKinley had been "more than cordial," but what concerned him most in the letter to Henry Cabot Lodge was that he found himself "in horrible disfavor with Edith." He was so busy, he said, he had not been able to write more than "fragmentary letters" to her.

Eventually, Edith gathered up fourteen-year-old Alice, Ted, and Kermit for an overnight visit. Roosevelt thrilled the boys by letting them sleep in his tent. Pretty Alice turned the heads of the younger officers.

It was a time for reunions, as well, with men who considered themselves Rough Riders even though they had remained at Tampa throughout the war. Moved up to Camp Wikoff to be mustered out, they brought two of the regiment's mascots who also had been left behind, an eagle and the ill-tempered mountain lion, Josephine. The eagle was let loose to walk the camp streets or wing overhead, always returning. Although the big cat was kept tied up, in part to keep her from making a meal of the bird, she managed one escape and wound up creeping into bed with a sleeping Third Cavalry man. A greatly amused Roosevelt recorded that the trooper "fled into the darkness with yells, much more unnerved than he would have been by the arrival of any number of Spaniards."

No longer deprived, the men lived high. They had milk, eggs, oranges, and all the tobacco they desired. Roosevelt enjoyed the luxury of spare time. Finding himself with two or three hours on his hands, he summoned Woodbury Kane, Jack Greenway, and other officers to "gallop down to the beach and bathe in the surf, or else go for long rides over the beautiful rolling plains."

Peace also brought him leisure to pen longer letters than he had written from the battlefield. One of the lengthiest went to Lodge and indicated that his dissatisfaction with the secretary of war's performance was unabated. He grumbled, "I am very much afraid with Alger the trouble is congenital. He simply *can't* do better; he *can not* learn by experience."

The letter then turned from army affairs to personal ones:

If the popular feeling is strong enough, and steady enough, I shall be nominated and elected. If it is merely temporary, then I shall be neither; and I don't believe that any effort of mine would alter the result one way or the other. I have been very busy with the Regiment, and have to let the other matter attend to itself. If I am nominated, well and good; I shall try to be elected, I shall try to rise to the extremely difficult position in which I shall find myself. If I am not nominated, I shall take the result with extreme philosophy and with a certain sense of relief, and shall turn my attention to the literary work which is awaiting me.

He had in mind a book about the Rough Riders. Since taking the oath of allegiance as Lieutenant Colonel Roosevelt on May 6, he had been one of them for 121 days. Now, with only memories of the drilling at Camp Wood, the commandeered trains of Texas and Tampa Bay, the hijacking of the *Yucatan,* the nearly disastrous landing at Daiquirí, the battle of Las Guasimas, and the charges up the San Juan Heights, he bore the responsibility to see that the Rough Riders were properly disbanded and sent home.

Doing exactly that by wading through paperwork in his tent on a sunny afternoon in mid-September, with the mustering out a few days away, he was asked by Lieutenant Colonel Brodie to step outside. Expecting to confront a problem, he left the shade of the tent for the brightness of the autumn sun. Squinting through his noseglasses, he found the entire regiment formed in a hollow square, with the officers and color sergeant in the middle.

Before them on a table stood something large and bulky and draped with a blanket.

Private William S. Murphy, formerly of Caddo in the Indian Territory and now a member of Troop M, stepped forward.

"A very slight token of admiration, love and esteem," he said as his voice choked.

The blanket was whipped off the mysterious object.

Gleaming in the sun and appearing a little misty in Roosevelt's teary, nearsighted eyes stood a bronze cowboy hanging on for dear life on a wildly bucking mustang. Roosevelt's old friend Fred Remington had sculpted it before the war and had given it the title *The Bronco Buster.* The troops had chipped in to buy it.

Stroking the horse's metal mane, Roosevelt swallowed hard, but after a moment a gift that never failed him—words—spilled from the wealthy mouth:

> Nothing could possibly happen that would touch and please me as this has. . . . I would have been most deeply touched if the officers had given me this testimonial, but coming from you, my men, I appreciate it tenfold. It comes from you who shared the hardships of the campaign with me, who gave me a piece of your hardtack when I had none, and who gave me your blankets when I had none to lie upon. To have such a gift come from this peculiarly American regiment touches me more than I can say. This is something I shall hand down to my children, and I shall value it more than the weapons I carried through the campaign.

Advancing to ranks of men he recognized by face and name, he said, "I want to say goodbye to each one of you in person."

One soldier felt a handshake was insufficient. He later admitted, "I wanted to hug him." But that would have been unmanly, not a thing for a Rough Rider to do.

On September 15, 1898, the 133d day since Roosevelt went to war, Color Sergeant A. P. Wright took down the flag for the last time. Horses, rifles, and the rest of the regimental property had been turned in. Men who now took one another by the hand for the last time had received for their services in donning the uniform of their country so as to drive the Spaniard out of the New World the sum of $77 each.

Now they scattered, as Roosevelt put it in his book about them, "to their homes in the North and the South, the few going back to the great cities of the East, the many turning toward the plains, the mountains, and the deserts of the West . . . as gallant fighters as ever wore the United States uniform."

A letter from John Hay had provided a handy and apt catchphrase for all they had done and all that had happened. "It has been a splendid little war," he wrote, "begun with the highest motives, carried on with magnificent intelligence and spirit, favored by that Fortune which loves the brave. It is now to be concluded, I hope, with that fine good nature, which is, after all, the distinguishing trait of the American character."

The man who had come to epitomize, embody, and exemplify that trait had stood before the Rough Riders during one of Chaplain Brown's Sunday services to deliver a sermon with what he called "a hortatory character." It included a last order and a warning: "Don't any of you get gay and pose as heroes. Don't go back and lie on your laurels. They will wither."

Epilogue

Children of the Dragon's Blood

Laurels in the form of votes turned Colonel Roosevelt into Governor Roosevelt, though he would beam with pride and pleasure whenever he was addressed as Colonel, as he was in a letter he received in December from a teacher in an academy in the Indian Territory, some of whose former pupils had been in the regiment. Alice Robertson wrote:

> Did you hear any echoes of our Indian war whoops over your election? They were pretty loud. I was particularly exultant because my father was a New Yorker and I was educated in New York, even if I was born here. So far as I can learn, the boys are taking up the dropped threads of their lives as though they had never been away. Our two Rough Rider students, Meagher and Gilmore, are doing well in their college work.
>
> I am sorry to tell you of the death of one of your most devoted troopers, Bert Holderman, who was here serving on the Grand Jury. He was stricken with meningitis in the jury-room and died after three days in delirium. . . . The words of commendation which you wrote upon Bert's discharge are the greatest comfort to his friends. They wanted you to know of his death, because he loved you so.
>
> I am planning to entertain all the Rough Riders in this vicinity some evening during my holiday vacation. I mean to have no other guests, but only give them an opportunity for reminiscences. I regret that Bert's death makes one less.

The first of several postwar deaths of comrades had been that of Nathaniel Adsit of Buffalo, who died of typhoid fever on August 1 at his home, and Trooper Alfred Judson, who died of it on that date at Montauk. Thomas Newnbone, a private from Phoenix, Arizona, died

279

of typhoid three days later at Fort MacPherson. Stanley Hollister, who had survived a wound received on July 2, passed away in the army hospital at Fort Monroe, Virginia, on August 17, also of typhoid, as did Private Wallace Anderson of Pasadena, California, two weeks later in St. Peter's Hospital in Brooklyn.

The only known suicide among the regiment had been Harry De-Vol, who had come through all the battles only to shoot himself in the head at Camp Wikoff.

Others who died after the peace treaty were John O'Neill, of dysentery; Frank Booth, of complications from his wounds, at Key West on August 30; J. Knox Green, of an unspecified sickness, and Eugene Lutz, of yellow fever, both at Camp Wikoff; Frederick Gosling and Edwin Eugene Casey, from causes unspecified; and Gerard Ives at home in New York City, of typhoid.

On August 26, William Tiffany died. As a memorial for him, several of Roosevelt's New York friends, including August Belmont, Major Austin Wadsworth, and Stanley and Richard Mortimer, donated funds to assist Rough Riders who found themselves in difficult financial straits.

Many had gone home to find that they had lost their prewar jobs. Some had been too weak to return immediately to work. Almost all were reluctant to accept help until Roosevelt, "by the exercise of a good deal of tact," persuaded them to take the money as "a memorial of poor young Lieutenant Tiffany."

A few Rough Riders demonstrated no reluctance when it came to appealing to Governor Roosevelt for state jobs and, later, to President Roosevelt for posts in the federal government. For many veterans, he remained their chief and only adviser and friend. In 1906, when Secretary of War William Howard Taft asked for the nomination of a Yale man, George Walker, to a government position in the Southwest, Roosevelt wrote, "I guess Yale '78 has the call, as there seems to be no Rough Rider available and every individual in the Southern District of the Indian Territory (including every Rough Rider) appears to be either under indictment, convicted, or in a position that renders it imperatively necessary that he should be indicted."

This jocular reference to misdemeanors (or worse) by former Rough Riders did not mean that an ex-trooper found himself barred from Roosevelt's largesse because of his misdeeds. Ex-Sergeant Benjamin Franklin Daniels, the one-time sheriff of Dodge City, found that even a stint in a penitentiary could not prevent him being looked on favorably as a U.S. marshal in Arizona. The problem, however, was that at that time Daniels was in another prison on a charge of murder. Yet even this could not overcome Roosevelt's admiration for Daniels's battlefield record of bravery. When ex-Lieutenant Colonel Alexander Brodie was selected by President Roosevelt to be governor of the Territory of Arizona, Roosevelt got him to give Daniels a job that would not require the advice and consent of the U.S. Senate— Brodie installed Daniels as warden of the penitentiary in which Daniels had been an involuntary guest.

John Hay's reaction upon hearing of this was "I believe the proverb runs, 'Set a Rough Rider to catch a thief.' "

Roosevelt accused Hay of "a brutal absence of feeling."

In June of 1900, when he was still governor but being boomed by some to challenge the renomination of William McKinley and run for president himself, he took time away from politics to go to Las Vegas, New Mexico, to help mark the anniversary of the Battle of Las Guasimas with a reunion of the Rough Riders.

Accompanying him as he crossed Kansas by train was reporter William Allen White. The editor of the *Emporia Gazette* found in him "a great, roaring, jocund tornado of a man."

Though Roosevelt denied any presidential longings, White did not overlook the fact that at each stop en route, Roosevelt was greeted by enthusiastic crowds. Neither could the object of this adulation. Roosevelt wrote to Lodge that at every stop "I was received by dense throngs exactly as if I had been a presidential candidate." When the Roosevelt tornado had departed Kansas, White advised the readers of his paper that Roosevelt was "more than a presidential possibility in 1904, he is a presidential probability." Not only that, he predicted, Roosevelt "is the coming American of the twentieth century."

For this reunion of rough and tough men, there could be no more fitting spot than Las Vegas, New Mexico. Into that dusty old town in September 1879 had ridden Wyatt Earp, straight from Dodge City, to rendezvous with his brothers and Doc Holliday, en route to another small town in Arizona with a daunting name: Tombstone. Earlier, Las Vegas had been a stopping-off point for Robert Ford. The man who had shot Jesse James in the back and killed him had hoped to succeed in the saloon business but failed and moved on.

In these storied and bloodied surroundings, Roosevelt passed thirty-six hours with his beloved, carousing Rough Riders. They and he would meet in other reunions. The last to be scheduled was in

1969; only three of the regiment were still around, two being too feeble to celebrate their past glories.

Between reunions, Roosevelt's prime source of information on what the former Rough Riders were up to in their civilian lives was the ex-captain of Troop G, Bill Llewellen, whose valor, service, and friendship had been rewarded with the rank of major and the position of U.S. attorney in New Mexico. His locale and job afforded him the rich opportunity to know the worst and tell it in his singularly bemused fashion. One letter noted:

> I have the honor to report, that Comrade Ritchie, late of Troop G, is in jail at Trinidad, Colorado, on a charge of murder. It seems that our comrade became involved in a controversy and it appears that the fellow he killed called him very bad names, even going so far as to cast reflections on the legitimacy of our comrade's birth. He killed the fellow instantly, shooting him through the heart.
>
> Also have to report that Comrade Webb, late of Troop D, has just killed two men at Bisbee, Arizona. Have not yet received the details of our comrade's trouble but understand that he was entirely justified in the transaction.

Another communication related that while "out at the penitentiary yesterday" he had had "a very pleasant visit with Comrade Frank Brito, whom you will remember was sent to the penitentiary from Silver City for killing his sister-in-law. He is very anxious to get out. You will doubtless recall that he was shooting at his *wife* at the time he killed his sister-in-law. Since he has been in the penitentiary, his wife ran away with Comrade Coyne of Troop H, going to Mexico. This incident has tended to turn popular sentiment strongly in Brito's favor."

Roosevelt delighted in these updates from Llewellen, whom he described to Hay as "a large, jovial, frontier Micawber type of person with a varied past which includes considerable man-killing."

Affectionately calling the former Rough Riders his "great big, goodhearted, homicidal children" and "children of the dragon's blood," he wrote his memoir of leading them. He published *The Rough Riders* in serial installments and then as a book. When it appeared, no less an authority on literature and history than Finley Peter Dunne's fictional Mr. Dooley reviewed it.

"If I was him," he wrote, alluding to Roosevelt's ego, "I'd call th' book 'Alone in Cubia.'"

Roosevelt's letter to Dunne was double-edged. "I regret to state that my family and intimate friends are delighted with your review of my book."

Others also had been writing about the war. In April 1899 General Wheeler protested to Roosevelt about one of these books that had attempted "to take credit from the cavalry brigades." Roosevelt replied to Fighting Joe, "I do not think you and I need to pay any attention to all these vermin. If any of them gets in my way I stamp on him."

He did just that in an appendix of *The Rough Riders.* Still smarting over suggestions that the Rough Riders had been ambushed at Las Guasimas, he dismissed as "wholly erroneous" assertions in articles "by newspaper-men who were in the rear and utterly ignorant of what really occurred." But he launched a long broadside at Stephen Bonsal, author of *The Fight for Santiago,* citing page after page of errors by a writer who "was not present at the fight [and] never at any time was with the cavalry in action."

To bolster his own objections, he included a lengthy letter from Richard Harding Davis. "If it is to be ambushed when you find the enemy exactly where you went to find him," he wrote, "and your scouts see him soon enough to give you sufficient time to spread five troops in skirmish order to attack him, and you then drive him back out of three positions for a mile and a half, then most certainly, as Bonsal says, 'L Troop of the Rough Riders was ambushed by the Spaniards on the morning of June 24th.' "

After the reunion in New Mexico, Roosevelt returned to New York with the announcement that he would not be a candidate for president that year. He urged the renomination and re-election of McKinley. However, in his private conversations with Henry Cabot Lodge, he indicated that he would grudgingly replace old, ailing Vice President Garret Hobart as McKinley's running mate, although he preferred to bide his time in fulfilling William Allen White's prediction and become president and "the American of the twentieth century" starting in 1904.

Nominated and elected, he took the oath as vice president on March 4, 1901. Then a man with a gun speeded up Roosevelt's timetable and history by assassinating McKinley in September.

As the forty-three-year-old President Theodore Roosevelt occupied the Executive Mansion that he would formally name the White House, he could look back two years to the Rough Riders following his

waving polka-dot scarf up the San Juan Heights and define it, right-
fully, as "the great day of my life."

Yet even after Roosevelt won the presidency in his own right in
the election of 1904, William Llewellen's letters had a knack for bringing him back to the Rough Rider days. On December 27, 1904, he
wrote about "Comrade Johnson, late of Troop G," who had been converted and was now "a full-fledged Evangelist, laboring in the Lord's
vineyard among the Swedish and Norwegian sailors."

The letter concluded, "You will doubtless be glad to know that at
least one of the men of your regiment is not in the penitentiary or a
candidate for office."

Sources

I was delighted that you did not use footnotes. I believe they distract from
the narrative.
                                                      —Roosevelt to another author

Anyone setting out to write about why and how Theodore Roosevelt went to war
must stand on others' shoulders, beginning with his. His memoir, *The Rough
Riders*, is the touchstone of the regiment's saga and a treasure of insights into
him. To understand his thinking before the war and for a history of what he called
"America the Unready," one must begin with his autobiography, published in 1913.
Views of almost any subject are contained in the body of his work as an author,
beginning with *The Naval War of 1812*.

For an appreciation of his embrace of the views of Captain Alfred Thayer
Mahan, there are the reviews of his two books in the *Literary Essays*, published
in 1926 by Scribner's. His analysis of Brooks Adams's exposition on social Darwinism, *The Law of Civilization and Decay,* first published in *The Outlook*, January
1897, was included in *American Ideals,* a compendium of his social and political
essays by G. P. Putnam's Sons, also 1897.

The spectrum of his ideas, thoughts, feelings, ambitions, and disappointments in both his public and private affairs are in his letters, collected and edited
by Elting Morison from Roosevelt archives located primarily at Harvard University. Other material has been preserved at the Theodore Roosevelt birthplace in
New York City and at Sagamore Hill at Oyster Bay, as well as in the National
Archives, the Library of Congress, and the New York Public Library.

In search of an overview of his life and times, a writer finds an abundance of
biographies, including the extraordinary *The Rise of Theodore Roosevelt* by Edmund Morris and Nathan Miller's *Theodore Roosevelt, a Life.* Two memoirs of
Roosevelt during the period leading up to, throughout, and after the war that
provide insights and anecdotes are those of Jacob A. Riis and Owen Wister.

For the history of Roosevelt "shot on the wing" by contemporary journalists,
there are the reminiscences of Richard Harding Davis and the almost daily reporting on the activities of the assistant secretary of the navy and leader of the Rough
Riders in the era's newspapers, yellow and otherwise.

As for this book, when their inclusion would not interrupt the flow of my
narrative, I have noted sources within the text. The origins of other data are cited
in the following pages.

Prologue

The history of Newport, Rhode Island, and its role as seaside resort for the
rich are drawn from *Baedeker*'s guide to America (1893) and society notes in contemporary magazines and newspapers. Several naval histories provide the details

of the founding of the Naval War College. Roosevelt's speech received wide circulation in the press; the text used is found in his collection of essays published by Putnam's.

PART I By Jingo

Chapter 1

Detailed summaries of events in Roosevelt's life prior to the war years are found in numerous biographies, including David McCullough's *Mornings on Horseback* and Morris's *The Rise of Theodore Roosevelt*. His work and woes as head of the New York City Police Department are covered in this author's *Commissioner Roosevelt*. Tales of Roosevelt's pugnacious nature may be found in his autobiography and in early chapters of Owen Wister's account of his friendship with Roosevelt, starting in the gymnasium at Harvard.

Chapter 2

Valuable insights into the Pleasant Gang are found in "Marching as to War" in *The Spanish War, An American Epic—1898*, by G. J. A. O'Toole, various Roosevelt biographies, his own memoirs, and his letters. Material regarding Roosevelt's admiration for Leonard Wood threads through all of Roosevelt's accounts of the war period. His relationship with Secretary Long is described in their diaries and letters.

Chapter 3

The role of the naval militia in this period is recorded in Charles Oscar Paullin's *History of Naval Administration,* a resource that proved invaluable throughout the writing of this work, as did Paolo E. Coletta's *The American Naval Heritage*. The breadth of Roosevelt's fondness for torpedo boats is found in his memoirs and letters, as is his often testy relationship with Secretary Long.

Chapter 4

Roosevelt treats the subject of the weakness of the U.S. Navy at length in his autobiography, along with his fascination and advocacy of a battleship-led fleet. His admiration for Alfred Thayer Mahan is attested to in a posthumous tribute to Mahan in *The Outlook,* January 13, 1915. Helpful material on him and William Sampson is found in James C. Bradford's *Admirals of the Steel Navy*. A wellspring of fact and fancy regarding the rise of yellow journalism comes from my friend Hy B. Turner, a lifelong "ink-stained wretch" and expert on the history of New York City newspapers.

PART II The Noble Elk

Chapter 5

Praise for Commodore George Dewey abounds in Roosevelt's writings, and Dewey's debt and gratitude to him are found in his own autobiography. For an overview of Dewey's life, I relied on *The Admiral* by Laurin Hall Healy and Luis Kutner.

Chapter 6

Gratitude for the portrait of Roosevelt at the age of thirty-nine is owed to Owen Wister's fond memoir of their friendship. The tangled web of Navy Department personnel problems is detailed in Paullin and discussed in Roosevelt's autobiography. Roosevelt's scolding of Jacob Riis and Lincoln Steffens for asking him if he yearned to be president of the United States is in Steffens's autobiography.

Chapter 7

Roosevelt's review of Mahan's exposition on the influence of seapower upon history is contained in Roosevelt's collected literary essays, along with the review of Mahan's biography of Lord Nelson, the invincible British admiral whose order to rake the enemy's ships with fire impelled Roosevelt to lead the second charge atop the San Juan Heights. Helpful in plumbing the philosophy and philosophers of social Darwinism as they pertained to American expansionism in the 1890s is Ivan Musicant's *The Banana Wars*. Roosevelt's own analysis of Brooks Adams's *The Law of Civilization and Decay* is found in his book of essays, *American Ideals*.

PART III   No Place for Mercy

Chapter 8

Newspapers of the era brimmed with stories of filibusterers and the difficulties they created for the McKinley administration in its efforts to avoid a war with Spain. Roosevelt's views on the Monroe Doctrine as being a matter of living policy are replete in his writings.

Chapter 9

The role of William Randolph Hearst in fanning the flames of crisis has been detailed in W. A. Swanberg's biography. It provides helpful guidelines in writing about Hearst's role in the events leading up to and during the war, as did Hy B. Turner's research regarding the exchange of messages between Remington and Hearst. The complete story of the career of Richard Harding Davis may be found in Charles Belmont Davis's biography and a collection of Davis's letters, as well as in a biography by Scott Compton Osborn and Robert L. Phillips. Except for Jacob Riis, no journalist won the respect and affection of Roosevelt more than Davis, although some journalism historians feel that Davis sacrificed his integrity by becoming a Roosevelt apologist, particularly his change of mind regarding the question of whether the Las Guasimas battle began with the Rough Riders being ambushed. An excellent biography of Hearst's chief newspapering rival is *Joseph Pulitzer and His World* by the last city editor of the *World*, James Wyman Barret, published in 1912.

Chapter 10

A concise analysis of McKinley's policy of peace is found in Walter Millis's 1931 book, *The Martial Spirit* (chapter 4). Despite Roosevelt's misgivings about the strength of McKinley's backbone in the election of 1896, in an address on January 27, 1903, at a banquet in McKinley's hometown of Canton, Ohio, in honor of McKinley's birthday, Roosevelt said, "It was given to President McKinley to take the foremost place in our political life at a time when our country was brought face to face with problems more momentous than any whose solution we have ever attempted . . . and it was under his leadership that the nation solved these mighty problems aright."

Chapter 11

Sources for most of the material in this chapter have been cited in the text. Other data are drawn from memoirs, biographies, histories, and newspaper accounts. Admiral Dewey's autobiography provides information on his visit to the emperor of Japan.

PART IV   A Name to Remember

Chapter 12

Vivid accounts of the fate of the *Maine* have been written in the century since she blew up and sank under mysterious circumstances. An almost minute-by-minute version on which I relied is *A Ship to Remember,* by Michael Blow, whose grandfather was one of her officers.

Chapter 13

History owes a debt to journalists for capturing the confusion and horror in Havana harbor as the *Maine* burned and sank. A number of histories and memoirs provide other details, including the chapter on the *Maine* in Walter Millis's *The Martial Spirit;* Captain Charles Sigsbee's serialized version, "My Story of the Maine," in *Cosmopolitan* in July and August 1912; and George Bronson Rae's "The Night of the Explosion in Havana," *Harper's Weekly,* March 5, 1898.

Chapter 14

The activities of William Randolph Hearst on the night of the blowing up of the *Maine* and of his newspaper in the days that followed are described in Swanberg's *Citizen Hearst*. Almost a century after the disaster, the debate remains unsettled as to the cause. Was it the accidental hitting of a Spanish mine? A torpedo? Sabotage? Might an American have done it in order to start the war? Could William Randolph Hearst have been behind such a scheme? As in all the great disputes of history, exactly what happened on the night of February 15, 1898, will continue to be argued.

Chapter 15

Sources have been cited in the text. The report of the investigation into the disaster is in the archives of the Senate Committee on Foreign Relations. The cry of "Remember the Maine" is indelible in the pages of American history, while the *Maine* itself has been remembered in the form of a huge monument in (ironically) Columbus Circle in New York City. It was erected at Hearst's urgings. The ship also is honored through the preservation of her two masts. One serves as a flag staff at the U.S. Naval Academy at Annapolis. The second flies the flag over the graves of heroes from all the armed forces in the Arlington National Cemetery.

Chapter 16

Sources have been cited in the text.

Chapter 17

Sources have been cited in the text.

Chapter 18

The actions of Dewey, Sampson, and Roosevelt are preserved in their memoirs. Naval statistics and other data are drawn from naval histories, especially Bradford and Paullin.

PART V Cowboy Cavalry

Chapter 19

As ever in the life and career of Theodore Roosevelt, newspapers flocked to cover him as he went to war. As always, he was acutely aware of the value of the press as a means of affecting the public's perception of him, as evidenced by the story in the *New York Times* in which Roosevelt expressed misgivings about the public seeing the Rough Riders as a circus. New York newspapers were especially fascinated by the young men of the city's high society who rushed to follow him to war and by the unlikely mingling of these sophisticated and moneyed youths with the rawhide men of the frontier who made up the bulk of the regiment.

Chapter 20

Events surrounding Roosevelt's departure for Texas are taken from Riis and newspaper accounts, as well as from Roosevelt's *The Rough Riders*. The activities of the naval and land forces are found in numerous histories of the war. Because this work centers on Roosevelt's activities and does not pretend to be an overall history of the Spanish-American War, the grand strategies and detailed activities of the other forces engaged in the conflict have been described only to the extent to which they were needed to provide background and context for the activities of Theodore Roosevelt and his Rough Riders.

Chapter 21

This chapter relies primarily on Roosevelt's book for the events and personalities during the organization of the regiment in Texas.

Chapter 22

This chapter's primary source is *The Rough Riders,* chapter 1, "Raising the Regiment."

Chapter 23

This chapter's primary source is *The Rough Riders,* chapter 2, "To Cuba." Other material is drawn from newspaper accounts, chiefly the *New York Times*. The arrangements at Tampa are found in stories filed by Richard Harding Davis and other journalists, as well as in pertinent passages of Michael Blow's *A Ship to Remember*. The letter from Roosevelt to his children is taken from Joseph Bucklin Bishop's *Theodore Roosevelt and His Times* but may also be found in Elting Morison's collection of Roosevelt's correspondence.

Chapter 24

The main source of this chapter is *The Rough Riders,* chapter 2, "To Cuba." The army and navy activities are culled from numerous histories.

Chapter 25

The primary sources are *The Rough Riders,* chapter 2; Richard Harding Davis; and Frederic Remington. The history of the founding of Vitagraph is found in *The Film Encyclopedia* by Ephraim Katz. The advent of the newsreel camera on the battlefield is recorded by John D. Hemment in his memoir, *Cannon and Camera,* published in 1898.

PART VI   Three O'Clock Courage

Chapters 26–32

The chief source for these chapters is *The Rough Riders,* chapters 3–5. Other sources are cited in the text. Accounts of the actions of the navy and the Spanish are derived from numerous histories, memoirs, and biographies of the participants, as well as from newspaper coverage.

PART VII   Crackerjacks

Chapter 33

This chapter's primary source is *The Rough Riders,* chapter 6, "The Return Home." Other sources are cited in the text.

Chapter 34

In addition to *The Rough Riders,* chapter 6, Roosevelt's confrontation with the Department of War and Secretary Alger over the withdrawal of the army from disease-ridden Cuba is found in his letters. The face-off between Dewey and the German admiral is found in several naval histories and in Dewey's memoirs.

Chapter 35

The primary sources for this chapter are *The Rough Riders,* chapter 6, "The Return Home," and Roosevelt's letters.

Chapter 36

The primary sources for this chapter are *The Rough Riders,* chapter 6, "The Return Home," Roosevelt's autobiography, and contemporary newspaper accounts.

Epilogue

The primary source here is *The Rough Riders,* chapter 6. The names and circumstances of the deaths of the troopers named are to be found in appendix A, which lists the mustering-out roll. Other sources are cited in the text.

Bibliography

Abbot, Lawrence F. *Impressions of Theodore Roosevelt*. Garden City, N.Y.: Doubleday, Page and Company, 1922.

Alden, John D. *The American Steel Navy*. Annapolis, Md.: Naval Institute Press/American Heritage Press, 1989.

Barret, James Wyman. *Joseph Pulitzer and His World*. New York: Vanguard Press, 1941.

Beale, Howard K. *Theodore Roosevelt and the Rise of America to World Power*. Baltimore, Md.: Johns Hopkins University Press, 1956.

Bishop, Joseph Bucklin. *Theodore Roosevelt and His Time*. New York: Charles Scribner's Sons, 1973.

Blow, Michael. *A Ship to Remember: The Maine and the Spanish-American War*. New York: William Morrow and Company, 1992.

Bradford, James C., ed. *Admirals of the New Steel Navy*. Annapolis, Md.: Naval Institute Press, 1990.

Brown, Charles H. *The Correspondents' War: Journalists in the Spanish-American War*. New York: Charles Scribner's Sons, 1967.

Burton, David H. *Theodore Roosevelt*. New York: Twayne Publishers, 1972.

Busch, Noel. *T. R.: The Story of Theodore Roosevelt and His Influence on Our Times*. New York: Reynal and Company, 1963.

Chadwick, French Ensor. *The Relations of the United States and Spain: The Spanish-American War*. New York: Russell and Russell, 1911.

Coletta, Paolo E. *The American Naval Heritage*. Lanham, Md.: University Press of America, 1987.

Coston, William Hilary. *The Spanish-American War Volunteer*. Freeport, New York: Books for Libraries Press, 1971.

Davis, Charles Belmont. *Adventures and Letters of Richard Harding Davis*. New York: Charles Scribner's Sons, 1917.

Davis, Richard Harding. *The Cuban and Porto Rican Campaigns*. New York: Charles Scribner's Sons, 1898.

Dewey, George. *Autobiography of George Dewey*. Annapolis, Md.: Naval Institute Press, 1987.

Dunne, Peter Finley. *Mr. Dooley in Peace and in War*. New York: Charles Scribner's Sons, 1898.

Freidel, Frank. *The Splendid Little War*. Boston: Little, Brown and Company, 1958.

Harbaugh, William. *Power and Responsibility*. New York: Farrar, Straus and Cudahy, 1961.

Harlow, Alvin. *Theodore Roosevelt, Strenuous American*. New York: Julian Messner, 1943.

Healy, Laurin Hall, and Luis Kutner. *The Admiral*. New York: Ziff Davis Publishing Company, 1944.

Howland, Harold. *Theodore Roosevelt and His Times*. New Haven: Yale University Press, 1921.

Hunt, John Gabriel, ed. *The Essential Theodore Roosevelt*. New York: Gramercy Books, 1994.

Iglehart, Ferdinand. *Theodore Roosevelt—The Man as I Knew Him*. New York: Christian Herald, 1919.

Jeffers, H. Paul. *Commissioner Roosevelt: The Story of Theodore Roosevelt and the New York City Police—1895–1897*. New York: John Wiley & Sons, 1994.

Jones, Virgil Carrington. *Roosevelt's Rough Riders*. Garden City, N.Y.: Doubleday, 1971.

Lewis, Wm. Draper. *The Life of Theodore Roosevelt*. New York: United Publishers of the United States and Canada, 1919.

Lodge, Henry Cabot. *Selections from the Correspondence of Theodore Roosevelt and Henry Cabot Lodge—1884–1918*. New York: Charles Scribner's Sons, 1925.

Mahan, Alfred Thayer. *The Influence of Sea Power Upon History*. Boston: Little, Brown and Company, 1890.

Mason, Gregory. *Remember the Maine*. New York: Henry Holt, 1939.

Miller, Nathan. *Theodore Roosevelt, A Life*. New York: William Morrow and Company, 1992.

———. *F. D. R., An Intimate History*. New York: New American Library, 1984.

Millis, Walter. *The Martial Spirit: A Study of Our War with Spain*. Boston: Houghton Mifflin Company, 1931.

Morison, Elting E., ed. *The Letters of Theodore Roosevelt*. Cambridge, Mass.: Harvard University Press, 1951.

Morris, Edmund. *The Rise of Theodore Roosevelt*. New York: Coward, McCann and Geoghean, 1979.

Morris, Sylvia Jukes. *Edith Hermit Roosevelt: Portrait of a First Lady*. New York: Coward, McCann and Geoghegan, 1965.

Musicant, Ivan. *The Banana Wars: A History of the United States Military Intervention in Latin America from the Spanish-American War to the Invasion of Panama*. New York: Macmillan, 1990.

Osborn, Scott Compton, and Robert H. Phillips Jr. *Richard Harding Davis*. Boston: Twayne Publishers, 1970.

O'Toole, G. J. A. *The Spanish War, An American Epic—1898*. New York: W. W. Norton & Company, 1984.

Paullin, Charles Oscar. *Paullin's History of Naval Administration, 1715–1911*. Annapolis, Md.: Naval Institute Press, 1968.

Pringle, Henry F. *Theodore Roosevelt, A Biography*. New York: Harcourt, Brace and World, 1931.

Riis, Jacob. *The Making of an American*. New York: Macmillan, 1923.

———. *Theodore Roosevelt, the Citizen*. New York: Outlook, 1904.

Roosevelt, Theodore. *American Ideals and Other Essays, Social and Political*. New York: G. P. Putnam's Sons, 1897.

———. *An Autobiography*. New York: Macmillan, 1913.

———. *Literary Essays*. New York: Charles Scribner's Sons, 1926.

———. *The Naval War of 1812*. Annapolis, Md.: Naval Institute Press, 1987.

———. *The Rough Riders*. Williamstown, Mass.: Corner House Publishers, 1979.

Southworth, John Van Duyn. *The Age of Steam: Part One, The Story of Engine-Powered Naval Warfare, 1783–1936*. New York: Twayne Publishers, 1970.

Spears, John R. *Our Navy in the War with Spain*. New York: Charles Scribner's Sons, 1898.

Swanberg, W. A. *Citizen Hearst: A Biography of William Randolph Hearst*. New York: Charles Scribner's Sons, 1967.

Trask, David F. *The War with Spain in 1898*. New York: Macmillan, 1955.

Weems, John Edward. *The Fate of the Maine*. New York: Henry Holt, 1958.

Wister, Owen. *Roosevelt, The Story of a Friendship*. New York: Macmillan, 1930.

Index